The Mutual-Aid Approach to Working with Groups

*Helping People Help
One Another*

Second Edition

D0048556

THE HAWORTH PRESS
Titles of Related Interest

Rebuilding Communities: Challenges for Group Work edited by Harvey Bertcher, Farris Kurtz, and Alice Lamont

Group Work: Strategies for Strengthening Resiliency edited by Timothy B. Kelly, Toby Berman-Rossi, and Susanne E. Palombo

Social Work with Groups: Mining the Gold edited by Sue Henry, Jean East, and Cathryne Schmitz

Crossing Boundaries and Developing Alliances Through Group Work edited by Jocelyn Lindsay, Daniel Turcotte, and Estelle Hopmeyer

Social Work with Groups: Social Justice Through Personal, Community, and Societal Change edited by Nancy E. Sullivan, Ellen Sue Mesbur, Norma C. Lang, Deborah Goodman, and Lynne Mitchell

Stories Celebrating Group Work: It's Not Always Easy to Sit on Your Mouth edited by Roselle Kurland and Andrew Malekoff

The Social Work Student's Research Handbook by Dominique Moyse Steinberg

The Mutual-Aid Approach to Working with Groups
Helping People Help One Another

Second Edition

Dominique Moyse Steinberg, DSW

Routledge
Taylor & Francis Group

NEW YORK AND LONDON

First published by

The Haworth Press, Inc., 10 Alice Street, Binghamton, NY 13904-1580.

Transferred to Digital Printing 2010 by Routledge
270 Madison Ave, New York NY 10016
2 Park Square, Milton Park, Abingdon, Oxon, OX14 4RN

Cover design by Jennifer M. Gaska.

Library of Congress Cataloging-in-Publication Data

Steinberg, Dominique Moyse.
    The mutual-aid approach to working with groups : helping people help one another / Dominique Moyse Steinberg.—2nd ed.
        p. cm.
    Includes bibliographical references and index.
    ISBN 0-7890-1461-0 (hard : alk. paper)—ISBN 0-7890-1462-9 (soft : alk. paper)
    1. Social group work. 2. Self-help groups. I. Title.
    HV45.S783 2004
    361.4—dc22
                                                                        2004007025

Dedicated with unending gratitude to Roselle Kurland,
my teacher, mentor, friend

And special thanks to my husband, Irwin Steinberg,
for always *being there* for me

ABOUT THE AUTHOR

Dominique Moyse Steinberg, DSW, CSW, ACSW, has been a faculty member at the Hunter College School of Social Work, where she served as field advisor to MSW and BSW students, supervised social work interns, and offered private research and writing tutorials to doctoral students. She has provided services to various organizations, including the New York Family Reception Center (policy/practice); the Child Welfare League of America and the New York Academy for Educational Development (program design); the Children's Defense Fund, Manhattan Teen Pregnancy Network, and the Parsons-Sage Institute (program design/practice); and Bronx-Lebanon Hospital and the New York Sisters of the Good Shepherd (practice).

Dr. Steinberg is an editorial board member of Social Work with Groups; a Fellow of the Academy of Certified Social Workers; a member, former board member, and former Chair of Endowment for the Association for the Advancement of Social Work with Groups; a member of the NYC/New England chapters of NASW; and a former consultant to the NASW Committee on Inquiry. After teaching at NYU and Hunter College for several years, Dr. Steinberg now commutes between New York City and New England, where she teaches group work practice, research, and writing for publication at Smith College School of Social Work in Northampton, Massachusetts.

CONTENTS

chapter 1
chapter 2
chapter 3
4
5

Foreword   xi
    Roselle Kurland

Preface   xiii

Introduction   1
    Key Concepts of This Chapter   1
    The Purpose of This Book   1
    The Mutual-Aid Approach   3
    The Theoretical Basis for Mutual Aid   4
    The Conditions for Mutual-Aid Practice   4
    Implications for Practice   7
    How This Book Is Organized   8
    Recommended Further Reading   10

THEME   13

**Chapter 1. The Mutual-Aid Approach in Social Work
    with Groups**   13
    Key Concepts of This Chapter   13
    Mutual Aid Defined and Described   15
    The Mutual-Aid Mind-Set   21
    The Primary Functions of Mutual-Aid Practice   22
    The Notion of Group-Specific Skillful Practice   28
    Key Points of This Chapter   31
    Recommended Further Reading   32

**Chapter 2. The Nine Dynamics of Mutual Aid
    and Their Implications for Practice**   35
    Key Concepts of This Chapter   35
    Sharing Data   36
    The Dialectic Process   38
    Discussing Taboos   41
    All in the Same Boat   42

Mutual Support   44
Mutual Demand   45
Individual Problem Solving   48
Rehearsal   49
Strength in Numbers   50
Key Points of This Chapter   52
Recommended Further Reading   53

Chapter 3. Pregroup Planning with Mutual Aid in Mind   **55**

Key Concepts of This Chapter   55
Setting the Stage   55
The Role of Group Purpose in Mutual Aid   64
Key Points of This Chapter   73
Recommended Further Reading   74

Chapter 4. Early Group Goals and Norms   **77**

Key Concepts of This Chapter   77
Goals to Emphasize in the First Session   79
Norms to Emphasize in the First Session   84
Key Points of This Chapter   90
Recommended Further Reading   90

Chapter 5. Mutual Aid, "Time and Place," and the Role of the Worker   **93**

Key Concepts of This Chapter   93
Time and Place   95
The Changing Role of the Worker   120
Key Points of This Chapter   122
Recommended Further Reading   123

Chapter 6. Individual Problem Solving from a Mutual-Aid Viewpoint   **125**

Key Concepts of This Chapter   125
Prologue   125
Common Problem-Solving Strategies   129
The Mutual-Aid Approach   132
What Needs to Happen to Catalyze Mutual Aid   140
Key Points of This Chapter   143
Recommended Further Reading   144

Chapter 7. Mutual Aid and Authority   **145**

Key Concepts of This Chapter   145
Having a Real Say and the Group's Need for It   147
Authority and Group Development   153
Helping the Group Exercise Its Say Along Humanistic
    As Well As Democratic Lines   156
Professional Reflection   158
Group-Specific Skills for Decentralizing Authority
    and for Helping Maintain a Democratic-Humanistic
    Climate   161
Key Points of This Chapter   163
Recommended Further Reading   164

Chapter 8. The Role of Conflict in a Mutual-Aid System   **167**

Key Concepts of This Chapter   167
Keys to Using Conflict for Mutual Aid   169
Group-Specific Skills for Helping a Group Use Conflict   181
Key Points of This Chapter   182
Recommended Further Reading   183

VARIATIONS ON A THEME   **185**

**Chapter 9. Mutual-Aid Practice with Single-Session
Groups**   **193**

Key Concepts of This Chapter   193
Time and Place Issues of the Single-Session Group   196
Implications for Practice   198
Key Points of This Chapter   204
Recommended Further Reading   206

**Chapter 10. Mutual-Aid Practice with Short-Term
Groups**   **207**

Key Concepts of This Chapter   207
Time and Place Issues of the Short-Term Group   208
Implications for Practice   211
Key Points of This Chapter   218
Recommended Further Reading   220

Chapter 11. Mutual-Aid Practice with Open-Ended Groups   **221**

Key Concepts of This Chapter   221
Time and Place Issues of the Open-Ended Group   222
Implications for Practice   225
Key Points of This Chapter   231
Recommended Further Reading   233

Chapter 12. Mutual-Aid Practice with Very Large Groups   **235**

Key Concepts of This Chapter   235
Time and Place Issues of the Very Large Group   237
Implications for Practice   239
Key Points of This Chapter   244
Recommended Further Reading   246

Chapter 13. Conclusion   **247**

Key Concepts of This Chapter   247
All Things Considered   248
Group-Specific Skills for Helping a Group Evaluate
    Its Mutual-Aid Development   253
End Note   254
Key Points of This Chapter   255
Recommended Further Reading   255

Bibliography   **257**

Index   **267**

Foreword

Mutual aid is at the very heart of good group work practice. The expectation that members of a group will be able to help one another—in fact, that they will be expected to do so—is a statement to each person in the group that she or he has strengths to offer to others. It is empowering. It lets each person know that she or he has something to give to the group, not just to get from it. That belief is deeply rooted in group work practice. Yet, that message is not heard by many clients with whom we work in social work. Mutual aid means that client strengths are called upon and emphasized, a feature that makes group work special and unique and wonderful.

This book examines mutual aid in depth so that practitioners can maximize its use in their work with groups. Its premise, that mutual aid is relevant to and possible in all work with groups whatever the setting or population or length of time, is very sound.

The work of Bertha Reynolds* is quite applicable to this book. She identified five stages of learning, and described the final stage as "the ability to teach what one has mastered." The depth of Dr. Steinberg's understanding of mutual aid, as it is demonstrated in this book, surely is an indication of her mastery of the subject and of her ability to teach it.

Bertha Reynolds was also an advocate of clear, nonjargonized language. "The real test of knowing a thing well enough to apply it," she said, "is being able to say it in simple language." Dr. Steinberg does just that.

Complex language is not synonymous with complex ideas. In fact, just the opposite. The flow and ease of Dr. Steinberg's writing dem-

---

*The works cited are, respectively, *Learning and Teaching in the Practice of Social Work* (New York: Russell and Russell, 1965, p. 83) and *Social Work and Social Living* (Washington, DC: National Association of Social Workers, 1951, p. vi).

onstrates her mastery of the subject of mutual aid in all its complexity. It makes this book a joy to read, even as it increases readers' understanding and grasp of mutual aid and their enthusiasm to want to skillfully help group members help one another.

Roselle Kurland
Hunter College School of Social Work

Preface

Do it right because it is beautiful and you love it.

> Blanche Honegger Moyse,
> Artistic Director and Founder,
> New England Bach Festival, to her Chorale

Welcome to the second edition of *The Mutual-Aid Approach to Working with Groups.* To the extent that groups vary in form, practice must also vary in its application of theory and principles so that our work with groups can have real-world logic, not just theoretical propriety. Integrated into this second edition, therefore, are four new chapters that provide implications for practice with group types that differ in some significant way from the classic long-term, closed, and stable system upon which the fundamental theories, concepts, principles, and skills of mutual-aid work are based. These chapters focus on single-session, short-term, open-ended, and very large groups. In each of these new chapters the context of time and place is carried over from Chapter 5 as a framework for examining the extraordinary obstacles to mutual aid in each group type and for identifying the extraordinary challenges to practice—*extraordinary* in this case signifying obstacles that exist *in addition to* those routinely faced by any group. These four group types also have more in common than meets the eye at first glance, however, and the common within which their particular obstacles occur is outlined in the introduction preceding the chapters of *Section II: Variations on a Theme.*

Other variations on the theme of the small, closed, long-term group exist today as well, of course, such as telephone or video-conference groups, Internet chat rooms, and Web-based bulletin boards, to name but a few. However, their impact on mutual aid, and thus implications for mutual-aid practice, is just being discovered, and their discussion is left to the future. Meanwhile, some of the current thinking on these and other such new forms is included at the end of this preface.

At the time of the first edition of this book five years ago, I thought it was both the best and the worst of times for groups, to borrow a phrase from Charles Dickens. I am still under that impression. It is still the best of times because one can hardly open a telephone book or magazine or newspaper without finding a group to join. As someone who believes so strongly in the ability of group life to enhance quality of life, but who sees an ever-greater degree of work life take place in front of a home computer, I am delighted to know that opportunities to be *en companie,* whatever the reason, still exist. However, I think it is the worst of times as well, because formal and informal evidence continues to suggest that it is still the dwindling of human service resources and poorly conceptualized managed-care policies that are causing the proliferation of groups, rather than any true understanding of or respect for the healing power of groups or skill in the group-work method. In addition, I continue to believe that there is a fundamental misunderstanding of mutual aid among those who are forming and leading all these groups. I still hear people who work with groups wonder if mutual aid is really relevant to their particular settings or say that it's a great idea but doubt whether it can really work in their setting or with their population.

Clearly, as I discuss specifically in Chapter 1, in Chapter 3, and periodically throughout this book, a relationship exists between setting and mutual aid. But as I also repeatedly note, setting never dictates the *capacity* of a group to become a mutual-aid system, only the *kind* of mutual aid that might be catalyzed. In other words, no group is ever devoid of potential. Mutual aid is the *normal* stuff of groups; and as Clara Kaiser (1958) indicated, helping groups develop their unique potential is a question of how we approach our work, not where we do it or with whom. If it seems as if a group is not acting as a mutual-aid system, then I continue to believe that the most likely explanation is lack of skill on the practitioner's part; and I continue to hope that the manner in which theory and practice are joined in this book will make a difference.

RECOMMENDED FURTHER READING

Finn, J. (1995). Computer-based self-help groups: A new resource to supplement support groups. *Social Work with Groups* 18(1):109-117.

Heckman, T., Kalichman, S., Roffman, R., Sikkema, K., Heckman, B., Somlai, A., and Walker, J. (1999). A telephone-delivered coping improvement intervention for persons living with HIV-AIDS in rural areas. *Social Work with Groups* 21(4):49-62.

Kaslyn, M. (1999). Telephone group work: Challenges for practice. *Social Work with Groups* 22(1):63-78.

Meier, A. (2000). Offering social support via the Internet: A case study of an online support group for social workers. *Journal of Technology in Human Services* 17(2/3):237-266.

Meier, A., Galinksy, M., and Rounds, K. (1995). Telephone support groups for caregivers of persons with AIDS. *Social Work with Groups* 18(1):99-108.

Regan, S. (2002). Building bridges over troubled waters: A bridging model for teleconferencing group counseling. In *Social Work with Groups: Mining the Gold,* eds. S. Henry, J. East, and C. Schmitz, pp. 199-130. Binghamton, NY: The Haworth Press.

Rittner, B. (2001). "Re-conceptualizing group process: Computer-based chat rooms and discussion boards group development." Paper presented at the 23rd Annual Symposium of the Association for the Advancement of Social Work with Groups. Akron, OH, October.

Schopler, J., Galinsky, M., and Abell, M. (1997). Creating community through telephone and computer groups: Theoretical and practice perspectives. *Social Work with Groups* 20(4):35-54.

Wiener, L., Spencer, E., Davidson, R., and Fair, C. (1993). National telephone support groups: A new avenue toward psychosocial support for HIV-infected children and their families. *Social Work with Groups* 16(3):55-71.

Introduction

KEY CONCEPTS OF THIS CHAPTER

Aggregational Therapy of Individuals (Hartford 1978)
Capacity to Communicate and Interact
Casework in a Group (Kurland and Salmon 1992)
Democratic-Humanism (Glassman and Kates 1990)
Exchange of Strengths
Group Purpose
Group As a Second Client
Groupness (Middleman and Wood 1990a)
Group-Specific Skill
Practitioners As Workers, not Leaders
Multiple Helping Relationships
Mutual Aid
Open-Ended Groups
Setting the Stage for Mutual Aid
Sharing Authority
Short-Term Groups
Single-Session Groups
Thinking Things Through
Very Large Groups

THE PURPOSE OF THIS BOOK

Groups abound today, and although an impressive body of professional literature on social work testifies to the centrality of catalyzing mutual aid in practice with groups, what has been lacking is a resource for making the link between the descriptive and prescriptive of mutual-aid practice, for bridging theory (i.e., the descriptive component of professional practice) with practical information (i.e., the prescriptive component of mutual-aid practice). The purpose of this book is to provide such a link.

By describing and discussing theories, concepts, and practice principles specific to mutual aid, this book provides a foundation for practice. Although many books offer a foundation for practice with groups, most of them are so comprehensive that mutual aid is usually assigned only partial attention along with other aspects of practice. In contrast, *The Mutual-Aid Approach to Working with Groups* makes mutual aid its principal subject. It encourages further study in each of the key areas of mutual-aid practice by referring the reader to specific literature at the end of every chapter. In addition, it attempts to combine the *why* of mutual-aid practice with the *how-to* in some immediately useful manner by offering case examples of practices that are both productive and counterproductive to mutual aid.

This is the first book to bring under one cover the most salient historical and contemporaneous discussions on the role of mutual aid in social work with groups. Until now it has been necessary to sift through mountains of literature merely to understand the ways in which mutual aid has been conceptualized throughout decades of professional growth— a tedious and unwieldy task. For example, as a social group-work concept, the term *mutual aid* was first coined by William Schwartz (1961). The process, however, has been recognized as an important group-work dynamic since the early 1900s by such professional leaders as Coyle, Hart, Newstetter, Lieberman, Slavson, and Cantor, all of whom, among others, have struggled to identify and articulate a specific knowledge base and scientific body of practice principles for systematic and purposeful social work practice with groups.

Through many rich examples of actual practice interventions, some of which were gathered through an empirical study (Steinberg 1992) and others that were collected through informal dialogues with colleagues, *The Mutual-Aid Approach* aims to help people who work with groups understand the essential and distinctive dynamics of an approach to practice that seeks to help people help one another. Furthermore, in contrast with books that tend to offer only examples of "correct" practice, *The Mutual-Aid Approach* juxtaposes examples of interventions that are counterproductive to mutual aid with those that are productive in order to illustrate the impact of various professional behaviors on small-group process.

THE MUTUAL-AID APPROACH

The mutual-aid approach to practice is based on the belief that we work with groups precisely because of their potential for mutual aid. What is mutual aid, exactly? Unadorned by professional jargon, mutual aid simply refers to people helping one another as they think things through. Helping people engage in mutual aid is no simple matter, however. In addition to the need for knowledge about small-group dynamics, mutual-aid practice takes a certain vision to exploit group process as the powerful helping medium it can be. It calls for a shift in the way we regard and use our authority, and requires the purposeful use of group-specific skills—the application of a whole body of skills that extend beyond those we use in work with individuals.

In its utilization of group process as the primary means for helping and so in direct contrast to the "individual-work-in-a-group" style that overwhelms much of practice today, mutual-aid work is truly group work. Not only are the individual members our clients but also the group as a system is our client—our *second* client (Shulman 1999). Thus, while one eye looks to the needs of the individual to help members shape and use process toward mutual aid, the other eye attends to the nature and quality of that process.

Whenever people come together there is always group process at work, of course, whether we attend to it or not (Middleman 1978). Process can take on many different looks, however, not all of which promote mutual aid. For example, mutual aid relies on spontaneous communication and interaction among members and has little room to develop when they interact primarily with the worker while others watch and listen (Middleman and Wood 1990b, Papell and Rothman 1980, Kurland and Salmon 1992). It also relies on the exchange of strengths and thus has little room to develop when the practitioner is regarded as the principal helper (Newstetter 1935; Trecker 1955; Hartford 1964; Schwartz 1976; Northen and Kurland 2001; Breton 1990; Middleman and Wood 1990a; Shulman 1999). Finally, mutual aid needs a *democratic-humanistic* culture (Glassman and Kates 1990), an environment in which everyone has the right to be heard and in which everyone's needs and feelings are taken into account in all of the group's decision-making processes.

THE THEORETICAL BASIS FOR MUTUAL AID

As the recommended further readings at the end of each chapter and the bibliography at the end of this book make very clear, the theoretical justification for mutual-aid work with groups is rooted in social work. In fact, in no other profession does mutual aid play such a pivotal role (Glassman and Kates 1990). Nonetheless, although using group process specifically to catalyze mutual aid is a unique social work mandate, the practice skills that we use to help people engage in mutual aid are useful for work with any and all groups that aim to maximize their human resources. In other words, mutual aid is just as relevant to organizational committees and social-action groups, children's activity or sports groups, and political coalitions, for example, as it is to groups formed expressly for therapeutic or socialization purposes of helping.

THE CONDITIONS FOR MUTUAL-AID PRACTICE

What about the fact that we practice in so many different types of settings? Can mutual aid be developed in any setting, in any group, under any conditions? Yes. It is true that work with a wide variety of groups in different settings demands many areas of content and setting-specific expertise; but it is also true that enough generic group-work skills have been identified to help maximize the mutual-aid potential of any group with which we work. Henry Ford used to say, "Coming together is a beginning. Keeping together is progress. Working together is success." Although Ford was referring specifically to corporate teamwork when he said this, the principles to which he alluded most certainly speak to the value of mutual aid.

Mutual aid happens at many intensities and in many ways, both during the life of one group and across different groups (Gitterman and Shulman 1994). Furthermore, some groups experience all of the dynamics of mutual aid (see Chapter 2), while others experience only some aspects. Although one group may experience mutual aid very intensely, others may experience it to a lesser degree. A reminiscence group of elderly persons may experience *all in the same boat* more than it does *mutual demand,* for example. Or individuals in groups for disabled or severely ill persons may be so highly preoccupied with their own health or well-being that they can interact only at a fairly superficial level. Or a group for persons with mental illness may engage in much *debate* while another group experiences this dynamic less than *mutual support*. Does this mean that mutual aid is not playing a significant role in these groups? Absolutely not! Does it mean that one of these groups is experiencing more or even a more "serious" level of mutual aid than another? Again, absolutely not! What these nuances reflect is that mutual aid comes in many shapes and sizes, and a group need not experience the full range of possibilities or interact at only the deepest affective levels in order to qualify as a mutual-aid system. Just as J. S. Bach wrote some "lovely little pieces" for early piano study in addition to his architectural masterpieces, there exists a wide range and variety of and potential for mutual aid. We might not think that Bach's "little" piano pieces are as musically intense as his B Minor Mass, but we would nevertheless not suggest that they are not music. Likewise, mutual aid may come from intense debate, but it can also come from a better understanding of difference, a pat on the back, a glance of understanding, or a quiet but comfortable sense of belonging. Thus, all groups have the potential for mutual aid; the central issue for practice is that whenever an opportunity for it arises, the worker should be able to recognize it and help members seize that opportunity.

On the other hand, a few conditions do need to coexist for mutual aid. To begin with, we need to be willing to consider ourselves as only one of many possible helpers in the group (Middleman and Wood 1990a). It is not by accident that social work with groups refers to the practitioner as a *worker* rather than a *leader* (Trecker 1955). Yes, the practitioner brings his or her own expertise to the group, but so does every other participant in some unique way, and it is those areas of expertise that form the basis for mutual aid. The more we assume the role of the group's only or even primary helper, therefore, the more difficult we make it for members to identify the strengths they might use to help themselves and one another.

Mutual aid also requires a *democratic-humanistic* culture (Glassman and Kates 1990), in which everyone has a real say in the group's affairs and in which everyone's feelings are taken into account when decisions are made. Hence, the practitioner also needs to be willing to share authority with the other participants so that whatever leadership skills members possess can be used to the group's advantage. How do we share our authority? Very simply, we encourage and help members take part in all of the group's decision-making processes (see Chapter 7).

Furthermore, members need to have some capacity to communicate and interact with one another (Newstetter 1935; Trecker 1955; Hartford 1964; Schwartz 1976; Breton 1990; Middleman 1982; Middleman and Wood 1990a; Shulman 1999). Therefore, although we would not prevent a person with limited communication skills from participating, since helping people develop such skills is one of the great benefits of group membership, neither would we expect persons with no capacity to interact, verbally or nonverbally, to come together for purposes of mutual aid.

In addition, it is important that the group have a purpose, a common cause that binds members' individual goals to one another (Kurland 1978; Lowy 1976; Galinsky and Schopler 1977; Papell and Rothman 1980; Northen and Kurland 2001; Glassman and Kates 1990). Only through a sense of community or we-ness will members come to acknowledge and accept one another as potential sources of help. In fact, the precise nature of their common cause matters less than the fact that they have one, since mutual aid can be useful for achieving all types of tasks and goals, be they labeled support, insight, action, education, or recreation. True, conscious and specific attention to process may slow down task achievement to some extent, but we have only to look at Japanese industrial protocol to see how mutual aid in action on a large scale benefits all of the participants in production-oriented ventures. We have all heard the old joke that a camel is a horse designed by a committee. Clearly, that was no mutual-aid committee!

Finally, no matter how genuinely we may desire it, mutual aid requires group-specific skill. Only through the purposeful use of such skill can we help a *group* become a *Group,* as Margaret Hartford (1978) put it. If we do not have the skill to attend to group process or, as Middleman and Wood (1990b) state it, to attend to the *groupness* of a group, we may end up doing more harm than good (Galinsky and Schopler 1977; Hartford 1978; Tropp 1978; Meddin 1986; Glassman and Kates 1990). Thus, we need skill that goes beyond what we use in individual work—skill to help the vision of mutual aid take on real-world characteristics.

Thus, if we relinquish the role of sole or even primary helper, if we encourage a democratic-humanistic culture, if we work with persons who can interact with their peers, if the group has a common purpose, and if we have group-specific skill, we can help any group actualize its particular mutual-aid potential. Setting and population provide us with a framework in which we need to carry out our planning process, yes (see Chapter 3); but in the end, as Clara Kaiser (1958) argues, mutual-aid practice is more a question of how we approach our work than where we do it.

One problem with many approaches to working with groups today is that they do not, in fact, attend specifically to group process. In fact, even those who claim to believe in mutual aid still tend to focus on individuals in the group (Rooney et al. 1981; Birnbaum et al. 1989; Middleman and Wood 1990b; Wayne and Garland 1990; Steinberg 1992). However, labeled long ago as *aggregational therapy of individuals* (Hartford 1978) and, more recently, as *casework in a group* (Kurland and Salmon 1992), this type of work is actually "mutual-aid-less"! (Kurland and Salmon 1992, p. 8).

Perhaps practitioners misunderstand the concept of mutual aid. Or perhaps they lack the skill to bring it about. In either case, when we merely carry out individual work against a group backdrop, we attend neither to the quality nor the capacity of the material at hand (Phillips 1957).

IMPLICATIONS FOR PRACTICE

A mutual-aid approach to group work carries many implications for practice. We need to

- understand the theoretical basis for conceptualizing groups as mutual-aid systems and the many different dynamics, or facets, of mutual aid;
- adopt a mindset in which we are neither the be-all nor end-all of any group process;

- take the time to set the stage for mutual aid by specifically working toward group goals and norms that most promote mutual aid;
- appreciate the relationship between group development and mutual aid;
- understand how our participation influences group process and progress;
- know how to set into play and keep in motion the kind of problem-solving process that most harnesses a group's mutual-aid capacity;
- understand the impact of group autonomy on its ability to develop mutual aid as well as the impact of its decision-making process on climate;
- help each group reach beyond its particular obstacles to its own unique mutual-aid potential;
- help a group discover its potential for common ground, help it reach that common ground, and help it use its differences constructively; and
- adopt a consumer-based and process-oriented framework for evaluating the group's success as a mutual-aid system.

HOW THIS BOOK IS ORGANIZED

This book has thirteen chapters, eight of which are devoted to a key component of basic mutual-aid practice and collectively guide the reader through the fundamentals of thinking about practice with groups from a mutual-aid point of view to actually evaluating a group's success as a mutual-aid system. Four chapters, new to this edition, describe and discuss the special challenges to mutual-aid practice with groups whose characteristics do not resemble those of the classic system upon which most of the fundamental theories, principles, and skills are based.

Chapter 1 offers a *theoretical justification* for using mutual aid as a framework for practice by reviewing the historical development of mutual aid in social work with groups, by discussing its role in social work with groups today, and by articulating the professional mind-set needed for helping any group become and function as a mutual-aid system.

Chapter 2 discusses in some detail the different facets, or *dynamics,* of mutual aid. The particular group-specific skills that best help set into motion and sustain each of the dynamics are also identified.

Chapter 3 examines the impact of *pregroup planning* on a group's ability to develop a mutual-aid climate and identifies specific pregroup planning skills as well, giving particular attention to the concept of group purpose.

Chapter 4 identifies those *early group goals and norms* that best set the stage for mutual aid. It also describes the ways in which working toward certain goals and helping the group to establish certain norms helps create a climate for mutual aid in the new group. The chapter also identifies group-specific skills at our disposal for helping a group work toward certain goals and establish certain norms.

Chapter 5 describes the relationship between *group development* and mutual aid, with a special focus on how the passage of time generally governs a group's ability to make use of the dynamics. The worker's role and expectations are also addressed in this chapter.

Chapter 6 proposes a shift in thinking about and in approaching the use of group time for *individual problem solving* and offers cases in point and counterpoint to make explicit the implications for practice of such a shift.

Chapter 7 discusses the relationship between the worker's exercise of *authority* and a group's capacity to develop mutual aid. This chapter also identifies group-specific skills for helping a group both assume responsibility for its affairs and carry out its decision-making processes according to *democratic-humanistic* values (Glassman and Kates 1990).

Based upon the assumptions that (1) the members of any group inevitably bring with them some manner of *difference* and (2) that those differences can help them think about new ways of being and doing, Chapter 8 presents a few keys for helping a group use its differences to work toward, rather than away from, its mutual-aid potential.

In recognition of the role and value of and need for time-limited practice in many settings today, Chapter 9 outlines the special considerations of catalyzing mutual aid in *single-session groups,* and Chapter 10 speaks to working with *short-term groups.* Each chapter identifies group-specific skills for working with the respective systems.

Chapter 11 describes and discusses the special obstacles in helping *open-ended groups* develop and maintain a mutual-aid rhythm in spite of constantly-changing faces and offers a number of group-specific skills for helping each *groupe du jour* realize its unique potential.

Based on the growing use of *very large groups* in some settings, Chapter 12 describes the special obstacles to mutual aid in working with large systems and identifies a number of group-specific skills to help promote a climate that is both *humanistic* and *democratic* (Glassman and Kates 1990).

Finally, Chapter 13 proposes a consumer-based and process-oriented approach to *evaluating the group's success* as a mutual-aid system. Group-specific skills are identified for helping group members carry out that process.

RECOMMENDED FURTHER READING

Falck, H. (1988). *Social work: The Membership Perspective.* New York: Springer.

Finn, J. (1995). Computer-based self-help groups: A new resource to supplement support groups. *Social Work with Groups* 18(1):109-117.

Gitterman, A. and Shulman, L., eds. (1994). *Mutual Aid Groups and the Life Cycle.* New York: Columbia University Press.

Glassman, U. and Kates, L. (1990). *Group Work: A Humanistic Approach.* Newbury Park, CA: Sage Publications.

Heckman, T., Kalichman, S., Roffman, R., Sikkema, K., Heckman, B., Somlai, A., and Walker, J. (1999). A telephone-delivered coping improvement intervention for persons living with HIV-AIDS in rural areas. *Social Work with Groups* 21(4):49-62.

Kaslyn, M. (1999). Telephone group work: Challenges for practice. *Social Work with Groups* 22(1):63-78.

Meier, A. (2000). Offering social support via the Internet: A case study of an online support group for social workers. *Journal of Technology in Human Services* 17(2/3):237-266.

Meier, A., Galinksy, M., and Rounds, K. (1995). Telephone support groups for caregivers of persons with AIDS. *Social Work with Groups* 18(1):99-108.

Middleman, R. and Wood, G. G. (1990). From social group work to social work with groups. *Social Work with Groups* 13(3):3-20.

Regan, S. (2002). Building bridges over troubled waters: A bridging model for teleconferencing group counseling. In *Social Work with Groups: Mining the Gold,* eds. S. Henry, J. East, and C. Schmitz, pp. 119-130. Binghamton, NY: The Haworth Press.

Schopler, J., Galinsky, M., and Abell, M. (1997). Creating community through telephone and computer groups: Theoretical and practice perspectives. *Social Work with Groups* 20(4):35-54.

Schwartz, W. and Zalba, S. (1971). *The Practice of Group Work.* New York: Columbia University Press.

Wiener, L., Spencer, E., Davidson, R., and Fair, C. (1993). National telephone support groups: A new avenue toward psychosocial support for HIV-infected children and their families. *Social Work with Groups* 16(3):55-71.

Chapter 1

The Mutual-Aid Approach in Social Work with Groups

KEY CONCEPTS OF THIS CHAPTER

Common Cause/Group Purpose
Communication
Dual Focus
Group Building
Group Climate
Group-Specific Skillful Practice
Harnessing Strengths
Holistic Use of Groups
Mutual Aid
Mutual-Aid Mindset
Psychosocial Practice with Groups
Purposeful Use of Self
Shared Authority
Strength-Centered Practice

* * *

Although not the first to identify mutual aid as the key to social group work, William Schwartz (1961) was the first to introduce the term into social work. By the time he adopted the term, however, not only had the concept long been recognized as central to social group work, it had been used in other fields as well. For example, mutual aid had already been used as a framework for thinking about biological evolution (Wilson 1979), as well as for analyzing social advancement (Kropotkin 1908). "Beside the 'law of Mutual Struggle,'" Petr Kropotkin wrote,

> there is in Nature the "law of Mutual Aid," which, for the success of the struggle for life, and especially for the progressive evolution of the species, is far more important than the law of mutual contest. *I* obviously do not deny the struggle for existence, but I maintain that the progressive development of the animal kingdom, and especially of mankind, is favored much more by mutual support than by mutual struggle. (p. *x*)

Mutual aid is not a fabrication of social work; nor is it a modern passing notion. The idea of people helping one another has been acknowledged for a long time as a human dynamic of some biological and social import.

In terms of professional work with groups, a review of the literature reveals very clearly that mutual aid has always been at the heart of social group work practice. (See, for example, Breton 1990; Coyle 1949; Gitterman 1989; Gitterman and Shulman 1994; Glassman and Kates 1990; Hartford 1964, 1971, 1978; Konopka 1964, 1983; Kurland and Salmon 1992; Middleman 1978, 1987; Middleman and Wood 1990a,b; Newstetter 1935; Northen and Kurland 2001; Papell and Rothman 1980; Phillips 1964; Schwartz and Zalba 1971; Shulman 1999; Wilson and Ryland 1949.) In the latter part of the nineteenth century and the early years of the twentieth, for example, settlement houses used mutual aid to help groups of immigrants acclimate themselves to new ways of life that included new fights and new expectations by helping them help one another meet all manner of social, educational, vocational, and recreational needs. Today, mutual aid is acknowledged as the hallmark of social work with groups, as we have come to see that helping people engage in mutual aid meets several of the profession's most powerful mandates for practice. By attending to both personal and interpersonal needs, we carry out its mandate for a psychosocial perspective (Glassman and Kates 1990; Northen and Kurland 2001; Papell and Rothman 1980). By attending to the group as a system as well as each individual in the group, our practice reflects a holistic use of groups (Newstetter 1935; Shulman 1999)—a duality of focus that greatly distinguishes social work with groups from other approaches (Glassman and Kates 1990; Hartford 1964; Middleman and Wood 1990a; Shulman 1999), Finally, by focusing on people's strengths instead of limitations, the mutual-aid approach reflects a strength-centered way of helping people (Breton 1990; Glassman and Kates 1990; Middleman 1978; Newstetter 1935). In fact, group work is particularly well suited for meeting this last mandate, for in direct contrast to casework protocol, which requires that people assume and maintain a help-seeking position, mutual aid requires that they exercise and extend their strengths to help others as well as themselves.

MUTUAL AID DEFINED AND DESCRIBED

So, what exactly is mutual aid? Mutual aid tends to be so misunderstood that we should begin with what it is not. Mutual aid is not a process of problem identification followed by the gift of advice—an all-too-common phenomenon of so-called helping groups. Composed of several possible dynamics (Shulman 1999), mutual aid can be said to have many different faces or looks (see Chapter 2).

Often, when people think of mutual aid, they think of it as a process, and even more specifically as a particular kind of problem-solving process, but while mutual aid is a process, problem solving is only one of its dynamics; there are many other dynamics as well, such as *sharing information* and *mutual support.* When one group member offers a comember a simple touch of comfort or nod of understanding it reflects a dynamic or dimension of mutual aid. When a group comes together as a force of advocacy or change, that is mutual aid. When members talk about issues considered taboo in other groups, that is mutual aid. When a group provides a safe haven for its members to explore differences and to try new ways of thinking, being, or doing, that too reflects mutual aid.

In addition to being a process, mutual aid is a result. To the extent that it is comforting to be with others who share common concerns, when group members realize that their comembers do share common feelings, needs, or concerns, for example, that result reflects mutual aid. Or to the extent that any one member's concerns have been resolved through the group's collective problem-solving efforts, that result may be said to reflect mutual aid. To the extent that group members emerge from some process having gained greater insight into themselves or a greater capacity for empathy, that result is mutual aid. Or to the extent that one member's cause has been advanced through collective social action, that result, too, is mutual aid.

We have a substantial philosophical and epistemological foundation for conceptualizing mutual aid as the key to social work practice with groups. And although implications for practice have been developed from a variety of perspectives (such as composition, stage theory, self-determination, communication, decision making, relationships, group building, structure, or a social worker's skill, to name but a few), all theoretical fingers point to mutual aid as cause and effect of social work with groups. As cause, mutual aid is why we use groups as a helping medium, why we plan our work with groups the way we do, and why we intervene in group process the way we do. As effect, mutual aid is the result of our interventions; that is, it is what people experience as a result of having participated in the group. In essence, then, mutual aid is why we do what we do, and it is what happens as a result of what we do.

"But there's more to social work with groups than mutual aid, isn't there?" someone once asked me. Still a doctoral student in search of a dissertation, I had not yet fully digested the vast body of social group-work literature and so, not overly secure of my position, I responded, "Oh, of course." I still regret that response, for I have come to believe that exactly the opposite is true—that mutual aid is, in fact, the sine qua non of work with groups. In one form or another and at various levels of intensity, the opportunity for mutual aid exists from the moment a group meets ("Where do we hang up our coats?") to the moment it ends ("Must we say good-bye?"). At the same time, mutual aid does not come about automatically. It needs communication. It needs a certain kind of climate. And it is most easily actualized in groups that are formed around a common cause.

Mutual Aid and Communication

Before mutual aid can be a result, it must reflect a process. And because mutual aid occurs through direct member-to-member contact, group members must have both some capacity and an opportunity to communicate and interact with one another. Further, they must have the freedom to do so if and when they believe they have a contribution to make to the process.

Not all forms of group process are conducive to mutual aid, as Middleman and Wood (1990b) point out. In fact, we can often gauge the value assigned to mutual aid by the way in which the members of a group do interact. For example, when the worker talks primarily to members individually, one by one, they are effectively denied any opportunity to talk with one another spontaneously and directly. This classic didactic style, labeled a *maypole* pattern of communication by Middleman and Wood (1990b), reflects the antithesis of the process most conducive to mutual aid. Or when group members are asked to take turns talking in relation to any given subject, for example, they may have occasion to respond to what others have said, but they are still denied the spontaneity so crucial to mutual aid. No matter if ideas spark other ideas, in other words, group members must simply "hold that thought" until it is their turn to talk. Thus, we would say that this style of communicating, labeled *round robin* by Middleman and Wood (1990b), also closes many windows of opportunity for mutual aid. The hot-seat syndrome (Middleman and Wood 1990b), which has also been coined *casework in a group* (Kurland and Salmon 1992), can unfold into two slightly different scenarios, neither of which promotes mutual aid. In the first scenario, the worker engages in dialogue with a particular group member about that person's issues while others listen and presumably learn through osmosis. Because there is little room for member-to-member interaction in this scenario, there is little occasion for mutual aid. Sometimes, on the other hand, group members are also engaged in this process, and while this latter scenario may promote interaction and spontaneity, the quality of interaction can often become, as many group-shy people would undoubtedly testify, harshly confrontational and less than helpful.

The only communication style that fully promotes mutual aid is a free-floating one (Middleman and Wood 1990b). By establishing a norm of speaking when there is something to say regarding to the subject at hand, a free-floating pattern of group interaction permits members to both interact directly with one another and to contribute spontaneously to the group's discussion.

Of course some room exists for groups to use a variety of communication styles, the choice of the moment depending on the developmental needs and skills of individual members (e.g., age), the needs and skills of the group as a system (e.g., how long the group has been together), and on the nature of the particular issues at hand (e.g., the type and intensity of the issues under discussion). It might not make sense for a problem-solving discussion to be carried out in round-robin fashion, for example, but it might make sense for the members of a new group to use such a format for introductions.

Thus, although there may be moments in which other patterns of interaction make some sense, the free-floating pattern is still the most conducive to mutual aid as a group norm.

The Mutual-Aid Climate

Although group members need freedom to interact, the quality of that interaction also needs to be conducive to mutual aid. It may be the quantity of interaction that sets the stage for mutual aid, but it is its quality that sets the tone for it. It is the quality of its processes that sets the mutual-aid system apart from, on the one hand, the social tea group in which politeness reigns supreme and, on the other hand, other types of so-called helping groups in which personal attack reigns supreme. In fact, as Lang (1986) claims, it is the very quality of group interaction that determines whether people will be able to build a community or whether they are destined to remain in a state of mere aggregation.

Therefore, the climate of mutual aid may be said to be one of balance. Scales are weighted on one side with freedom to express real feelings and ideas, but they are equally weighted on the other with an obligation to respect the feelings and ideas of others. That is, we want group members to feel safe to express their honest opinions and attitudes without the fear of being so harshly judged that having done so once they never dare to do so again, but we would also ask that they listen to what others have to say with an open mind and sensitivity. A mutual-aid climate is generous in spirit, then, but its generosity is tempered with the demand for serious attention to those issues of common cause around which the group was formed in the first place.

The mutual-aid climate is also one in which the need and desire for mutuality, cooperation, and companionship is balanced with the need and desire for individuality. Thus, while we discourage one-upmanship due to its inherent counterproductivity to community building, for example, we would still recognize, appreciate, and use group members' individual skills to help strengthen the group as a whole.

One of the best uses for a group is to help people try out new ways of being, thinking, and doing. Thus, the mutual-aid climate is also one of creativity. Brainstorming is encouraged. All possible courses of action, no matter how implausible, are entertained, and through such activities as role play, psychodrama, various art forms, or even discussion, group members explore ways of being that make them uncomfortable or about which they disagree or they adopt positions and counter positions in their struggle to locate their own way. At the same time, since the creation of new possibilities is always carried out with real-world living in mind, mutual aid also demands a measure of reality testing so that the passage into new territories is always balanced with an eye to real implications and real consequences.

Finally, the mutual-aid climate balances structure with flexibility. If the group decides that its purpose as originally defined no longer reflects its common bond, for example, it needs to have the freedom to redefine its bond so its process does not become "beside the point." Mutual aid is most likely to develop in a group with a clearly defined purpose, therefore, but a mutual-aid system still requires the freedom to change its purpose should a redirection seem to be in order. Or should we be prepared to help the group carry out a particular manner of content or activity, for example, only to discover that members have changed their minds in favor of another form of content, we need to be flexible enough to entertain that possibility. Thus, although mutual aid requires a framework for practice composed of such factors as nature of practice setting, membership needs, group purpose, composition, and number, length, and timing of meetings, it also requires the freedom to evaluate that framework and to entertain the possibility of change.

The Need for Common Cause

Over the years one of the most pervasive myths about group work has been, as Margaret Hartford stated it in 1978, that "if a worker collects an aggregate, that is, gets people together in the same place, and responds to them individually in the presence of each other, something significant and helpful will occur" (p. 9). Experience working with groups and analysis of that work has taught us, however, that although something significant and helpful may indeed occur under those circumstances, it usually does so haphazardly. Individual work on the part of the practitioner in the presence of others may be an acceptable norm in some groups, therefore, but if we want to establish a norm of mutual aid, we need to take a more planned approach. We need to offer new group members a common denominator that is both clear and compelling enough to draw them together and keep them invested in helping one another. We need to offer them a common cause, or, as it will be referred to from now on, a group purpose.

The concept of group purpose is central to the social group work method (Galinsky and Schopler 1977; Glassman and Kates 1990; Hartford 1978; Kurland 1978; Lowy 1976; Northen and Kurland 2001). It represents the mission of the group as a system, and reaches beyond the scope of individual goals. Only when a group purpose has been established does a basis exist upon which members can develop mutual-aid relationships. In fact, mutual aid is less a reflection of the goodness of fit between method and population than a reflection of the goodness of fit between group members' needs and the group's purpose. Too often, however, group purpose is perceived as a relatively amorphous idea around which individuals collect none too neatly to realize their own loosely formulated goals, rather than as the powerful nucleus that, like the atom, tightly binds group members to one another and around which all things should happen. The problem of not having a group purpose, then, is that individual goal achievement takes center stage and, as a result, the group simply becomes a context for *casework in a group* instead of one for group work.

Although purpose is tentatively identified through individual dialogues with potential members about their needs and concerns, it is actualized as a group concept through *en groupe* dialogue or, as Middleman and Wood (1996) have coined it, "multilogue." That is, it is brought to life for the group through in-group discussion about the commonality of members' needs and desires. Without this kind of dialogue, they are left to divine or fantasize about how they are each related to the others, the essence of what brings them together in this particular group stays unclear, and the group has difficulty locating a basis for group building. In short, the very foundation for mutual aid remains vague.

Speaking about the importance of group purpose might cause some to argue that it is "Standard Practice 101" to ask the members of a group to discuss their needs and desires when they first meet. But a purposeful and specific dialogue about how those individual needs and desires bind group members in common cause does not appear to be standard practice. The fact that so many practitioners articulate content (*what* members will talk about) when asked to describe group purpose (*why* the group will do what it will do) suggests that the concept of purpose is often misunderstood altogether.

THE MUTUAL-AID MIND-SET

From the very first group meeting, the social worker thinks about working herself out of a job. That is to say she enables the group to increase its autonomy to its greatest potential. Although therapy can be the content . . . some clinical work will fall outside the realm of social work, especially if the focus of the practitioner is limited to the treatment of individuals—casework in a group. (Middleman and Wood 1990a, p. 11)

The *mutual* dimension of mutual aid reflects the belief that when we help others, we also help ourselves by giving ourselves the pleasure of confirming and sharing ways of being and doing that have served us well or by providing ourselves with opportunities to review and improve those that have not served us so well. The mutual-aid mind-set, therefore, conceptualizes the group as a forum for helping people do just that—for helping them review their own needs and goals as they help others do the same and for helping them discover ways in which they can in fact be of help to one another. It expects that group members will contribute to the process whenever they believe they have something to contribute. It also expects that they will take from it whenever they believe there is something to take. Inherent in this position is the belief that everyone in the group brings expertise of some kind and that it is the right of each and every participant to integrally affect the shape and direction of the group (Breton 1989, 1990; Coyle 1937, 1949; Galinsky and Schopler 1977; Gitterman 1989; Glassman and Kates 1983, 1990; Lowy 1978; Middleman and Wood 1990a; Newstetter 1935; Northen and Kurland 2001; Schwartz and Zalba 1971; Trecker 1955). The worker is not seen as either the central helper or authority figure in the group. Rather, his or her primary task is conceptualized as helping the group engage in ongoing assessment of its affairs while providing the framework within which it may or must operate (Phillips 1957).

The existence of an inextricable interdependence between people's need for individual expression and their need for membership is also presupposed by the mutual-aid mind-set (Breton 1989; Coyle 1937; Falck 1989; Newstetter 1935; Schwartz 1961). Thus, while mutual-aid practice attends to members as individuals, it also attends to them as members of a system. We make the group our second client, as Shulman (1999) puts it. In that way, all of its resources—individual and collective, personal and interpersonal—may be exploited to its mutual-aid advantage. How do we do that? How do we actually make the group as a system a client? We use our eyes and ears. We use one eye and ear to monitor how well each individual in the group is doing, and we use the other eye and ear to monitor how well the group is doing as a system—that is, how well it is working toward its purpose and the extent to which it is using its mutual-aid potential to do so.

THE PRIMARY FUNCTIONS OF MUTUAL-AID PRACTICE

Working with groups from a mutual-aid point of view involves three primary functions. The first is to help members identify the strengths they bring to the group (harnessing strengths). The second is to help them use those strengths to build a community conducive to mutual aid (group building). The third is to teach them to engage in mutual aid (teaching purposeful use of self).

Harnessing Strengths

> Strengthen me by sympathizing with my strength, not my weakness.

> A. Bronson Alcott, "Sympathy," 1877

To a great extent, our approach to practice reflects our approach to life in general. Do we usually see the glass as half empty or half full? If we usually see the glass as half empty, we tend to devote our energy to mourning what is gone, to fretting over what is missing. If we see it as half full, on the other hand, we devote our energy to appreciating what we still have.

Our practice can also focus on what is missing—that is, on people's limitations, on their weaknesses, on what they do not have enough of, in which case we concentrate on what is wrong with members, on what is broken, on what needs to be "fixed." Or it can focus on what people have going for them—that is, their talents, special skills, and personal ego-based and other strengths that they might use to their own advantage and to the advantage of others. In short, it can focus on what people have going for them, on those ways of being and doing that help them successfully negotiate their world. This is the approach of mutual-aid practice.

We are sometimes hard pressed to discern a person's strengths, but everyone has something working to his or her advantage, even if it is as simple as a sense of humor or as basic as the ability to survive in a seemingly indifferent world. By focusing on developing and exploiting those strengths, mutual-aid practice helps to reinforce those skills that contribute to both personal and interpersonal well-being while offering the possibility of learning new skills as well.

Sometimes, of course, qualities that might be considered strengths become woven into the fabric of our character such that they become faults, as it were, or to a degree of which they get in our way. For example, with people who are generous to a fault, generosity nears the point of self-sacrifice, while some people seem so sensitive and fragile that we are afraid of engaging them in real talk. Still, with a bit of reframing, many such characteristics can be considered strengths, and if we do not adopt a strength-centered approach to practice, we will inevitably end up frustrated over what is missing or cannot be done instead of appreciating what is present or can be done.

When we consider people's habits of thinking, feeling, being, and doing, then, we need to ask how these might be positive, useful, or helpful to the group. How might they be conceptualized as strengths rather than limitations?

Take the case of the so-called talkative group member. We can regard that person as a monopolizer and wish he or she would be quiet, or we can interpret his or her behavior as demonstrating a willingness to participate. Being willing to participate, to venture forth and risk the judgment of others is a strength when we commit to a group; not only can we now regard this trait as a strength but we can also, by using it as a model, exploit it as a strength or skill for the whole group.

From the other side of the coin, consider the quiet member. Rather than regard him or her as unwilling to participate, for example, we can reconsider this person as appearing to have good listening skills or even good sharing skills. The ability to listen in a group or to share are also strengths, thus we have at our disposal even more strengths to exploit to the group's advantage. Although the group can provide an opportunity for this person to model his or her ability to listen or to share, it can also provide an opportunity to learn from the person who is not afraid to talk. The result? Mutual aid!

What about people who seem to create conflict in groups? Can we really turn the tendency to create friction into a strength? Yes, in fact, we can. Although conflict is often taboo in groups, it is not unusual for the exploration of difference to be the very thing that helps a group deepen the level of its interaction and expand its potential for mutual aid. It may well be that some people need help to express themselves in ways that get their messages across to others in a form that doesn't put people on the defensive, but both the courage to be different and the courage to express that difference can certainly be regarded as strengths. Only when we are prepared to do such reframing will we begin to be prepared for mutual-aid practice.

What does it mean to harness strengths? It means that when we invite people to join a group, we ask that in addition to using membership as a need-meeting strategy, they also commit their personal talents to building the group's pool of resources in order to help others meet their needs as well. When we identify and encourage the contribution of those talents, we say that we harness them. As noted previously, even the differences that inevitably arise among group members can be harnessed and used as sources of strength (Glassman and Kates 1990; Papell and Rothman 1980).

This strength-centered approach requires that all of the participants, not just the worker, be acknowledged and appreciated as human resources. In addition to acknowledging the capacity of others to be helpful, then, we also share our authority over group affairs so that everyone may contribute to and take from the group according to his or her needs and abilities. In this way (in direct contrast to process that focuses only on what members need) people are given the opportunity to experience, as Margot Breton (1990) puts it, the "fulfillment and deep delight" (p. 27) that comes from knowing that they contribute to as well as take from their environment. As a result, they become better members of all groups to which they belong.

Group Building

> We must indeed all hang together, or, most assuredly, we shall all hang separately.
>
> Benjamin Franklin

Shulman (1999) identifies one of the obstacles to mutual aid as the difficulty people have identifying their self-interest with the interests of others. As a result, one of the primary tasks of mutual-aid practice is to help group members come to feel a sense of their *we-ness,* and since new members are likely to feel unsure about whether or not their real selves, as it were, will be accepted by others, our early goals are to help them accept one another, help them identify the ways in which they might help one another, and help them develop their *we-ness.*

How do we help people come to develop a sense of *we-ness?* Essentially, we do it by helping them identify those issues, needs, concerns, desires, and goals that will bind them as a community. In the language of mutual aid, this process is called *group building* (Papell and Rothman 1980).

Group building involves two tasks. The first is to promote a sense of community by using every occasion to point out all of the commonalities that exist among members. In early sessions, for example, we use skills such as *visual scanning, reaching for information links,* and *reaching for affective links* to emphasize what group members have in common, and help them discover their common ground. Later, when the bond of commonality is strong enough to withstand differences, we might *reach for and promote variety, demand some reality testing, support respectful confrontation,* and in other ways help the group accept and integrate its differences as well as its commonalities for purposes of mutual aid.

The second task is to encourage group autonomy by sharing as many leadership functions with the group as it can support (Middleman and Wood 1990a). Every time there is a decision to be made that affects the group, we turn that responsibility over to the group—even, as Middleman and Wood suggest, when members appeal to our supposedly superior knowledge. We do this out of a sense of practice ethics as well as logic. Our sense of ethics suggests that when we ask members to commit to the group as a mutual-aid venture, we do not have a right to ask them to partialize that commitment. We cannot say, "Hold it! You should *help* one another, but you may *not* take part in deciding what this group should do and how it should do it." Our sense of logic tells us that if we espouse the philosophical belief that two heads are better than one, then we need to put this philosophy into practice whenever the occasion presents itself. When we ask people to contribute their strengths to the group so that it may develop into a mutual-aid system, then, we are essentially asking for the *full* participation of *each* member in *all* aspects of group life.

The notion of shared leadership as a desirable group norm is not new. As early as 1937 Grace Coyle recognized its value to mutual aid, while in 1955, Harleigh Trecker declared that the label *worker* rather than *leader* should be used purposefully to confirm the desirability of and potential for leadership flexibility.

Throughout the years group building has been conceptualized in the following ways: as helping to *set the stage or to provide the suitable environment* (Newstetter 1935); as *helping group interaction as well as activities contribute to growth* (Coyle 1949); as *helping a group take charge of its corporate affairs* (Wilson and Ryland 1949); as setting in motion a process *with the greatest degree of consideration for and utilization of the quality and capacity of the material*

(Phillips 1957); as *helping group members collaborate in decision making* (Northen and Kurland 2001); as *attending to the groupness of the group* (Middleman and Wood 1990a); as *furthering linkages between members* (Papell and Rothman 1980); and as *enabling the group to become a Group* (Hartford 1964). Regardless of context, however, be it planning, stages, norms, communication patterns, decision making, program, or membership rights and responsibilities, what remains clear is that group building is central to helping people develop a mutual-aid system.

Teaching Purposeful Use of Self

Know Thyself.

Inscription, Oracle of Delphi

Mutual aid occurs through a particular process called purposeful use of self, a process intended to prevent people from engaging in that all-too-intellectual and empathically effete process of advice giving so prevalent "helping" groups today—a process to which many of us are highly allergic.

Purposeful use of self can occur in many contexts. Regardless of context, however, it always connotes the same thing: the intentional use of who one is, what one knows, what one has experienced, and what one feels. Even the circus clown who trips and tumbles on purpose, claims Virginia Robinson (1942), is engaging in purposeful use of self when he does it at just the right moment to make people laugh.

There are two dimensions to the purposeful use of self. The first, self-reflection, refers to the process of thinking about one's own life and experiences. This dimension helps group members reflect upon their own ways of being and prevents them from focusing solely on those of others. In other words, by causing them to search within, it forces them to find and make connections, helping to put them into the same boat. The second dimension, self-reference, refers to the process of talking about one's own life and experiences. By sharing their own stories with one another—both those that confirm jobs well done and those that identify jobs perhaps not so well done—self-reference helps group members discover the various ways in which they can be of help to one another.

Purposeful use of self sets into play what might be referred to as a *me-too* syndrome, a story-sharing process through which members make use of their personal experiences as gateways to insight, empathy, and innovation (see Chapter 6). Although we are often irked by people who constantly respond to us with, "Oh yeah? Me too!" it is precisely this norm that prevents a group from entering the *aggregational therapy of individuals* (Hartford 1978) or into *casework in a group*. It is essential to mutual aid, therefore, that story-sharing be refrained from reflecting a process of egocentricism and guided toward providing a way for people to work toward common ground.

The *me-too* syndrome is set into motion through analogic thinking, as group members seek personal analogies to the situations or feelings they are hearing about. They may not always be able to reach back to analogous situations, but they can always reach analogous feelings. Through the story-sharing process, group members have opportunities to clarify (and even change) their own feelings and attitudes, achieve a better understanding of one another, and develop empathy for others. In sum, purposeful use of self is a process through which people revisit their histories and use their own lives and experiences to contribute a variety of perspectives for view and review. And while previous success stories are confirmed on the one hand, opportunities to learn new skills are provided on the other, through the reconsideration or reworking of failures as personal stories. In either case, mutual aid occurs.

THE NOTION OF GROUP-SPECIFIC SKILLFUL PRACTICE

Helen Phillips (1954) stated that although she was most fearful of skill without dedication, she also feared dedication without skill. We too need to guard against the temptation to believe that good will is enough to bring about a mutual-aid process. Neither an intellectual understanding nor even a heartfelt appreciation for the power of mutual aid is enough to develop a mutual-aid approach to practice. If we want our interventions (i.e., our attempts to influence group process) to encourage mutual aid, then our practice needs to be group-specific skillful.

What does it mean to be group-specific skillful? Grace Coyle (1959) states: "It seems to me that the primary skill [of the group worker] is the ability to establish a relationship with a group as a group . . . as well as to become a part of the relationships and to affect them" (p. 100).

Group-specific skillful practice has two components, then, according to Coyle. First, since it is the multiplicity of relationships in a group that quantitatively and qualitatively influence its capacity for mutual aid, group-specific skillful practice consists of relationship-building skills. Second, since we know that groups can exert tremendous negative as well as positive pressure on their members, it also consists of skill at influencing the nature and direction of those relationships.

In spite of evidence to the contrary, however, a few myths about working with groups still abound. One is that group workers are merely "naturals," a myth that leads some to believe that work with groups cannot be learned. Another is that if you know how to work with individuals, then you know how to work with groups, which suggests that work with groups need not be learned. Finally, another myth implies that groups are simply for "happy campers" (i.e., only for recreational purposes), a myth that devalues the therapeutic potential of group membership altogether. The truth is that a substantial body of knowledge belonging to group work has existed for quite awhile. As Margaret Hartford (1978) pointed out in her separation of facts from fancies about group work to those who would listen:

> It is a fact that groups can and do exist, that there is a body of knowledge that can be understood, and that understanding this knowledge can lead to planned and deliberate behavior on the part of the social worker. . . . This is not a myth, nor a fancy. . . . The knowledge is there—we have but to reach for it, and to incorporate it into our practice and our teaching. (p. 121)

Essentially, the vision in the world will not help us catalyze mutual aid if we lack group-specific skill. In fact, research suggests that even with a genuine desire to use mutual aid, a group can easily become hazardous to the health of its members without group-specific skilled intervention (Coyle 1949; Galinsky and Schopler 1977; Glassman and Kates 1990; Konopka 1983; Phillips 1954; Steinberg 1992). We may appreciate mutual aid in action whenever we experience it, but without skill we are powerless to make it happen again. Just as the blend of a conductor's artistic vision and musical skill helps transform a stage full of musicians into an orchestra, it is the worker's artful blend of vision and skill that helps transform a *group* into a *Group*. As Margaret Hartford (1964) stated, it is an entity whose potential is greater than the sum of its individual parts.

For almost half a century now, scholars and practitioners have studied the way in which social workers work with groups and examined their rationales for intervening in the ways they do. As a result, a number of group-specific skills have been identified and articulated (see, for example, Brandler and Roman 1991; Gitterman 1989; Glassman and Kates 1990; Hartford 1964; Middleman and Wood 1990b; Shulman 1999; and Trecker 1955). Those that most promote mutual aid generally focus on enlisting group members as allies in effecting and affecting group process (identifying and harnessing strengths), on encouraging group members to accept one another as mutual-aid resources (group building), and on helping group members use their own stories rather than advice to help themselves and others (teaching purposeful use of self).

Some skills, such as helping people express themselves, helping them make use of available services, and using professional judgment in selecting interventions, are generic to the helping process. Still, because of their attention to the group as a system, many other skills are clearly group-specific. Consider scanning, which refers to a visual roaming over the entire group when we talk or listen. Scanning is used to make sure we pick up all nonverbal as well as verbal reactions to what is being said or done, and is therefore an important group-building skill. In contrast, if we were to allow our eyes to roam the room as we worked with an individual, not only would our behavior look mighty peculiar, it would also suggest that we were uninterested. Or consider the skills of assessing and recording developmental process and progress. Although we certainly use similar skills in working with individuals, we do so only with regard to the individual's development and to our working relationship with that individual. When we work with a group, however, we have the additional task of assessing the development of the whole group as it progresses through its own developmental stages (Berman-Rossi 1993; Galinsky and Schopler 1989; Garland et al. 1978; Hartford 1971; Northen and Kurland 2001; Schiller 1995; Schwartz 1963; Shulman 1999). Many group-specific skills exist, then, and are both available to and necessary for helping us help groups actualize their potential for mutual aid.

KEY POINTS OF THIS CHAPTER

1. The concept of mutual aid has long been recognized as central to social work with groups.
2. A mutual-aid approach to work with groups represents a psychosocial approach to professional practice. It reflects a holistic use of groups, and it is a strength-centered way of helping people.
3. Although thinking about, planning, and working with groups have been discussed from a variety of perspectives, all theoretical fingers point to mutual aid as cause and effect of social work with groups.
4. Mutual aid is both a process and a result. As a process, mutual aid is what group members do together to be helpful. As a result, it is what group members experience from having interacted with others in a particular way.
5. The opportunity for mutual aid exists from the moment a group meets until the moment it ends, but it does not come about automatically. It needs communication. It needs a certain kind of group climate, and it is most easily actualized in groups that have been formed around a common cause.
6. The mutual-aid approach to working with groups presupposes that people who have the capacity to interact also have the capacity to help and, in helping others, people also help themselves.
7. The expectation that group members will contribute their strengths to the group is as powerful an expectation of the mu-

tual-aid approach as is the expectation that they will use the group to meet their needs.

8. A dual focus is needed to help a group develop into a mutual-aid system; one of the worker's eyes and ears needs to be on the process and progress of each individual in the group, and one needs to be on the process and progress of the group as a system.

9. Shared authority over group affairs is both a right and an obligation of membership in a mutual-aid system, and each person is expected to integrally effect and affect the group's affairs.

10. Mutual-aid practice has three primary functions: helping the group identify the strengths of each of its members, helping it use those strengths to build a community open to mutual aid, and teaching group members the process of purposeful use of self so that they might actually engage in mutual aid.

11. A number of group-specific skills have been identified that attend to the group as a system.

12. Group-specific skillful practice involves two types of skills: relationship-building skills and skills aimed at influencing the nature and direction of those relationships.

RECOMMENDED FURTHER READING

Bernstein, S. (1976). Values and group work. In *Further Exploration in Group Work,* ed. S. Bernstein, pp. 145-179. Boston: Charles River Books.

Coyle, G. (1949). Definition of the function of the group worker. *The Group* 11(3):11-13.

Falck, H. S. (1995). Central characteristics of social work with groups—a sociocultural analysis. In *Group Work Practice in a Troubled Society: Problems and Opportunities,* eds. R. Kurland and R. Salmon, pp. 63-72. Binghamton, NY: The Haworth Press.

Gitterman, A. (1989). Building mutual support in groups. *Social Work with Groups* 12(2):5-21.

Hartford, M. (1978). Groups in the human services: Some facts and fancies. *Social Work with Groups* 1(1):1-10.

Middleman, R. and Wood, G. G. (1990). From social group work to social work with groups. *Social Work with Groups* 13(3):3-20.

Newstetter, W. (1935). What is social group work? *Proceedings of the National Conference of Social Work,* pp. 291-299. Chicago: University of Chicago Press.

Northen, H. and Kurland, R. (2001). *Social Work with Groups.* New York: Columbia University Press.

Phillips, H. U. (1957). *Essentials of Social Group Work Skill.* New York: Association Press.

_____ (1964). Working definition of social group work. In *Working Papers Toward a Frame of Reference for Social Group Work,* ed. M. Hartford, pp. 48-51. New York: National Association of Social Workers.

Roberts, R. and Northen, H. eds. (1976). *Theories of Social Work with Groups.* New York: Columbia University Press.

Schwartz, W. (1961). The social worker in the group. *The Social Welfare Forum,* pp. 146-171. New York: Columbia University Press.

Shulman, L. (1999). *The Skills of Helping Individuals, Families, Groups, and Communities.* Itasca, IL: Peacock.

Trecker, H. B. (1955). *Social Group Work: Principles and Practices.* New York: Whiteside.

Tropp, E. (1978). Whatever happened to group work? *Social Work with Groups* 1(1):85-94.

Wilson, G. and Ryland, G. (1949). *Social Group Work Practice.* Boston: Houghton Mifflin.

Chapter 2

The Nine Dynamics of Mutual Aid and Their Implications for Practice

KEY CONCEPTS OF THIS CHAPTER

All in the Same Boat
Dialectic Process
Discussing Taboos
Individual Problem Solving
Mutual Demand
Mutual Support
Obstacles to Mutual Aid
Rehearsal
Sharing Data
Strength in Numbers

* * *

Mutual aid is often misconstrued as either "sympatico" behavior (i.e., commiseration) or the exchange of advice. As the literature reveals, however, mutual aid is a much more elaborate process than either the expression of sympathy or the giving of advice. It has many facets and embraces many types of interaction, including those that might at first glance appear less than helpful.

Lawrence Shulman (1999) suggests that helping group members work through the obstacles to mutual aid is what helps to define the role of the worker. He identifies these obstacles as the complexity of the tasks involved in creating a mutual-aid system (hence the need to harness members' strengths), the difficulty group members have in identifying their self-interest with that of others (hence the need to open avenues of communication and appreciation for the possibility of mutual aid through group building), and the difficulty with which people communicate honestly (hence the need to teach members how to engage in the purposeful use of self, an empathy-based helping process composed of self-reflection and self-reference).

As articulated by Shulman (1999), understanding the dynamics of mutual aid can help us recognize when it is and is not taking place; can put us in a good position to formulate appropriate expectations of group members, of ourself as the worker in a mutual-aid system, and of the group as a whole; and can help us articulate what we do and why we do it to interested others, such as prospective members, their significant others, our colleagues, and our students.

SHARING DATA

> Whether . . . specific tips . . . or values or ideas about relation-
> ships, each member can contribute to the common pool. The
> worker will also contribute data which when combined with that
> of the others provide a rich resource for the members. (Shulman
> 1999, p. 303)

People bring all manner of information, knowledge, wisdom, and experience to the group, and one way of harnessing their strengths is by calling on that fund. How do we call on it? How do we set this data-sharing dynamic in motion? As with all other dynamics, we set it in motion during our very first contact with prospective group members by voicing our desire for this kind of norm. In describing and discussing our expectations, for example, *we state very clearly that one of our expectations is that the group will be a forum for the exchange of information.* By letting prospective members know that sharing information of all types will be an integral component of the group, we begin to help them assess the goodness of fit between what they think would be helpful to them and what we envision. They can begin to imagine what at least some part of the process will look like. And they can also begin to think about and explore the strengths that they envision bringing to such a group. In other words, they begin to think of themselves as potential data resources. It might be said, then, that this dynamic reflects the networking aspect of mutual aid.

Once the group begins, we continue to develop this mutual-aid dynamic by *turning all issues,* from the not-enough-chairs dilemma to the more important issues, *back to the group* at every possible opportunity—even when the group calls on our supposedly superior knowledge (Middleman and Wood 1990b). We reach for information linkages among the members by asking them to think about the ways in which one person's idea or experience relates to that of another. Because everyone who wishes to take part in this dynamic must have the opportunity to do so, we *visually scan the group* while we talk and listen for nonverbal reactions to what is being said or done at any given moment. When necessary we help members hear what others have to say by *amplifying overly soft* or *toning down overly loud* messages. In short, we consistently encourage members to look for ways in which they can exchange information and ideas.

Consider the case of Maria, who had agreed to join a new group for single mothers:

> Just before the first meeting began, Maria came to me and said that although she wanted to be in this group, her babysitter had just backed out of her commitment. She had only come because her mother had agreed to watch the kids tonight, but Maria knew she could not count on her mother to be free every Tuesday night, and she knew of no one else who could watch her children. I asked Maria if she had time to stay this evening and talk to the group about her child care problem. Maria said that because her kids were at her mother's tonight, she could stay this time. When we started I asked Maria to be the first to introduce herself, and I also asked her to tell the others about her child care dilemma. It was great! Within a few minutes, she had two solid leads for child care and one other possibility to explore.

We too have information and knowledge to share with the group and contribute to its data-sharing process, but we do not force our own contributions onto center stage, even if we like our own ideas best. If our ideas predominate, we imply that when all is said and done, it is still what *we* have to offer that is more valuable to the group than what *others* have to offer. Thus we begin to set a norm for the practice of individual work in a group context rather than group work and mutual aid. Once members experience the value of this dynamic of mutual aid—both in terms of being helpful to and being helped by others in the group—they will begin to take ownership of this process by initiating it for themselves.

To some extent, the group's freedom to become a data-sharing system is affected by the nature of the work setting, generally, and organizational policy, more specifically (Kurland 1978). In a closed system in which self-determination is restricted, for example (such as prisons or institutions in which those being helped have little power over what happens to them), a group may have the freedom to problem solve and explore ideas but less freedom to try out different ways of acting outside the group. It is imperative, therefore, that we understand the implications of the setting in which we carry out our work—its history with regard to working with groups (an organization's tradition with regard to the use of groups, for example); its current attitudes toward groups (whether an organization appears to value or is threatened by formally organized groups); and its general philosophy regarding the use of groups as a helping medium (the ways in which groups are used). Only when we understand systemic or organizational restraints can we help a group understand its data-sharing potential and define its acceptable range of data-sharing possibilities (see Chapter 3).

THE DIALECTIC PROCESS

> An important debate of ideas can take place. . . . Group members can risk their tentative ideas and use the group as a sounding board—a place for their views to be challenged and possibly changed. (Shulman 1999, p. 305)

If group members are expected to debate and, even further, if they are expected to take some risks by debating real feelings, real ideas, and real attitudes, then the group must be perceived as a place where people can express themselves freely and safely and challenge others freely and safely. Not only is it useful to share data, it is also useful to examine its implications.

The *dialectic* process is set in motion when we *voice our expectation* to prospective group members *that not only will the exploration and debate of different perspectives* (regardless of how farfetched they may seem) be a norm of the group we have in mind but also the *examination and exploration of differences that emerge* in the group *will actually be encouraged.*

The idea of a forum for debating ideas often appeals to prospective group members, but most of us are not very skilled at this process. At one extreme, so-called polite social debate tends to be carried out at a superficial level, guided by good manners and such restraint that true positions and feelings are often left unrevealed. As a process whose goal would seem to be to keep all feathers unruffled, this kind of debate—if it could even be called that—might be labeled as "all form, no substance." At the other extreme are debates in which feelings and positions are expressed with such bad manners and lack of restraint that, while viewpoints are made quite clear, the total lack of interest in hearing other opinions is equally clear. Although we would also be hard pressed to refer to this exchange as debate, if we had to label it for the sake of comparison to polite tea talk, we would refer to it as "all substance, no form." Somewhere in the middle of these two extremes, and much like the conversations at some dinner tables, talk often comes from all corners at once, focused more on "a good time was had by all" than on any real exchange of ideas or understanding of others or of synthesis.

The idea of debate may be appealing, but the demand for authentic and respectful expression is not always easily met. Some people, afraid of being judged harshly, may be reluctant to reveal their true feelings. Others, afraid of finding themselves alone in their positions, may also be reluctant to reveal their real attitudes. And still others, oblivious to the sensitivities of their listeners, may find it difficult to express what they think or feel without alienating those around them. Nevertheless, to the extent that it helps people try to deal with difference and understand where others are coming from, debate is one of the most valuable aspects of mutual aid.

Because debating is such a difficult process, when the group begins we focus our efforts on helping it balance authentic expression with respecting the sensitivities of its members. We do this by attending to two tasks at once: we *help group members express themselves* whenever they indicate the desire to do so, and we *help the group adopt a structure* for the safe examination and exploration of its differences. In a new group, for example, we *restate or reframe* overly aggressive or understated communication, or *ask that group members help one another find new words* to express sentiments, and we ourselves *model a sensitive and open manner* of presenting our views and listening to those of others. Later, however, when the group's sense of community is stronger and better able to withstand dissent and make use of its differences, we take a back seat and *encourage members to provide whatever structure and norms* they think are necessary for *examining, exploring, understanding, and making use* of their differences.

It is often when we are helping group members debate issues and stick with them rather than give in to the temptation to move away from painful, thought-provoking, or otherwise disconcerting discussion that our skill of *being there* for all members at all times (Middleman 1987) takes on its greatest meaning, for it is precisely during these moments that we need to balance *empathy* for everyone in the group with *demand* from everyone as well. Consider again the case of Maria's group of single mothers:

> At our fourth meeting, some differences emerged as the women started to talk about the pros and cons of working outside the home. Tina said her mother had worked and talked about some of the ways she felt her mother had been an excellent role model. Jeannette said she felt her mother, who had also worked, had never been around when she needed her and said if she were still married, she'd stay home with her kids. Tina said she thought the issue had to do with quality time, not quantity time—at which Jeannette raised an eyebrow, and Gloria sighed and said she wondered if what they thought even mattered, since they all had to work whether they wanted to or not anyway . . . so . . . what was the point of even talking about it?
>
> After a few moments of silence, I said that I thought there seemed to be many different experiences among the women, but that each of those experiences, even though they were different, seemed to be placing some real burdens on them in terms of their own present situations. They agreed and started to talk again, but while they had first focused on their feelings as daughters, they now started to talk about their feelings as mothers.

The group's discussion eventually revealed that those who had expressed the opinion that mothers should be able to work outside the home actually had mixed feelings about not being ready with cookies and milk for their children at the end of the school day. And those who had expressed the opinion that mothers should stay home felt bad about having to work whether they wanted to or not. In this case, then, *being there* for all group members by not placing judgments on any viewpoint or position helped them continue to explore their differences (histories, experiences, and cultural norms and expectations). It gave them opportunities to hear about other ways of being, doing, and thinking, and it helped them discover some common denominators (such as feeling guilty for not being able to "do it all" and mourning their loss of choice) that transcended their differences.

DISCUSSING TABOOS

> [T]he group recreates in this microsociety the "culture" the members experienced outside. Thus, direct talk about such subjects as authority, dependency, and sex is experienced as taboo. . . . As [group members] experience positive work, they are given permission to enter the formerly taboo area. (Shulman 1999, p. 305)

As demanding as it might be to engage in straight talk, it is even more so when we approach those areas we define as taboo. When people greet us, for example, it is taboo to tell them how we really feel. What should I do when my physician first asks how I am? Should I respond politely first and go from there? Or should I skip the polite altogether and immediately plunge into why I have come to her office? Even in situations we know to be more than merely social, in other words, we often still feel pressured to behave in certain socially prescribed ways.

Many topics, such as income, sexuality, prejudice, or attitudes toward authority, to name but a few, are taboo topics in our culture, and we do not expect to discuss them under any but the most necessary circumstances (such as with our accountant or physician, for example) or the most lighthearted circumstances (such as in joke telling, for example). On the other hand, taboo issues are what often bring people to a group in the first place, and it is more often than not, therefore, precisely into taboo territory that many groups need to venture.

How can we help the group make this journey? Two tasks are called for. The first is to *model the process,* by being honest with prospective group members about our own perceptions of their needs and concerns and by discussing with them the ways in which we think their needs could be met through the group we have in mind.

Modeling is particularly important to the new group, because it helps members know that when we said we wanted the talk in this group to be real, we meant it. At the same time, it is a task that we continue throughout the life of the group *by being responsive* when real talk takes place, by *encouraging the expression and exploration* of members' needs and concerns, and even by *raising taboo issues for discussion* if we think it would be useful and no one else is doing so.

The second task is to *explicitly discuss* in the group how it may be different from others to which members currently belong or to which they have belonged in the past. In this group, we state, we will deal with real and sometimes sensitive issues. And although members may find themselves in a state of mutuality regarding some issues, it is also likely that at other times they will find themselves in a state of conflict. Regardless of which particular dynamic is in play at any given moment, and although the sensitivities of all group members will be treated with respect, we add, it will be a norm of this group to address all issues useful to the helping process and to helping it achieve its purpose.

Since taboo issues are kept secret, we rarely have occasion to measure our own thinking and attitudes against those of others. Through the mutual-aid process, however, people are given exactly such an opportunity. And while the expression of commonalities can be comforting, differences can be useful. Commonalities can let people know that they are not alone—that others share similar concerns or have similar problems, but the expression of differences gives people an opportunity to examine their own beliefs or attitudes and often provides a corrective experience. In either case—whether members have occasion to experience commonality or difference—it is usually refreshing to participate in a group in which speaking about the normally unspeakable is acceptable.

ALL IN THE SAME BOAT

> We do not mind our not arriving anywhere nearly so much as our not having any company on the way.
>
> Frank Moore Colby,
> *The Margin of Hesitation,* 1921

Discovering that feelings are shared by other members of the group can often be the beginning of freeing a client from their power [and] can be one of the most powerful forces for change resulting from the mutual aid process. (Shulman 1999, p. 306)

People often believe that being in a boat with others who share similar issues, needs, or problems will prevent anyone in that boat from arriving anywhere. But group members must share a boat in some important respects if they are to bond together in common cause. Consequently, an early task of mutual-aid practice is to help people imagine how the group we have in mind will mobilize rather than immobilize its members. How do we do that? We use *examples of mutual aid in action* to help them understand our vision of mutual aid, both as a process and as a mission or result. And we *share our vision* of the group as a strength-centered joint venture, using the group purpose we have in mind as the reference point for helping them understand what participating in such a group will mean for each of them. Although it is true that members' needs, issues, and goals are in the same boat, let us not forget that their strengths are now in the same boat as well. Hence, while we *use introductions to help group members see how they are connected to a common purpose,* for example, we also use that time to *help them identify their individual strengths and skills.* In fact, it is often during this process that group members begin to understand how being in the same boat can lead to another mutual-aid dynamic: *strength in numbers.*

Our own attitude toward groups generally, toward their therapeutic potential more specifically, and toward people's capacity for mutual aid even more specifically, is most revealed by the way we articulate this particular dynamic. People can usually imagine receiving comfort and support from being with others of similar ilk, yet they often have difficulty understanding how change or action can also come about in such a case, particularly if they are accustomed to thinking about groups as forums for sharing deficits or problems. To help people overcome this hurdle, therefore, we need at the very least to believe in mutual aid. Beyond that, we also need knowledge. We need to know about small-group theories, specifically those theories that have evolved with mutual aid in mind (such as theories about planning, composition, group development, and interaction). We need to know about small-group dynamics, particularly those that affect and effect mutual aid (such as which communication patterns or group-management or decision-making norms are most conducive to mutual aid). We also need to know about the mutual-aid process itself (that is, the nature of each of its dynamics) so that we will know when mutual aid is or is not taking place. If we too are not sure how people in the same boat can help one another; or if we, like some, tend to conceptualize groups primarily as an efficient backdrop for working with individuals; or if we do not know how to translate the ideal of strength-centered practice into action, then we will be hard pressed indeed to offer examples to others that reflect this dynamic.

MUTUAL SUPPORT

> [The] acceptance and caring of the group can be a source of support during a difficult time. . . . At crucial moments in a group one can sense a general tone or atmosphere, displayed through words, expressions, or physical posture which conveys the caring of the "group" for the individual. (Shulman 1999, p. 308)

One of the most appealing dynamics of the mutual-aid system is its capacity to provide support, caring, and empathy for its members, norms that evolve from the emotional commitment people make in themselves, in one another, and in the group as a whole. Even when ideas, feelings, and perspectives differ, which they inevitably do, there is great comfort in being surrounded by people who we believe accept and understand us or, if they do not fully understand us, are at least willing to hear where we are coming from. This dynamic is frequently cited as a group's primary value.

However, *mutual support* is not always extended to its fullest potential. All too often, group members support one another in good times when the support is easy, such as when everyone agrees, but then tend to fall short in hard times, such as when differences emerge and what is needed is empathy rather than sympathy. All too often, instead of exchanging mutual support in such moments, people become harsh and critical, chiding those who disagree or take a different position (Konopka 1990). It is, however, precisely in such times of strife that a supportive atmosphere is most needed.

Thus, while we discuss with prospective members the group's potential for providing support, we set this dynamic in motion when we *explain that* in the group we have in mind, *mutual support includes empathy as well as sympathy.* We set it in motion when we *ask that prospective group members make an emotional commitment* beyond the one they might normally make to their own growth or well-being in a therapeutic process—that is, when we ask them to commit to the support, growth, and well-being of the other group members as well as their own. And we set it in motion when we *ask members* of the group *to extend their emotional commitment to the well-being of the group as a whole.*

Although it is up to the group members to make such a commitment, it is up to the worker to create an appropriate opportunity for commitment by initiating the norms of acceptance and empathy. Early on, therefore, we *use every occasion* to help group members come to know one another, care about one another, and care about what happens in and to the group as a whole. We model and *demonstrate our acceptance, support, and compassion* through our purposeful choice of caring words, expressions, and gestures. Our constant and consistent message is that in this group, people will really feel for one another—not only when times are good but also when times are difficult; and in this group, if we disagree, it does *not* mean that we do not care for one another; it just means that we disagree.

MUTUAL DEMAND

> Another group expectation can be that the members will work on their concerns. At moments when clients feel overwhelmed and hopeless exactly this expectation may help them take a next step. (Shulman 1999, p. 308)

Similar to its counterpart of mutual support, *mutual demand* also tends to be misunderstood. In some cases, the demand that group members work on issues of concern takes the shape of the "hot-seat" syndrome, during which one member is badgered by the worker and comember "assistant therapists" (see Chapter 1). In other cases, either under the guise of sensitivity or the need for equal time, problem solving is carried out in so cursory a manner and at such a superficial level that no meaningful exploration of problems, possibilities, or implications can take place (see Chapter 6). Whichever the case, such processes reflect more a misconception of mutual aid than its *worth*.

Often requiring deep self-reflection and reorganization of thought, meeting personal and interpersonal needs, working out issues of concern, and resolving problems can be slow, painful, and difficult processes. But if the group is going to be a forum for work, however that has been defined by its purpose, then the expectation that it will be a place where people really do grapple with issues rather than merely scan them needs to be clear. Further, if it is going to be a forum for *group* work rather than individual work in the presence of others, then the expectation that members will work on issues cooperatively rather than individually and/or adversarially also needs to be clear.

Setting mutual demand in motion occurs when we first discuss with prospective members what they hope and expect to receive from being in the group. In that dialogue, we *examine the relationship* between their hopes, needs, and desires and the purpose of the group we have in mind. And while we *acknowledge* that work may sometimes take the form of shaking old ways of thinking and doing, we also *reassure* them that work will always take place in a supportive and empathic atmosphere. Even when—or perhaps *especially* when—we find ourselves in disagreement with arguments, positions, or points of view, we will *be there* for all group members at all times. That is, we will make sure there is an opportunity to voice and explain all feelings and positions in the group. In essence, then, we ask that prospective group members pledge themselves to the serious examination of issues that bring them together and, in turn, we pledge to provide a safe structure for that process (Gitterman 1989; Schwartz and Zalba 1971).

The worker is usually the first to make a demand for work from the group, to set the tone of work, to let members know that working, however that has been defined by the group's purpose, will be an integral part of membership. In fact, group purpose plays a central role in this dynamic, for if a clear, collective purpose does not exist, the group will have no reference point for its work and, as a result, the question of what it is that members have in common to work *toward* will always plague them.

When the group first meets, it will need some help to talk the talk of mutual aid, to "dig deeper," to identify and stretch its thinking-through skills. Hence, in the new group, the worker's primary role is to demonstrate what work looks like. We model the *action* dimension of this dynamic by *being thoughtful before we speak,* for example, and by *taking a few moments to collect our thoughts and words* to demonstrate our own efforts into the contributions that we ourselves wish to make to the group's process. At times, we *share our own thinking* with the group to initiate or confirm the norm of using the group to help think things through. We model the *reaction* dimension of this dynamic by being *visibly attentive and reflective* when we listen to others. We *scan the group* as we talk and listen to make sure that we pick up all contributions to the work process. We *ask for clarification or elaboration* whenever we find ourselves in doubt or making assumptions. We ask questions such as: "What do you mean, exactly?" "Can you give an example?" "Why do you say that?" "Do you really mean that?" "Do you know why you feel that way?" "Can you be more specific about what you mean?" "Can you be clearer?" "Can you say more about what you mean?"

By being thoughtful and by taking risks ourselves, we are inherently making a direct demand for work from the group as well. When we speak, we are demanding that group members listen to what we are saying and that they think about what we are saying. We are demanding that, like us, they think about what they are saying, that they not just "mouth off" or simply talk to hear themselves talk but that, just as we take care about what we say and how we say it, they take similar care. By scanning the group visually while we talk and listen, we are in effect demanding that all reactions, verbal and nonverbal alike, be expressed.

When we set mutual demand in motion, that is, once we initiate the norm of work, group members follow suit and make the same demands of one another. The following moment in an after-school group of teenagers is a good example of this dynamic in action:

One teen became so provocative we had to stop what we were doing. I asked the group to sit on the floor and said: "Okay, now, what are we going to do? How are we going to do a show with all this going on?" Some of the members started to talk about what Ben needed to stop doing, then he talked about what the others needed to stop doing. In fact they talked for a long time without much input from me, and after a while, they all agreed on what they had to do to work together better. The discussion went something such as, "You have to stop . . ." "Well, you have to stop . . ." "Well, okay, but if I stop . . . then you have to stop . . ." "Okay, but then you can't . . ." "Okay, but then you better not . . ." "Well, okay, but then you have to . . ." "Okay?" "Okay!" "Okay?" "Okay!"

INDIVIDUAL PROBLEM SOLVING

> The general learning of the group members can be enhanced through the specific problem-solving work done with each member. (Shulman 1999, p. 309)

As group members bring their hopes, needs, desires, and concerns to the group, they engage in a collective problem-solving process. Through examination, exploration, and elaboration of the issues at hand, they look to their own personal experiences *(self-reflection)* in the attempt to deepen their insight, build empathy, and ultimately, to be helpful to others as well as to themselves and share their personal stories with the group *(self-reference)*.

There is a tendency in groups to partialize the problem-solving process so that the issues of one group member remain, for all practical purposes, unconnected to those of the others. In such a case, we might think to ourselves, for example, "Well, it seems to me that Tom needs to work on issue X, Dick needs to work on issue Y, and Harry needs to work on issue Z." This partialization, or *individualization* of issues, often occurs when the group purpose—that is, the common cause that binds members' issues together—is unclear or when no common cause has been identified. It also tends to happen when the worker does not help members discover the ways in which their work is connected. It is absolutely essential to mutual aid, therefore, that we understand and are able to describe the *purposeful use of self* process, explain its role in individual problem solving from a mutual-aid point of view, and help the group adopt such a norm (see Chapter 6).

We first set in motion *individual problem solving* from a mutual-aid point of view long before the group encounters problems to tackle. We do it by *discussing* with prospective members *the concept of group purpose* and our understanding of *the relationship between group purpose and individual goals.* We also begin to set the stage for this dynamic by describing what the process looks like. We *talk about* the fact that it is *purposeful use of personal experience* rather than advice that will be the key problem-solving vehicle in the group we have in mind, and we discuss the processes of *self-reflection* and *self-reference* and describe how they can help the problem-solving process take on meaning for the entire group. When the group meets, we ask it to continue this discussion. In fact, the dialogue about group purpose never really ends, as we use every occasion to help members identify what they have in common and how the group purpose as it has been articulated both embraces and reflects their own personal needs and goals.

Finally, in addition to asking that the group become involved in any and all problem-solving processes, we also model how to participate in this unique approach to problem solving *through our own purposeful use of self* and by *seeking explanation, clarification, and elaboration* of all so-called individual issues until the ways in which they can provide meaningful whole-group food for thought is clear to everyone.

REHEARSAL

[T]he group becomes a safe place to risk new ways of communicating and to practice what the client feels may be hard to do. (Shulman 1999, p. 310)

New ways of looking at old pictures—of communicating, of interacting, even of thinking—are often identified as a result of the mutual-aid process. One of the ways a group can help its members think things through is by providing a sounding board for action as well as talk. In fact, helping people examine the implications of the way they act and react is one of the things a group does particularly well. In addition to helping the group identify alternatives through its problem-solving process, therefore, one of the major tasks of mutual-aid practice is to help members use the group to rehearse, either in fact or in imagination, those alternatives and their implications.

We set the tone for rehearsal by *helping* the group *develop an atmosphere conducive to risk taking*—an atmosphere in which taking chances and making mistakes is actually desirable. How do we do that? We ourselves take some risks. We praise group members for the risks they take. We *acknowledge our own mistakes.* When others make mistakes that are either visible or touch the group in some way, we acknowledge them as well and *help the group put the issues into perspective.* We ask group members to work *collaboratively rather than competitively.* We *ask them to show support* for one another's risk taking. Whenever occasions for trying out new ways of being, doing, or thinking present themselves, we *encourage* group members *to take advantage of those opportunities,* often using activity appropriate to the group's developmental stage, such as role playing, to help it happen (Garland et al. 1978; Middleman 1982). Finally, by *helping the group develop and maintain a sense of community* and *common ground* at all times, we help it provide a safe and supportive climate for rehearsal and risk taking. In these and other many other skills ways, we help members understand that in the group we have in mind, trying and failing will be assigned a higher value than not taking risks at all.

STRENGTH IN NUMBERS

High tides raise all ships.

John F. Kennedy

An individual's fears and ambivalence can be overcome by participating in a group effort as one's own courage is strengthened by the courage of others. (Shulman 1999, p. 312)

Undoubtedly, we gain strength, courage, and new resolve from feeling connected to other people who we believe share needs, hopes, and goals similar to ours. Although talk can be very supportive, this dynamic, as if *rehearsal,* is often played out in action as well. Strikes, demonstrations, class-action suits, and tenants' associations, for example, all reflect this dynamic on a large scale. It can provide powerful mutual aid on a smaller scale as well, however, through vehicles such as community boards, organizational committees, consumer-rights or advocacy groups, or neighborhood-watch groups. Furthermore, even if groups are not social-action groups per se, there are still many possibilities for their members to experience this dynamic. When a member of a cancer-recovery group goes to her physician's office to obtain new test results accompanied by one or more of her comembers, for example, this dynamic is being acted out. Not only is the individual strengthened by the presence and support of a comember, the whole group is strengthened by this process, strengthened by the need to reach for and use whatever skills it has to help a member face a special challenge. When the group uses its collective power to take action on behalf of one of its members (such as helping someone negotiate a complicated system) or even on behalf of the entire group (such as the collective presentation of demands regarding organizational policy) this dynamic is also in action. In each case, members are strengthened by the fact that they are both bonded and banded, that they are not alone. In each case, the power of the group itself is strengthened by the contribution of each of its members to whatever process is being undertaken.

We first set this dynamic in motion when we help prospective members understand what we mean by *strength-centered* practice. We *offer examples* of how *individual strengths* can shape and cultivate the power of the group. And we *offer examples* of how *group power* can strengthen each member. Once the group comes together, we encourage the development of its strength-in-numbers potential by *helping it experience its we-ness* at every possible opportunity. We also *help members think about* some of the ways in which their *particular skills* might strengthen the group. We *help the group take advantage* of those strengths. We *help it identify how it has been strengthened.* We *help members think* about some of the ways in which *their membership* might strengthen them. We *help them take advantage of the group's power* whenever such a need presents itself. We *help them articulate* the ways in which they feel they have been strengthened by being in the group. Finally, we *praise* the *strength in numbers* phenomenon every time we think we see it in action; that is, every time we see group members, as the French say, *se tenir les coudes,* or "hold each other up by the elbows."

KEY POINTS OF THIS CHAPTER

1. Understanding the nature of each of the nine dynamics of mutual aid helps us articulate our vision of mutual aid to others.
2. Understanding the implications for practice of each of the dynamics of mutual aid helps us formulate appropriate expectations of ourselves, of group members, and of the group as a whole.
3. We set the dynamics of mutual aid in motion long before the group begins when we discuss our ideas and tentative plans with prospective group members.
4. The *data-sharing* dynamic of mutual aid reflects a group's informational networking potential. When members share "data" they help one another by sharing whatever information, knowledge, and wisdom they have accumulated in their own personal lives.
5. The *dialectic* dynamic helps group members debate their ideas and examine and explore their differences, and it provides opportunities to hear about new ways of thinking, being, and doing.
6. Many of the issues and concerns that bring people to groups are considered taboo. The opportunity to *discuss taboos,* therefore, as well as opportunities to gain knowledge about issues not normally talked about and to debunk common myths, is an important dynamic of mutual aid.
7. People often feel as if they are alone in their concerns, that no one else feels as they do. When people spend time with others who they believe are in the *same boat,* they feel relieved and comforted by that company.
8. The dynamic of *mutual support* has two dimensions. The first is sympathy (e.g., "I've been there, and I know how you feel."). The second is empathy (e.g., "I haven't been there, but I think I can imagine how you feel.").
9. It is through *mutual demand* that group members carry out the group's work, however defined. This dynamic can be difficult for members to develop, because in many groups the right to demand work belongs only to the practitioner.

10. *Individual problem solving* from a mutual-aid point of view consists of a process called purposeful use of self, composed of self-reflection (thinking about personal experience) and self-reference (talking about personal experience). It is this mutual-aid dynamic that most helps a group stay away from *casework in a group* (Kurland and Salmon 1992).
11. The dynamic of *rehearsal* gives group members opportunities to practice, through talk or through action, new ways of thinking, being, and doing, either in imagination or in fact.
12. A group's *strength in numbers* potential is one of the most powerful dynamics of mutual aid and can be expressed in many ways, ranging from the use of group force to advocate on behalf of one of its members to the use of its collective muscle to promote social action.

RECOMMENDED FURTHER READING

Gitterman, A. and Shulman, L., eds. (1994). *Mutual-Aid Groups and the Life Cycle*. Itasca, IL: Peacock.

Middleman, R. (1982). *The Non-Verbal Method in Working with Groups*. Hebron, CT: Practitioners Press.

Shulman, L. (1999). *The Skills of Helping Individuals, Families, Groups, and Communities*. Itasca, IL: Peacock.

Chapter 3

Pregroup Planning
with Mutual Aid in Mind

KEY CONCEPTS OF THIS CHAPTER

Climate
Commonalities/Differences
Communication/Interaction
Content
Group Purpose
Individual Goals

* * *

Pregroup planning plays a major role in social work with groups (Kurland 1978), and regardless of where we work, the population with which we work, or the nature of the group purpose we have in mind, there are a few aspects of planning that pertain specifically to setting the stage for mutual aid: attending to the larger setting/system in which the group is to take place, giving some consideration to composition, and identifying and developing a relevant purpose.

SETTING THE STAGE

Setting the stage for mutual aid begins with pregroup planning, a process intended to help us think through the impact of both generic and contextual factors on our ability to get a group off the ground and to help it become a viable need-meeting and help-exchanging system (Hartford 1978; Kurland 1978). First we need to consider systemic factors, or the nature of the setting in which the group will operate (Galinsky and Schopler 1971; Hartford 1971; Kurland 1978; Schwartz 1976). All groups have the potential for mutual aid, but their setting will always have an impact on both the manner and degree of mutual aid they experience. Considering systemic factors, therefore, can help us keep our plans reasonable and feasible. Second, we need to give some thought to the degree to which prospective members have, or at least appear to have, some capacity to communicate and interact with their peers, even if on a nonverbal level (Bertcher and Maple 1996; Breton 1990; Glassman and Kates 1990; Hartford 1964; Middleman 1982; Middleman and Wood 1990b; Newstetter 1935; Schwartz 1976; Shalinsky 1969; Trecker 1955). Third, we need to consider whether the needs, desires, goals, and expectations of prospective members will provide a group purpose both clear and strong enough to bond them to one another and to outweigh whatever differences they will inevitably bring with them as well (Galinsky and Schopler 1971; Glassman and Kates 1990; Kurland 1978; Lowy 1976; Papell and Rothman 1980).

Systemic Factors to Consider

Although the setting in which we practice does not dictate whether a group can become a mutual-aid system, its history and current attitude toward groups generally and group work more specifically necessarily influence the extent to which a group can fulfill whatever mutual-aid potential it has (Hartford 1971, Galinsky and Schopler 1971; Kurland 1978; Schwartz 1976). A setting might assign theoretical value to mutual aid as an intragroup process, for example, meaning that it would place a high value on the concept of people helping one another as an internal group process but might assign somewhat less value to mutual aid as an external process, especially if mutual aid results in the group's making demands against the organization itself. Or a group might be given the freedom to exercise some aspects of mutual aid but less freedom to have a real say in shaping or reshaping its purpose. As Maeda Galinsky and Janice Schopler (1971) put it,

> Some groups are formed by an agency for one specific purpose, such as orientation, and they are confined to that purpose, re-

gardless of the desires of the members. Other groups have a wide range of choices open to them, and members may formulate a variety of goals, or at least choose one goal from a wide range of goals. Thus, latitude may be either restricted or open, depending on the constraints placed upon the group system. (p. 251)

The setting in which the group is to function has an impact, therefore, on both the kind of mutual aid a group may make use of and the degree of mutual aid it may experience. A group that offers opportunities to problem solve or rehearse new ways of being in the group itself may well receive organizational blessing, while any attempts to actualize its strength-in-numbers potential, for example, may be less welcome.

That setting has an impact on mutual aid does not mean that groups inherently can or cannot become mutual-aid systems, however. It only means that the *manner* of mutual aid (i.e., which dynamics are most likely to be experienced) and the *degree* of mutual aid (i.e., which dynamics are likely to be experienced most keenly) will vary from one setting to the next, from one purpose to the next. Some settings may primarily regard groups as efficient for the purpose of carrying on didactic activities with several persons at once. Psycho-education groups are good examples of this kind of mind-set, as are house meetings in residential settings. Although mutual aid is not precluded in such settings, our ability to form groups around a vision of mutual aid will depend a great deal on our status in the system and how clearly we are able to articulate to colleagues and administrative powers the need for, relevance of, and value of mutual aid in that *setting*—what's "in it" for them (Galinsky and Schopler 1971). If we attempt to form groups around purposes that cannot be reasonably realized because of organizational policy, for example, or expect members to assume responsibility over affairs in which they may not, in fact, exercise such responsibility, we simply set the group up for failure and disappointment. Consider the case of a group for mentally ill adults that meets in a community day-treatment center every week:

Shortly before the onset of summer, I reminded the group that I would be on maternity leave over the summer. I identified some of the alternatives for the group to consider and helped the members express their feelings and come to a decision about what to do over the summer. This process took some time, as some of them wanted to continue to meet as a group without me while others did not. What they did eventually agree on was that it would be all right with everyone if those who wanted to continue to meet as a group did and those who did not simply resumed when I returned in the fall.

What if the worker had helped members problem solve around the continuance of sessions only to discover that their decision was not acceptable to the agency? What if the agency had a policy against their meeting on their own, for example, or that groups whose workers left for any reason or period of time were to continue with other workers? In either case, members would have been led to believe that they could make certain decisions about the group's affairs when in fact they could not. They would have devoted precious energy to problem solving and thinking through possibilities that were not even viable in that setting, and they would have been disappointed over their inability to carry out their decision.

Thus, historical and contemporaneous philosophies and policies of the setting in which we practice are integral to planning groups with mutual aid in mind. They do not dictate whether or not a group can be a mutual-aid system, but they do dictate to a great degree the shape and extent of mutual aid that can take place. Some dynamics of mutual aid will be easy to actualize in any setting. Aspects of others, such as the extra-group dimensions of *rehearsing* or *strength in numbers,* will be more difficult to actualize. In some settings, groups will have complete freedom to determine their purpose, while in others, their raison d'être will be largely predetermined.

Compositional Issues to Consider

It is difficult to be completely theoretically "correct" when planning groups. Still, all too often, composition is dictated by irrelevant issues such as who can pay (granted, not necessarily irrelevant to the service provider), who attended on a rainy night, who signed up first, who has a pleasant personality, who has nothing else to do, who has a friend who is joining, who can fill a vacant seat, who has available transportation, and so on. Clearly, we cannot always maintain professional ideals with complete integrity in the real world of practice. Nevertheless, since mutual aid is based on both the quantity and the quality of member-to-member rather than worker-to-member interaction, the purposeful selection of persons for membership plays an important role in planning a mutual-aid system; and pregroup planning theory can offer substantial food for real-world thought, even as we struggle with the art of the possible.

One factor we need to think about is the goodness of fit between the needs and desires of the people we have in mind and the group purpose we have in mind. We need to consider whether purpose as we have tentatively formulated it speaks to the needs and desires of the people we are thinking of inviting into the group. If goodness of fit is absent, we may well form a group that is both unhelpful and off-target, which means that the group will have difficulty establishing a basis for mutual aid.

We also need to consider each person's capacity to communicate and interact, and how his or her ways of communicating and interacting are likely to look. In addition, we must make our expectations of participation reasonable (Phillips 1954, 1957). Even if we are considering highly verbal latency-age children, for example, is it still reasonable to expect them to interact through the same kind of talking-circle format we might expect from adults? What about people who are preoccupied with their own chronic illness? Can we expect them to become as fully involved with one another's welfare as we might expect of those who are well? To what extent can persons afflicted with Alzheimer's disease be expected to interact? What about people with language barriers? Or blindness? Or deafness?

The point here is not to suggest that there are people who can communicate and people who cannot. The point is that capacities and styles influence the nature and degree of mutual aid that takes place. Even if communication and interaction occur on a nonverbal level, the members of a mutual-aid system must have some capacity to relate not only to the worker but to their peers as well, and a major preplanning task is to discover that capacity.

Finally, we need to consider the ways in which the commonalities and differences of group members will enhance their ability to make connections with and help one another (Bertcher and Maple 1996; Kurland 1978; Shalinsky 1969).

Several salient questions must be asked about potential commonalities and differences. Might a difference in gender stand in the way of mutual aid? Might this difference make it difficult for members to reach common ground, or to offer one another mutual support, or to discuss taboo issues? Or, given the group purpose we have in mind, might such a difference help catalyze the group's mutual-aid potential? Perhaps we think significant differences in age might get in the way of mutual aid. What about commonalities and differences in race? Or culture? Or educational level? Might they advance potential? If so, exactly how?

In brief, we need to consider, as William Shalinsky (1969) says, "any factors that can influence such affective relationships and thus the degree of participation" (p. 46).

Research confirms the importance of attending to composition generally and to commonalities and differences more specifically in pregroup planning. A study of planned and unplanned groups in 1974 by Boer and Lantz, for example, concluded that the degree of commitment demonstrated by the members, the consistency of their attendance, and their satisfaction with the group's therapeutic results were determined as much by membership selection as they were by the nature of ongoing process. In 1977, Galinsky and Schopler found that giving careful consideration to issues of composition can actually help a group avoid "destructive interpersonal developments" (p. 92). These next sections take a closer look at the impact of desire to join a group, communication and interaction styles, and commonalities and differences on planning a system of mutual aid.

The Desire to Be There

Harvey Bertcher and Frank Maple (1996) argue that the most effective groups are those whose members want to be there and that a person's decision to join or not join a group, therefore, may be viewed as a *critical attribute* of composition, that is, the extent to which members want to be in the group can have a real impact on the group's ability to develop into a system of mutual aid. What are the implications of such an argument for pregroup planning? First, we need to be aware that groups composed of so-called captive audiences may have some difficulty developing into mutual-aid systems. Second, we must try to develop a clear and engaging group purpose in order to help people understand what will be "in it" for them as members.

The most effective strategy for making a group desirable to potential members is to give them an opportunity to talk about the purpose we have in mind and to examine its goodness of fit with their needs and desires. We need to meet with them, describe concrete examples of process, discuss our expectations, and then elicit their opinions and feelings. Only through such pregroup discussion will we be able to develop purposes that meet people's needs and desires.

Whether or not people join a group of their own free will, then, it is the relevance of purpose that will most determine how useful and helpful a group is perceived to be by its members. If worker and members (potential or actual) take the time to develop a relevant group purpose, then even those members who did not choose to be there are likely to come to see its value and take advantage of what it has to offer them.

The Capacity to Communicate and Interact

As stated earlier, not all people have to be highly skilled or even equally skilled at communicating or interacting, since one of the great gifts of group membership is the opportunity to improve those very skills. What is necessary is that they be able to communicate their ideas, feelings, opinions, and attitudes to others, even if they need help doing so. Even more necessary is that all of the group's participants, including the worker, have in common some communication method through which expression, understanding, and help can occur, be it verbal or nonverbal.

Since mutual aid requires real and thoughtful communication and interaction, the larger the group the more difficult it is generally for members to develop mutual aid at any but the most superficial levels. Some groups have fifteen or more persons, such as multifamily or residential groups. We might refer to such collections of individuals as groups, but in reality, chances are that a group of fifteen will not leave enough time or space for all of its members to contribute to the process in a significant way.

Members might be able to share information or provide some measure of support or feel strengthened by sheer size of membership. It will be more difficult, however, for them to debate issues in depth, to talk about normally taboo issues, or to explore and problem solve, except in smaller subgroups. Large groups do not completely preclude the potential for mutual aid, but by limiting the nature and degree of communication and interaction that can take place they have an impact on the nature and degree of mutual aid that can take place as well.

Conversely, it may also be difficult for a very small group—say, two or three members—to actualize mutual aid. Naturally, as soon as two people come together, the potential for mutual aid exists. Still, as with large groups, the potential of a very small system is limited by its size, albeit in a different way. A very small group may well offer its members support, for example, and provide the comfort of company and a forum for real talk about real issues. When it comes to such processes as networking, debating, brainstorming, problem solving, and the opportunity to compare ways of being and doing with those of others, however, it is helpful to have some variety—variety of feelings, of viewpoints, of attitudes, of situations, and of experience. In contrast to overly large groups, then, there may be enough time and space for all voices to be heard in very small groups, but those voices may not provide enough variety to keep it both stimulated and stimulating.

Is there an ideal size for mutual-aid systems? Probably not, at least not in absolute terms. What is most important is that there be a reasonable relationship among size of group, length of group session, expectations regarding participation, and purposes. The group should not be so large that there is never enough time for all members to express themselves, and it should not be so small that constant efforts need to be made to keep dialogue alive. A core membership (i.e., consistent attenders) of about five to seven people (usually meaning a group initially formed with about seven to nine people, plus the worker) is probably optimal.

Commonalities and Differences

Just as mutual-aid systems need their members to have a language in common, be it verbal or nonverbal, they also need commonality with regard to needs, desires, and hopes. Commonality helps group members discover their common ground and helps them become open to one another as potential resources. The more people sense that comembers can imagine how they feel, the more open they will be to sharing their real concerns and desires.

Commonality also helps sustain a sense of community in times of crisis. Take, for example, the crisis of participating in a new group. It takes time for members to come to know one another and to come to know the worker as a *group* worker, even if they know him or her on an individual basis. We may have *said* that strengths would be valued and needs and desires respected, but did we really *mean* it? New members cannot know for certain until the occasion to test that claim presents itself. Until then, they need to make a leap of faith regarding the acceptability of what they have to give to and take from the group. What will help them make that leap is the extent to which they feel that they are in the company of others who share common ground. The clearer their commonalities are from the very beginning, the easier it will be for them to make this leap of faith, and the easier it will be for them to pass through the new-group crisis.

Another example is conflict, which often occurs as group members become more comfortable with one another and feel increasingly free to express their feelings and opinions (see Chapter 8). Here again, commonalities play a key role in the mutual-aid process. If what members have in common provides them with a strong tie to one another, it is likely that they will be able to work through their differences and reach states of empathy (i.e., understanding of and sensitivity to other positions) if not sympathy (i.e., identification with other positions). If their differences outweigh their common ground, it will be difficult for the group to continue to think and act as a community. Once a group loses its sense of community, however, it also loses potential for mutual aid.

The needs and desires that members bring must also have enough commonality that individual problem solving can easily provide food for thought for everyone (see Chapter 6). Whatever issues or concerns are raised by one member must be perceived as interesting and personally relevant by other members. The less they have in common with regard to their needs and desires, the more difficult it will be for them to reach into own experiences for understanding and empathy as they try to help one another think things through.

In a research class I once taught I decided, given that my students had only one semester to develop a research proposal, it might be more useful to form their in-class work groups based on their differences. The groups I had formed in the past had centered on commonality of interest areas, but this time I hoped that composing the groups based on differences might stimulate thinking more quickly. I would not say the results were disastrous, but it was the only year in which students found this aspect of class less than helpful. Rather than providing stimulation, their differences so immediately overrode their commonalities that they became immobilized rather than helped by group process and were essentially incapable of using the groups to meet their learning needs.

That commonalities are important to mutual aid does not mean that differences are unimportant. To the contrary, differences also play a key role in mutual aid, particularly as the group matures. Although what they have in common helps members support one another, accept one another as resources, and sustain a sense of community in times of crisis, what they bring with them that is *different* helps keep the group stimulated and stimulating and helps them cultivate their skills of empathy.

What kinds of commonalities and differences should members have? Bertcher and Maple (1996) suggest that, keeping the group's purpose in mind, we organize commonality around descriptive attributes (such as age, culture, and education) so that members can quickly see what they have in common with their fellow members and organize differences around behavioral attributes (such as interaction styles) so that there will be some variety in the ways in which people interact, increasing the possibility that their ways of being and doing will be useful to others. When all members have similar attributes, have faced similar problems, and tried similar solutions, the group holds little promise of new possibilities.

THE ROLE OF GROUP PURPOSE IN MUTUAL AID

There is strong evidence, both from casework and psychotherapy research, that clients are most apt to continue in treatment when they and their therapists share similar expectations. (Briar 1966, pp. 25-26)

Developing a Group Purpose

Developing a group purpose speaks to one of the major obstacles of mutual aid—the initial difficulty that people have in identifying their self-interest with that of others (Shulman 1999). Nonetheless, a lack of understanding about the role of group purpose in group work generally and with regard to mutual aid more specifically often causes this concept to be neglected in the planning process. Efforts to formulate and develop a group purpose may be regarded as a form of manipulation, a violation of the rights of members to select their own goals. Or it may be regarded as carrying out a piece of work that members should be doing for themselves once the group begins. Sometimes, having even a tentative group purpose is seen as infringing on a group's rights to spontaneous process. Sometimes it is thought that the only structure a group should have to begin with is consistent attendance—that a group purpose is simply an imposition by the worker upon the group.

For a mutual-aid system, a clear conceptualization of purpose—one with which *all* the participants agree—plays an important and positive role in group development (Galinsky and Schopler 1977; Glassman and Kates 1990; Kurland 1978; Lowy 1976; Northen and Kurland 2001; Papell and Rothman 1980). First and foremost, it ensures that the consumers of our services are informed, that people understand what they have "gotten into." Second, even if as a result of our pregroup discussions, new members can say to themselves, "I know why *I'm* here," they are still likely to ask, "Why are we in this same group together?" A clear purpose, even if tentative, helps them answer that question. In other words, it helps them identify their common cause. A kind of centerpost around which members can bond, group purpose provides a reference point for establishing, developing, and evaluating mutual aid as both process and result. As Galinsky and Schopler (1977) argue,

> [w]henever a group initially lacks sufficient consensus on goals and has no restriction in goal selection, fairly lengthy exploration and bargaining phases can be expected. The unlimited range of alternatives offers the possibility of finding some common purpose which will resolve differences and be acceptable to a sufficient number of members. This freedom, however, may result in prolonged confusion. Without guidelines for goal selection, the group may interminably explore alternatives without ever reaching a decision on goals. (pp. 29-30)

Group purpose also plays an important role in three ways as the system matures. First, when strong differences emerge, members sometimes wonder about the fact that they are experiencing disagreement and ask themselves, "Why should I stay in this group?" and ask of one another, "Why should we stay together, really? What is in it for us?" In moments such as this, it is only the group's purpose that will remind them of what they *do* have in common—not just in terms of their needs and goals but in terms of the work they have completed as a group and the work they have yet to carry out as a group. The group's purpose will help them remember why they are in *this* particular group with *these* particular people; it will help them to continually identify what they have in common with one another and keep in sight the extent to which their common ground is greater than the sum of their differences.

Second, group purpose helps members make appropriate selections of content and keeps the process focused and relevant. When members need to make decisions about what they should do—that is, what kind of content (means) will be most suitable to achieve the group's end (e.g., "What should we do now? Should we talk? About what? Should we do an activity? If so, what kind? Or should we have a guest speaker? If so, who should it be?") The group's purpose that will help them make that selection. It is the group's purpose that will serve as their reference point for deciding *what* the work of the moment should be and for evaluating the wisdom of that choice (e.g., "So, did this activity help us think through some of the concerns we wanted to address today? If so, how?"). And when members find it difficult to make meaningful contributions to the process because the goal has become vague ("Why are we talking about all this again?") or has become lost altogether ("*How on earth* did we get to this point?!"), only a return to group purpose will help them regain their focus. It is their reflection on group purpose that will help them recapture the *meaning* of what they are doing ("Oh yes, we are talking about this because we are trying to figure out how to . . .").

Third, when members evaluate their success as a mutual-aid system, it is the group's purpose that will serve as their standard of measure. As they ask themselves whether the *group* is accomplishing or has accomplished what it sought to accomplish, they will make that assessment against the group's purpose. As they ask themselves whether *each* one of them is accomplishing or has accomplished what he or she sought to accomplish in the group, they will make that assessment against the group's purpose as well. Finally, as they attempt to measure whether what they have accomplished (either as a group or as individuals) is *as much as* they had hoped for, or whether there is yet more to be done, they will make that assessment against the group's purpose.

Thus, although the nature of a group's purpose needs to remain fluid enough to change over time to keep it relevant to the members' needs, group purpose that provides a place to begin working, a reference point for carrying out and evaluating process and progress.

Of course, a group's purpose is always tentative until members meet, discuss, and reach a consensus about it *en groupe*. Still, we need to have a purpose in mind to identify potential members and to give the new group a place to begin its thinking-through process. An important pregroup planning task, therefore, is to educate ourselves about the needs, desires, goals, and capacities of the people we have in mind for the group. Another is to read the relevant professional literature. If we hope to have referrals from colleagues, yet another is to discuss the group we have in mind with them and other organizational parties who have the power to help or hinder our plans. In addition, we need to test our initial perceptions and ideas with potential members through pregroup dialogues. As Julianna Schmidt (1969) puts it,

> [u]nless a client knows clearly how his worker views their respective roles in determining interview content and direction, he is not really in a position to make a free choice. To make a choice, he must first perceive that the choice is his to make. There is some evidence to suggest that a lack of clarity on this point confuses the client's perception of what his worker is trying to do. It is at least conceivable that in these cases, the client's attention and concern may be directed more toward deciphering the worker's intent than to ways in which he can involve himself in the planning and utilization of the helping process. (p. 801)

This process of aligning and realigning our thinking continues until all parties with a significant vested interest in the planned group arrive at a consensus. Then, a basis exists on which group members can make specific decisions about *what* to do together, *why* they should do what they do, and *how* they are going to do it.

Group Purpose versus Individual Goals

While individual goals refer to the personal needs and desires that each member brings to the group, group purpose refers to the common cause that binds members together. It is an umbrella under which individual goals can be achieved. For example, the purpose of a group of children might be stated as: "to help group members do better in school." Since all of the members would need to do better in school, they would share in this purpose. The ways in which this purpose is accomplished, however, may be different for each member. Joan might need to learn how to ask her teachers for help when she needs it, whereas Jim might need to develop more effective study habits, and Bob might need help resisting peer pressure to play hooky. These three members would have different individual goals, but they would be bound by the common thread of needing to do better in school. Therefore the group's problem-solving focus might well shift from one specific situation to another, but because members would be working toward a common purpose of doing better in school, all of the situations would give each of them interesting and useful food for thought.

The point here is that as long as there is common cause, the details of each person's individual goal can be different. As long as all group members need help to cope with loss, for example, it does not matter that the objects of loss are different; feelings of loss are similar for all of us. Or, if all members would like to learn to be more assertive, the details about how, when, or where they experience difficulty in being assertive do not matter. What matters is that they share a common basis for being in the group. Their commonality will help them bond with one another and become open to one another as resources. The details of their differences will help them be mutual resources by stimulating new ways of thinking, being, and doing.

In sum, group purpose is distinguishable from individual goals in this way: individual goals are those personal needs and desires that people bring to the group, and group purpose is the common cause that ties those needs and desires together.

Purpose versus Content

Group purpose is frequently confused with group content. That is, as the *end* to which the group has been formed in the first place, group purpose is often confused with its *means,* or *what* members do when they get together. Even people who have a long history of working with groups are often quite good at articulating content but quite poor at articulating a statement of group purpose, often articulating the group purpose by saying: "The purpose of this group is to talk about . . ." or "The purpose of this group is to learn about. . . ." These statements reflect content, not purpose. They only speak to what members will *do* together; they do not speak of the *ends* to which they will do it.

It is important to distinguish purpose from content for several reasons. If content is mistaken for purpose, the group will have difficulty deciding its raison d'être—that is, why it should make the mutual-aid efforts it is asked to make. When members lose their focus, even if they know *what* they are doing, they will have difficulty recalling *why* they are doing it—why they are being encouraged to explore normally taboo issues, for example, or being encouraged to talk about their differences. Finally, if content is mistaken for purpose, the group will have difficulty identifying the standard against which it can measure the success of its mutual-aid efforts. It might be able to evaluate mutual aid as a process, but it will not be able to evaluate it as a result (see Chapter 13).

To "talk about," then, is always the *means* through which the group is to achieve some broader goal, or its purpose. The *end* to which the group is to talk will always be its purpose. If the end is to help members cope with the stress of being single parents, then that is its purpose, regardless of how members choose to work toward that end. If it is to help prison inmates be more prepared for life outside prison, then that is the group's purpose, regardless of what each member needs to do to achieve that. If the end is to help members better manage their health, then that is the group's purpose, regardless of what members actually need or want to do to accomplish this.

Articulating a Statement of Purpose

Articulating a statement of purpose is not always easy. It is useful, therefore, to begin the process of defining an appropriate statement in this way: "The purpose of this group is to help its members to . . ."

The statement needs to incorporate several different personal goals, so it must be articulated at a broad enough level to do that. It should not be too abstract, however, or it will lack its real meaning to actual group process, making it difficult for members to refer to it for direction. A statement of purpose that would apply to any helping group we could envision (e.g., "The purpose of this group is to help members improve the quality of their lives" or "to provide support") would be too abstract, then, to serve as a centerpost around which members can bond. Such purposes would be very unlikely to help members regain focus, for example. A statement of purpose needs to be broad enough to encompass individual goals, therefore, without being positively cosmic. At the same time, it needs to be concrete enough that the group to which it belongs can use it as a framework for shaping and assessing its process.

A good way of testing whether or not a group purpose is conceptualized at an appropriate level of abstraction is to think about the potential members, make a list of the needs and desires that we anticipate such a purpose would meet, and ask ourselves a few questions:

- Would the potential members have the capacity to work toward such a purpose? If so, in what ways (content) might they do so?
- Is it conceptualized broadly enough to encompass a variety of individual needs and desires without being so global that it becomes meaningless in real terms?
- If the process were to become unfocused, for example, would a reiteration of that statement help members refocus their discussion or activity?
- Is it clear and concrete enough to serve as a standard for measuring the group's success as a mutual-aid system?
- Will members be able to use it to assess the extent to which mutual aid helped them achieve their goals?

We also need to consider how a group's purpose is likely to be received by our three major audiences: the system within which the group is to operate, our colleagues, and our potential members. Is the purpose engaging to everyone who may have a significant vested interest in the group's development and success? How so? Is such a purpose even feasible? Are colleagues likely to refer people to the group? Why or why not? Are potential members likely to be attracted to it? Why or why not?

The basic issues here are (1) the relevance of group purpose to its members, (2) the extent to which all who are significantly involved with the group understand and agree on it, (3) the extent to which we can provide a sound and reasonable rationale for such a purpose, and (4) how well it fits with the mission of its setting.

Skills for Helping a Group Agree on a Purpose and Work Toward It

We use several skills for helping a group work out and work toward its purpose. To help members discover their common ground and reach a consensus about the group's purpose, we *ask them to talk to one another directly* (e.g., "Talk to the group, Frank.") rather than talk only to us or to others *through* us. To help them develop their common ground, we *ask them to connect with what others in the group say and feel* (e.g., "Okay, so one thing you'd like from the group, Phyllis, is help to manage your time better. Weren't you alluding to that too, Lou, when you said . . .?"). And we *encourage them to build on one another's contributions* (e.g., "Okay Lou, so you have some really good ideas for working that out. Phyllis, can you imagine putting any of those ideas to use in your own situation?"). To help the group acknowledge and confirm its common cause, or purpose, we *encourage group members to work together* rather than alone or in competition (e.g., "All right, let's work together here. Any ideas about how we might go about this?"); we *encourage collective decision making* (e.g., "So, do we all agree that we should do this?"); and we *identify, explicitly note, and focus* on group themes (e.g., "Okay, so far it seems to me that we've identified at least three areas in common on which we might focus . . .").

We help make the group's purpose inclusive by *encouraging members to express directly to one another* their reactions to ideas and feelings about the group's purpose (e.g., "So, we haven't heard from you yet, Marty. What are your thoughts and feelings about what's been proposed so far?"); we *help them reveal their needs and interests* to one another (e.g., "Howard, do you have any ideas about what might be most helpful or useful to you?"); we *invite everyone in the group* to participate (e.g., "We haven't heard from everyone here, right?"); we *help those who have trouble speaking up join in the dialogue* (e.g., "Saul, jump in here—you look like you have something to say") and we *express our appreciation* for all of their contributions (e.g., "This has been just great! I'm not sure we've talked it all out, yet, but we've made a good beginning effort."). And to help group members reach a consensus about its purpose, we *ask them to share and discuss their understanding* of group purpose as it has been articulated and as it might be articulated from their points of view (e.g., "If you will recall, we talked about this group's purpose when we met individually before the group even began. Now, though, I think we need to talk about it all again as a group, so that we can bring it out in the open, say what we think and feel, and come to some agreement."). All the while, we *scan the group visually* to reach for nonverbal reactions to what is being said (e.g., "Judy, I noticed that you were smiling as Don was talking, just now . . .") and in particular for any differences of opinions, ideas, and feelings that may exist (e.g., "Cal, you look as if you're thinking along different lines . . .").

Then, to help the group work toward its purpose, we *focus on group themes* as we help members identify and work out their individual objectives (e.g., "So, when all is said and done, it seems that we are all talking about . . ."). We *constantly encourage group members to join forces in common* rather than competitive pursuits (e.g., "I think that's a really good idea, Joe. How can we do that together as a group, do you think?"). And we *make statements that reinforce the give and take of help* (e.g., "That's a really nice offer, Carol.").

We help the group recognize the importance of its purpose by *behaving in ways that reflect our own commitment to the group's purpose,* and by *making statements that reflect the high priority we assign to the group,* such as statements about the importance of regular attendance, punctuality, and participation (e.g., "It's really important that we all be on time," and "I know some people have a harder time than others, but in this group it's really important that we all participate. Let me know if you need help.").

Finally, to help the group recognize and assess the progress it is making toward reaching its purpose, we constantly *ask group members to reflect on the group's process* (e.g., "So, Alan, what do you think? Was this process helpful to you?"); *ask them to measure the quality of group process against its purpose* as they have defined it (e.g., "It was? Can you tell us how so?"); and *take stock of the work still to be done while noting the group's achievements* (e.g., "Okay, we did some really good stuff here today. Let's give ourselves a hand! Now let's talk about taking all this even further.").

KEY POINTS OF THIS CHAPTER

1. In planning a mutual-aid system, we need to consider the historical and contemporaneous attitude of the system within which the group is to operate.
2. The capacity of the persons to communicate and interact on some level is an important consideration in planning a mutual-aid system. Not all group members need to be highly skilled or even equally skilled at communicating or interacting. What *is* important, however, is that they are all able to engage in an exchange of ideas, feelings, and knowledge with peers. A group's purpose, therefore, needs to place reasonable expectations on members.
3. Both commonalities and differences among group members will influence the quality of mutual aid. Commonalities will help them bond with one another, while differences will help keep the group stimulated and stimulating.
4. The most effective groups have been found to be those whose members want to be there. Regardless of whether people join a group freely, however, it is the relevance of the group's purpose that will determine how useful it is perceived to be by its members.
5. In general, a group's purpose speaks to the needs and desires of the population we have in mind and, more specific, those of prospective members.
6. A statement of purpose should be broad enough to encompass all of the members' individual goals but not so abstract as to lose its meaning to actual group process.
7. A clear group purpose on which all of the participants agree ensures that members will be informed consumers of our services, helps them identify the common cause that binds them together, helps

them select content, provides a direction for work, strengthens the group in times of crisis, and provides a standard for assessing success.

8. Group purpose and content are frequently confused. What members do together to achieve a certain end (such as talk or activity) reflects content. The end to which they do what they do (*why* they are talking or engaging in a certain activity) reflects purpose.

RECOMMENDED FURTHER READING

Bertcher, H. and Maple, F. (1996). *Creating Groups.* Newbury Park, CA: Sage.

Brandler, S. and Roman, C. (1991). *Group Work: Skills and Strategies in Effective Interventions.* Binghamton, NY: The Haworth Press.

Brown, A. and Mistry, T. (1994). Group work with "mixed membership" groups: Issues of race and gender. *Social Work with Groups* 17(3):5-21.

Davis, L. (1995). The crisis of diversity. In *Capturing the Power of Diversity,* eds. M. Feit and J. Ramey, pp. 47-58. Binghamton, NY: The Haworth Press.

Galinksy, M. J. and Schopler J. H. (1971). The practice of group goal formulation in social work practice. *Social Work Practice,* pp. 24-32.

_____. (1977). Warning: Groups may be dangerous. *Social Work* 22(2):89-94.

Heap, K. (1984). Purposes in social work with groups: Their interrelatedness with values and methods—a historical and prospective view. *Social Work with Groups* 7(1):21-34.

Kurland, R. (1978). Planning: The neglected component of group development. *Social Work with Groups* 1(2):173-178.

Liu, F. W. C. L. (1995). Towards mutual aid in a Chinese society. In *Group Work Practice in a Troubled Society: Problems and Opportunities,* eds. R. Kurland and R. Salmon, pp. 89-100. Binghamton, NY: The Haworth Press.

Lowy, L. (1976). Goal formulation in social work with groups. In *Further Explorations in Group Work,* ed. S. Bernstein, pp. 116-144. Boston: Charles River Books.

Northen, H. and Kurland, R. (2001). *Social Work with Groups*. New York: Columbia University Press.

Papell, C. and Rothman, B. (1980). Relating the mainstream model of social work with groups to group psychotherapy and the structured group approach. *Social Work with Groups* 3(2):5-23.

Schmidt, J. (1969). The use of purpose in casework practice. *Social Work* 14(1):77-84.

Schopler, J. H. and Galinsky, M. J. (1981). When groups go wrong. *Social Work* 26(5):424-429.

Shalinsky, W. (1969). Group composition as an element of social group work practice. *Social Service Review* 43(1):42-49.

Wheelan, S. and McKeage, R. L. (1993). Developmental patterns in small and large groups. *Small Group Research* 24(1):60-83.

Chapter 4

Early Group Goals and Norms

KEY CONCEPTS OF THIS CHAPTER

Authenticity
Authority
Collaboration
Commitment
Human Connection
Interaction
Mutual Aid in Motion
Purposeful Use of Self
Safety
Self Reference/Self Reflection
Structure
Work Connection

* * *

We are pressed to attend to many things with the new group, and especially in the first session, such as putting members at ease, encouraging them to return for the next session, helping them to begin seeing their commonalities, and helping them begin to get to know one another. We cannot do everything at once, however, thus we need to develop priorities, and the goals and norms we choose to prioritize at this early time in the group's life will set the tone for its future (Glassman and Kates 1990; Lowy 1976; Newstetter 1935). For example, if we hope to set the stage for mutual aid, members must leave the first session with a sense of their human connection, which will help them begin opening up to one another as mutual-aid resources. If we want them to begin to see the commonalities among their needs, desires, and goals, then we also want them to leave the first session with a sense of their connection to the group's purpose.

The hope that members will find the group trustworthy at this early point is unreasonable, of course. Nevertheless, we want them to leave the first session feeling that the group has at least the potential to provide safety and support as they work toward their goals, which will encourage them to come to the next session. In fact, if we were completely honest, we would admit that an even greater fear than people not showing up at the first session is the possibility that they will not show up at the second one! Even if we usually articulate this goal tongue-in-cheek, it does reflect in a nutshell our hope that group members' interest will be piqued enough in the first session to make them want to return to the second one—that they will, in effect, have begun to see what's "in it" for them (Glassman and Kates 1990; Lowy 1976; Papell and Rothman 1980).

Finally, we want group members to leave the first session having experienced at least some taste of mutual aid, having had an opportunity to glimpse some of the ways in which they might help one another.

In addition to prioritizing certain group goals, we also need to pay close attention at this point to the norms we wish to see develop, since norms have such make-or-break power over mutual aid (Glassman and Kates 1990). In fact, norms are so strong in their capacity to dictate ways of being and doing that once they are put into play and adopted, they are "undone" only with great difficulty, even when they are acknowledged as counterproductive by the group itself.

In the first session, therefore, we need to explicitly encourage norms that will set the stage for mutual aid (such as the expression of real feelings and opinions, working cooperatively, and the giving of help), and discourage norms that are counterproductive to mutual aid (such as giving advice, being competitive, or relying on the worker as the only or central helper). If we want it to be normal to express real feelings, if we want it to be normal for people to think before they speak rather than simply talk to hear themselves talk, and if we want it to be normal for people to speak in ways that demonstrate respect and sensitivity, then in the first session we need to model these ways of being and encourage members to follow suit. From the start we need to do everything we can to establish norms that will catalyze mutual aid and prevent those that will impede it from taking root (Glassman and Kates 1990; Konopka 1983; Northen 1988; Papell and Rothman 1980; Schwartz and Zalba 1971; Shulman 1999). Only through our purposeful attention to working toward certain goals and establishing certain norms can we begin to provide a basic operating structure for the new group, help it understand the framework within which it may function, and help it shape its mutual-aid process.

The next two sections discuss each group goal and norm in greater detail.

GOALS TO EMPHASIZE IN THE FIRST SESSION

Since the greatest priority of the mutual-aid approach is that people discover their common ground as quickly as possible, *group building* (Papell and Rothman 1980) is the logical frame of reference for deciding which goals to prioritize with the new group. These goals are for group members to begin to establish a human connection with one another, to begin to sense a common purpose, to begin to feel a sense of commitment to the group, to begin to see the group as a safe place for real talk, and to have a taste of mutual aid.

The Human Connection

Since it is through their relationships that mutual aid will develop, it is important that new members begin to connect with one another on a human level as quickly as possible. Without such a connection, it will be difficult for them to become open to and respond to one another as mutual-aid resources. We need to devote some attention in the first session, therefore, to simply helping members get to know one another (Lowy 1976; Papell and Rothman 1980). If we had to choose, for example, we would postpone a discussion of "rules and regs," since it is better for people to leave the first session without a firm understanding of the group's structural details than it is for them to leave without a sense of the other people.

How do we help group members begin to connect on a purely human level? We *use introductions* to help them begin to share who they are. We *help them discuss their feelings* about being in this group. We *encourage them to share the nature of previous group experiences.* We *ask them to talk about what they hope to achieve in the group.* We *take every occasion*—both formal (through introductions and contracting, for example) and informal (through pregroup or postgroup moments of chitchat, for example) *to help group members get to know one another.* As we do these things, group members begin to experience their commonalities, form personal attachments, and feel their human connection.

A Sense of Purpose

Although mutual aid depends to a great extent on the quality of the human connection among group members, it also depends on their work connection, on their connecting with one another regarding the group's raison d'être, or purpose.

How do we help people connect around work? Again, *we use the introduction process.* We *ask them to talk about* the *issues* that have brought them to the group. We *ask them to share* with the others *what they hope to get* out of participating. We *help them* begin to *identify and articulate* the *commonalities* between their own goals and those of others. Furthermore, we *encourage them to identify the threads* that seem to bind of their individual goals to the group's overall purpose.

When we first meet with the new group, we will already have discussed with prospective members both the concept of group purpose and the reality of this group's purpose. Nevertheless, group purpose will not take on its full meaning or become truly accessible as a reference point for either shaping process or assessing progress until members have the opportunity to reach a consensus *en groupe* with regard to its meaning. Only when they have had the opportunity to do that will the group's raison d'être truly belong to them, and they will begin to feel connected to one another at the work level. Even if a consensus about the group's purpose is not reached by the end of the first session, which is very likely since there are so many competing goals, it is still essential to group building that some degree of dialogue around the work connection begin now.

Commitment

If we want group members to want to return for the next session, then they must leave the first session with some degree of commitment to the group. Even when we work with a so-called captive audience (i.e., people in the group against their will), it is best for them to want to return to the next session, for a group's process will always be much more useful if members become engaged in and committed to its work.

We help members in many ways to become committed to the group. At the most fundamental level, we *model commitment,* for example, by being on time, by assigning more importance to the group than to other activities that beg our attention, and by showing respect for content. In other words, by taking the group seriously we help members take it seriously as well.

We do more than model commitment, however. We *also talk about the importance of the group* as we see it (e.g., "You've all talked some at this point about the needs and desires that have brought you to this group, and I really believe that in this group we'll be able to do much to help you meet those needs and desires."). We *make statements that help us share our vision of mutual aid* for this particular group (e.g. in, "Let me tell you some of the ways that I already see, even at this early point, in which I think you can all be of help to one another."). And we use every opportunity to *identify the potential for mutual aid* when we do see it (e.g., "So, Frank, you feel like Estelle, then, right?").

Finally, we help new members become committed to the group by being inclusive, and we do that by *making statements and gestures* that include everyone in the group (e.g., "In this group, we will decide on things together."). Being inclusive helps people begin to see themselves as a community, and even if that self-image is one of a community in the making, it still helps them begin to feel invested in what happens in and to the group. To some extent, of course, it is the nature of their differences that will help them entertain new ways of thinking or doing, but at this early point, we are more concerned with helping people see their association as members and "in it together" than we are with focusing on their differences (Falck 1989).

Safety

Another major goal of the first session is that group members will begin to think of the group as a safe place to express what they really think and feel, a goal that requires two types of interventions: generic and stylistic.

Generic interventions refer to those behaviors that practitioners routinely assume to help new members become comfortable. *Taking risks* and *admitting our own mistakes,* for example, are generic interventions intended to model the desirability of taking risks and the acceptability of making mistakes. *Helping new members understand that in this group, not knowing will be just as acceptable as knowing* (either by explicit statements to that fact or through admitting when we ourselves do not have an answer) is also a generic intervention.

Many generic interventions can be used to help put new members at ease, all of which acknowledge the newness of the group and aim to help members express and explore whatever ambivalence they may feel about being in the group. We help the group *attend to issues of confidentiality* and *set in motion the norm of cooperation* while discouraging competition. We *adopt a trusting posture ourselves* and *respond sensitively* to individual concerns. We are *thoughtful before we speak.* We are *reflective as we listen.* And we guard the new group against premature intimacy by structuring discussion so that people do not disclose highly personal information because of anxiety, for example, before the group is able to tolerate it and respond appropriately, in kind, and meaningfully.

Stylistic interventions, on the other hand, refer to those ways of being and doing that, in addition to generic interventions, we personally believe are effective for helping new group members begin to feel safe. These might consist of using *specific words or deeds* we think reflect a friendly, genuine, and caring manner and that we would normally use to put people at ease regardless of the context, such as smiling, the purposeful use of humor, engaging in informal chitchat, or in some form of nonverbal communication such as a nod of support or even providing refreshments.

Whichever interventions feel right to us, our overriding goal is essentially the same: that group members leave the first session with a sense that we have shown our concern for and sensitivity to them—

that we have "been there" for each of them. We cannot provide instant safety, of course (see Chapter 5), but we *can* help the group begin to build a self-image as a place where people can give of themselves without fear of ridicule or attack.

Mutual Aid in Motion

Finally, we want group members to experience a taste of mutual aid in the first session. Clearly, the intensity of mutual aid will increase as time goes by, as members come to know and trust one another, and as they come to see how they can help one another (see Chapter 5). Still, just as we can help them begin to feel a sense of safety, we can help them experience at least some manner of mutual aid as well. How can we help them do that at such an early point?

First, we can set the stage for experiencing mutual aid by *taking the time to help group members understand how we define it* (e.g., "Here is how I see mutual aid . . .") *and how we anticipate it as a group process* (e.g., Here are some of the ways in which I see its being played out in this particular group . . ."). Not only will this process help the group develop a common set of expectations, it conveys our faith that the group can develop into a system of mutual aid while helping people new to the process become more alert to moments in which mutual aid is or is not taking place.

Next, we help members begin to imagine how they might engage in mutual aid by using bridging techniques to draw out their commonalities. We *encourage the dynamic of data sharing* (e.g., "Does anyone know where we might get that information?") and through that process help group members begin to see their potential as an information network. We *encourage them to identify with feelings* that are being expressed (e.g., "So, Brian, you feel pretty nervous about being here, right? I bet you're not the only one. . . .") so that they begin to experience *mutual support.* We *use whatever threads of commonality we perceive* as they begin to talk about their needs, desires, and hopes (e.g., "It seems to me that you are all saying, in one way or another, that you have some real trouble controlling your anger and would like to change that.") to help them begin to see their "all in the same boat" dimension.

In essence, by creating or making use of existing occasions to help group members begin to see the ways in which they might be helpful to one another, we can give them a taste of what it will be like to participate in a mutual-aid venture. By noting every time we see mutual aid in action, we can help the new group begin to develop its ability to recognize and repeat it as well.

NORMS TO EMPHASIZE IN THE FIRST SESSION

Because of their ability to make or break the mutual-aid process, norms play a major role in social work with groups (Galinsky and Schopler 1977; Glassman and Kates 1990; Hartford 1971; Konopka 1983; Northen and Kurland 2001; Papell and Rothman 1980; Schwartz and Zalba 1971).

Norms are often confused with rules and regulations. Contrary to norms, however, rules and regulations are formalized and usually static sanctions on behavior. They tend to be discussed and developed in a new group as a part of its contract and generally refer to expectations regarding attendance, punctuality, confidentiality, and other structural issues, such as meeting times, size of group, or whether it is to be open or closed. Rules and regulations might also refer to expectations regarding process issues, such as whether or not members should raise their hands in order to speak, or which type of communication format (see Chapter 1) will take place. Rules may be developed to address any aspect of membership, then, but regardless of their direction or substance, we generally think of them as formalized and proactive directives regarding appropriate behavior.

Although groups may and often do discuss norms, norms generally tend to evolve on their own, out of actual process. That is, they tend to become established reactively rather than proactively. Therefore, rules and norms both speak to behavior, but there is a key difference between them. Rules *dictate* behavior. Norms *are* behavior. Norms are ways of being and doing that, unless directed otherwise, evolve into standards of acceptable behavior and ultimately reflect a group's usual way of doing things.

Norms often evolve discreetly, but they set strong precedents for behavior, and once in motion are extraordinarily difficult to challenge, let alone change. For example, a poster on the wall may state that no food is permitted in the room in which the group meets, but the norm of that group may still be for members to bring and eat a snack. In spite of the admonition against eating, if the norm of snacking is challenged later in the group's life, we can be sure that members will cry, "But why now? After we've been doing it all along?!"

In sum, once a precedent for any norm has been set, a proposal to change it—and often just the mere idea of examining it—feels very threatening to the group. Changing an established norm feels like a loss, as if something is to be taken away. It is important, therefore, to encourage from the very beginning ways of being and doing that will promote mutual aid and discourage ways that are likely to impede mutual aid so that we do not find ourselves in the unhappy position of norm-busting! Norms crucial to mutual aid are related to collaboration, authenticity, use of self, use of comembers as helpers, decentralized authority, and free-form interaction.

Collaboration

If a group is to build a sense of community, its members will need to work together rather than compete for the limelight or special status.

Placing a high value on collaboration does not mean that people's individuality will not be valued. Quite the contrary; their individuality will play a great role in actualizing some of the dynamics of mutual aid, such as *mutual demand* and *problem solving.* Neither does it mean that their individual leadership skills, comic-relief skills, comforting skills, working skills, or other skills and strengths will remain unrecognized and unappreciated. Clearly, one member will assume leadership of process at some points, while at others another will do so in accordance with his or her particular strengths and skills. Still, if mutual aid is to take place, a spirit of communal achievement (e.g., "All for one and one for all.") rather than individual achievement (e.g., "I'm in this for me.") needs to prevail. If not, it will be difficult for members to identify their self interest with that of others, to group build, and to do anything but remain preoccupied with their own needs.

Many skills encourage a norm of collaboration. We begin to set it in motion by *sharing our expectations* of the group as a collaborative venture. We *purposefully use words such as our, us,* and *we,* to help give the group a sense of community. We *invite everyone to participate* in all of the group's activities all the time to give each member the message that his or her contribution is always valued. We *encourage members to engage in collaborative efforts* while we discourage competitive endeavors. We *ask members to reflect on the results* of collaboration, and we *encourage them to talk about the impact of collaboration on group climate.* All of these skills give members the message that in this group, it will be normal for people to think and act as members of a community.

Authenticity

Eventually, the group matures. It progresses beyond its "getting to know you" stage, and members feel increasingly safe to express their real ideas and feelings. When that happens, the group's capacity for mutual aid also increases and, therefore, helping the group establish a norm of authenticity, or "real talk about real things," is essential to helping it develop its mutual-aid potential.

How do we help this norm become established in the group? We begin to set it into play simply by *being authentic,* by taking risks, and by *sharing our own reactions* to what is being said or done in the group. We *encourage, accept, and praise the expression of real feelings and ideas*—even when we disagree with the substance of what is being expressed—and we *amplify* overly subtle messages and *tone down* overly loud messages so that everyone in the group can hear everyone else. In this group, these skills indicate, it will be *normal* for real feelings and real positions to be expressed, and it will be *normal* for differences to see the light of day.

Purposeful Use of Self

As stated in Chapter 1 and as will be discussed in great detail in Chapter 6, the purposeful use of self by group members is crucial to mutual aid. Purposeful use of self consists of two processes: *self-reflection,* which refers to the process of thinking about personal experiences, and *self-reference,* which refers to the process of sharing those experiences as a way of helping others. Use of self is a crucial norm of mutual aid for two reasons. First, it forces people to think about their own lives and experiences instead of focusing on those of others to escape the tasks of introspection and self-analysis. That is, it prevents the helping process from being purely intellectual or abstract. Second, through its story-sharing aspect, use of self helps the group discover its common ground and through that common ground expand its capacity for insight and empathy.

Several group-specific skills help us help people engage in use of self. We *ask them to think about their own lives and experiences* as they listen to those of others. And we *ask them to share stories* about their own experiences instead of offering advice. We *encourage them to always speak only for themselves and only about themselves* instead of speaking for or about others—in other words, to express their points of view rather than attack those of others. We *ask them to reach for experiential links* so that their common ground stays in view. And when their experiential common ground is shaky, we *help them reach for feeling links* so that the group remains connected at an affective level. These and other such skills help new members understand that in this group it will be normal for them to make *personal* rather than *intellectual* contributions to the helping process.

Use of Comembers As Helpers

Since mutual aid springs from the capacity of people to help one another, the norm of using comembers as potential resources also needs to be quickly established. How do we set this norm into play? First, from the group's beginning, we *turn back to the group* all problems and issues as they arise, even when we—or the members—think we have the right solution (Middleman and Wood 1990b). That is, we call on members to respond to one another rather than assume this responsibility ourselves. That is not to suggest that we never respond to questions. Of course we do, if we are in the most logical position to respond. At the same time, it is important that we help the group learn to look to its own resources rather than automatically turn to us as the expert. We *scan the group* visually, both while we talk and listen, to identify possible contributions to the group's work process. We *use every opportunity to help members feel their commonality* so that they can become open to one another as potential resources. We also *use every opportunity to note their personal strengths and skills* to help them identify ways in which they might make use of one another as resources. Turning issues back to the group and redirecting communication encourages members to think of one another as resources. Scanning lets them know that it will be normal for their reactions to one another to be sought, noted, and expressed. Helping them identify their common ground and individual strengths helps them use one another as resources.

Decentralized Authority

Although we take an active and direct leadership role with a new group, if it is to eventually develop its full potential for mutual aid, members need the freedom to identify, cultivate, and use all of their resources, including whatever internal leadership potential exists among them (see Chapter 7). Whatever leadership skills people bring to the new group, therefore, need to be identified and exploited, and the norm of shared authority over group affairs must be established.

How can we help a group share authority? To begin with, we *explicitly acknowledge our expectation that decision making will be a whole-group process* (e.g., "Let's work on this together."). Then we *help the group understand its parameters* (see Chapter 1) and keep decision making real and relevant (e.g., "I see where we're headed, but I think we need to keep a couple of things in mind. . . .") We can *periodically check for consensus* (e.g., "All right, let's see where we all stand at this point—what do we feel and think about what's been said so far?") to help the group exercise its authority in a way that is humanistic as well as democratic (Glassman and Kates 1990). We *remain open to the emergence of leadership* from within the group and *enlist internal leadership as an ally* in the group-building process rather than perceive it as an affront to our own authority (e.g., "That's a great idea, Anthony! I hadn't thought of that. Tell us more about your thinking.") We harness the group's internal leadership potential by *encouraging members to take responsibility* for some pieces of process (e.g., "Okay, should we talk about the issue of confidentiality? I have a sense it's probably on everyone's mind at this point. What are your thoughts and feelings?"). We can *encourage members to reflect on process* (e.g., "Okay, we're coming into the end of the session. Let's talk about how we spent our time together. . . ."). In this group, these skills suggest, it will be normal for all participants to share responsibility for what happens. Shared authority will not merely be an ideal, it will be a reality.

Free-Form Interaction

Not only does a mutual-aid system need to hear from all of its members if its process is to be meaningful and relevant, it also needs to hear from them when they have something to say (see Chapter 1). It is vital, therefore, that a norm of free-form interaction be established.

New groups may experience some difficulty with free-form interaction simply because they are new. Furthermore, children or people who have difficulty controlling their impulses, expressing themselves, or taking their fair share of space, for example, may find it especially difficult to establish such a norm. The capacities of people to engage in free-form interaction need to be taken into account, therefore. Still, exceptions notwithstanding, most groups have at least some capacity to work toward (if not establish right away) a norm of free-form expression, and although the members of any group should have the freedom to do so, the members of a mutual-aid system *must* have the freedom to do so.

How do we help establish such a norm? To begin with, we *make explicit our desire that members participate in process* whenever they feel that they have a contribution to make (e.g., "I hope you'll all speak up.") We *actively help them enter the discussion* when they are reluctant to express difference (e.g., "Barry, you look as if you might have something to say. . . .") to let them know that all contributions to the group's process are welcome. We *encourage and help members communicate directly* with one another rather than through us (e.g., "Talk to the group, Fran."). We *encourage them to build on one another's contributions* (e.g., "I'm not sure I understand, Philip. How does that relate to what Inez was just saying?"). And we *use our scanning skills* to make sure that everyone who wants to contribute has the chance to do so and to help those who have trouble speaking up (e.g., "Come on in, Joyce!").

What do these skills imply in terms of the value of free-form inter- action? Essentially, they imply that in this group, not only will it be normal for members to contribute to the process but also it will be normal for them to do so whenever they believe they have something to contribute.

KEY POINTS OF THIS CHAPTER

1. Many group goals vie for our early attention, and the way in which we prioritize them will set the tone for the group's future.
2. The goals we most need to emphasize in the earliest sessions are that new members will leave the first session feeling some con- nection on a human level, some connection to the group's over- all purpose, a beginning sense of commitment, some trust in the group, and having experienced some manner of mutual aid.
3. Once in play, norms set strong precedents and are not easily un- done, even when the group recognizes them as counterproductive to mutual aid. It is important, therefore, to immediately encour- age the establishment of some group norms and to discourage others.
4. Those norms that most help a group catalyze its mutual-aid po- tential are collaboration, authenticity, use of self, decentralized authority, and free-form interaction.

RECOMMENDED FURTHER READING

Galinsky, M. J. and Schopler, J. H. (1971). The practice of group goal formulation in social work practice. *Social Work Practice,* pp. 24-32.
_____. (1977). Warning: Groups may be dangerous. *Social Work* 22(2):89-94.
Glassman, U. and Kates, L. (1990). *Group Work: The Humanistic Approach.* Newbury Park, CA: Sage.
Hartford, M. (1971). *Groups in Social Work.* New York: Columbia University Press.

Konopka, G. (1983). *Social Group Work.* Englewood Cliffs, NJ: Prentice-Hall.

Lowy, L. (1976). Goal formulation in social work with groups. In *Further Explorations in Group Work,* ed. S. Bernstein, pp. 116-144. Boston: Charles River Books.

Steinberg, D. M. (1992). *The Impact of Group Work Education on Social Work Practitioners' Work with Groups.* New York: The City University of New York.

Chapter 5

Mutual Aid, "Time and Place," and the Role of the Worker

KEY CONCEPTS OF THIS CHAPTER

Educating the Group
The Ending Group
Facilitating Process
Group Development
The Mature Group
The New Group
Pacing the Mutual-Aid Process
Time and Place

* * *

To everything there is a season.

Ecclesiastes 3:1

The passage of time has a very real impact on a group's ability to engage in and experience mutual aid. Although it might be said that mutual aid is a logical consequence of group life, it cannot be said that it is an inherent condition of group life. It does not simply exist. Only its *potential* exists (Shulman 1999). Neither does mutual aid simply happen. It takes both time and effort on the part of every participant for a group to become a mutual-aid system. As members come to know one another better and as they come to more fully recognize the commonality of their needs and goals, they also become increasingly open to one another as potential resources. As they begin to see the many ways in which they can be helpful to one another, they come to recognize and appreciate the strength and capacity of their potential for mutual aid, and they become increasingly better at functioning as a mutual-aid system (Garland et al. 1978; Hartford 1978; Middleman and Wood 1990a; Newstetter 1935; Northen and Kurland 2001; Schiller 1995; Schwartz 1963; Shulman 1999; Toseland and Rivas 1995).

What is the worker's role in all of this? The worker helps all this happen by sharing a vision of mutual aid with the new group. The worker helps it learn about those ways of being and doing that will most catalyze whatever mutual-aid potential it has. The worker helps the group establish and engage in those ways of being and doing. In short, it is the worker who helps the group translate a vision of mutual aid into action (Berman-Rossi 1993; Coyle 1949; Gitterman 1989; Glassman and Kates 1990; Hartford 1978; Middleman and Wood 1990a,b; Newstetter 1935; Northen and Kurland 2001; Papell and Rothman 1980; Shulman 1999, Trecker 1955). What can be said, therefore, is that the potential for mutual aid always exists in a group, but as the group develops or matures over time, its capacity for mutual aid through the worker's use of group-specific skills develops.

Given that a group's potential for mutual aid unfolds over time, it is useful to have a time-based framework for looking at its process and for helping set appropriate expectations along the way.

There is a strong and still-growing body of theoretical literature on group development (see Recommended Further Readings at the end of this chapter). The purpose of this chapter is less to discuss developmental characteristics of groups according to any one theory than it is to examine the generic relationship between the passage of time and a group's capacity for mutual aid. Therefore, no one particular developmental theory has been used as a framework for this discussion. Instead, stages of group development are conceptualized simply in terms of beginnings, middles, and endings, and the developmental process is discussed in terms of maturity. The *new group* connotes a group in its beginning or "getting to know you" stage. The *mature group* connotes a group that has progressed beyond that point. The *ending group* connotes the group that has started its termination process. Thus, in contrast to Chapter 2, which describes the dynamics of mutual aid and how we set and keep them in play through the use of specific skills, this chapter carries the discussion of each dynamic one step further by examining how a group's ability to take hold and make use of each dynamic is influenced by its developmental stage or level of maturity.

We probably have all watched an interviewer on television strike an intimate pose, lean forward, and ask a person whose child just died, "How do you feel about that?" and been stung by the incompatibility of time and place in such a moment. Because mutual aid is a logical aspect of group life, we do not always realize how it too is influenced by time and place. However, the concept of time and place is very pertinent to setting the stage for and harnessing mutual aid.

TIME AND PLACE

It is not uncommon to hear people who work with groups complain that a group does not seem to be *really* coming together or *really* sharing or *really* talking or expressing *real* feelings or *really* working or *really* dealing with conflict. Although the groups in question may be experiencing any number of problems, it is quite possible that at least one of those problems reflects a poor fit between time and place and the worker's expectations.

The time and place for the exchange of any and all manner or degree of mutual aid in the small group is not necessarily always right. While it may be very "right" for members who have been together for some time to share their innermost thoughts and feelings, talk about normally taboo issues, or take significant risks with or on behalf of one another, for example, it is equally "right" for members of the new group to do all this either to a much lesser degree or not at all. It may be appropriate for people who have attained some degree of intimacy to trust one another with their most personal thoughts or take risks—either in front of (as in *rehearsal*) or on behalf of others (as in collective action)—but it is equally appropriate for people who are strangers or relative strangers to maintain some privacy and distance. This state of affairs holds true even when group members already know one another, as in the following case:

We (a staff of nine social workers) had been together for a few years and interacted in a friendly and informal way, both in work and outside. Our years in the program ranged from three to ten, with most having been there about five years. Still, because there was a great difference among us in amount of formal training in work with groups, and because we all worked alone at host sites and came to staff meetings for supervision only once a week, we agreed that some on-site training would be helpful. Our director hired an outside consultant—someone known by and agreeable to all of us—for a six-session seminar. We discussed and agreed on training content, recognizing that some areas would be old news for some of us but not for others.

We had two sessions that were very successful. Then, during the third session, the consultant suggested a role play and asked for a volunteer to assume the role of worker. No one volunteered. A few minutes went by, and the consultant made a remark about our apparent reluctance. We giggled a bit, but still none of us volunteered. He let a few more minutes go by and then made another humorous but pointed remark. We giggled again, but still no one volunteered. Several *more* minutes went by, and finally, when I reluctantly volunteered, my colleagues all smiled and shouted "Great!"

The members of this group had been together for some time, but even so, there was a real reluctance to take risks in front of one another. Talking about their work at staff meetings was one thing; showing how they did (or would) carry out that work was an entirely different matter. Although groups composed of people who already know one another can often establish a climate of safety and intimacy more quickly than those composed of strangers, the concept of time and place still has an impact on both the nature and extent of risks people are willing to take.

Perhaps it is because the vision of mutual aid is such a compelling one that people who work with groups often expect them to be instant communities, and that the impact of time and place so often seem to be neglected. Such neglect will not only leave the worker frustrated, however, because the expectation is unrealistic, it is also unfair to the group. It is unrealistic because it takes time for the group to build a base of trust, to build a sense of community, or, as Margaret Hartford (1978) put it, to progress from being a *group* to being a *Group,* or, as Ruth Middleman (1987) put it, to gain a sense of its *groupness.* It is unfair because it asks group members to place themselves in vulnerable positions without any kind of safety net, feeling at the mercy of rather than in the company of others.

If members of a mature group do not seem to be sharing their real feelings or really using one another as resources or really taking risks, then the group may be experiencing myriad problems. If, however, this is the state of affairs in a new group, then it may well be that it is simply functioning the way all new groups do, that the concept of time and place has not been attended to well enough (or understood, perhaps), and a rethinking of expectations by the practitioner is in order.

What does it mean to *attend* to the concept of time and place? Basically, it means that a new group needs to be thought of and approached as a work in progress. To a great extent, therefore, the worker's task is one of *pacing,* of helping the group pace its process and progress toward becoming a fully functioning mutual-aid system and of pacing his or her own expectations so that they are in sync with the group's developmental capacity.

Does the fact that mutual aid consists of dynamics whose potential must unfold over time mean that mutual aid only happens in a mature group? No, it just means that the maturation process and capacity for mutual aid have a synergistic relationship: the more one happens, the more it causes the other to happen—and even more important, to a greater degree. The new group's ability to act as a mutual-aid system is always limited to some extent by its newness, therefore, and even if members have had pregroup contact with one another or the worker, the sense of community is still tentative. Only as members gain a better grasp of their common ground—through such processes as introductions, clarifying and reaching consensus regarding the group purpose, and connecting their individual goals to that purpose—will they begin to see opportunities for mutual aid. Each time they experience success with one of those processes—however intense or casual the moment—the group's sense of community will become strengthened, and its capacity for mutual aid will become strengthened as well, with each process building upon the other.

The key to helping a group fully develop its potential as a mutual-aid system, therefore, is to incorporate into our approach to practice the recognition that its capacity for mutual aid is *incremental* (i.e., it is a mutual-aid community in the making) and that its ability to act as a mutual-aid system is *differential* (i.e., the group's ability to make use of its mutual-aid potential varies according to how strongly it feels its common ground). The practitioner who does not adopt such an approach is apt to end up, as Clara Kaiser (1958) put it, frustrated for what the group is not doing rather than aware and appreciative of what it can do and is doing.

The following sections take a closer look at the relationship between time and place and each dynamic.

Sharing Data

The ability of group members to think of their peers as valuable sources of information, knowledge, and wisdom generally increases over time as they gain respect for one another. It is unreasonable, therefore, to expect that a new group will recognize exactly how its members can be resources in this way and make full use of them as such. People may be open to the *idea* that all people bring useful life experience, but they may be somewhat less open to it in *fact*. Nevertheless, even new groups can engage in this dynamic if members' areas of expertise are fairly evident. Some expectations that the new group engage in this dynamic are not, therefore, totally out of order. A good case in point is the example of Maria's single mothers' group offered in Chapter 2. When Maria's child care falls through and she needs help to find a new babysitter so that she can attend the group regularly, there is little question that her comembers, who are also single mothers needing child care, are the perfect resources to help her do that.

When it comes to so-called serious stuff, however, such as issues regarding group purpose or protocol, new members tend to think of and turn to the practitioner as the "real" expert. Unless counteracted quickly, this syndrome of turning to the worker as the only or real expert tends to continue over time, as in the following example:

> Monica said her parents used to make her get undressed down to her underwear and kneel down in the living room, sometimes for a whole hour. Jeanne said her father used to send her to the closet. Isabelle said her father keeps a big leather belt on a series of hooks in the kitchen where everybody can see it, and every time he gets mad, the belt comes down a hook. And when it gets down to the lowest hook, watch out—the next person he gets mad at gets the belt! She said even her mother was afraid of the belt—and they all seemed to identify with that whole scene. I was kind of horrified, even though I'd heard stories like this before, but I tried not to show it. After a while, I asked them what they do with their own kids. Most of them said they wouldn't do what their parents did, but they did agree that sometimes you (parents) have to hit little ones who don't understand in order to get the point across—didn't I think so? Well, I don't believe in any kind of hitting, and I wanted to say that, but instead I suggested we play with some "what ifs" (hypothetical scenarios in which discipline was called for). It was a lot of fun, and they came up with quite a few ideas on their own. I think they even surprised themselves!

Here, even though the group of teen mothers has progressed beyond its beginning stage, when it comes time to talk about child-rearing issues such as discipline, members turn to the worker who appears to them, if not as the only expert, then certainly as a more obvious and legitimate one than they.

Thus, even as members become increasingly open to one another over time and their mutual respect strengthens, helping a group make full use of this dynamic still presents an ongoing challenge, especially when it comes to information around issues on which members' expertise is not immediately apparent. The challenge to new members is to become open to the input of their peers, whereas for the more mature group it becomes one of remaining open to peers as tasks become more demanding and as the group becomes confronted with new or increasingly complex issues that, at first glance, seem to require the worker's input. The challenge for the worker remains essentially the same over the life of the group, but it is a challenge that becomes increasingly easy to meet. It is to constantly resist the temptation of taking on the role of be-all and end-all of the group. For example, it would not necessarily be inappropriate for the worker in the teen mothers' group to teach them some disciplinary methods, but while that approach might help them expand their child-rearing repertoire, it would not help them identify their own strengths. Turning the question back to them, however, does exactly that.

From the group's beginning, therefore, members need to be encouraged to think of themselves and one another as capable of contributing in this way. From the very first time a question arises and all heads turn in our direction, we need to turn those questions back to members, even when they appeal to our supposedly superior knowledge and even when we believe we have the "right" solution or the "best" way to go (Middleman 1987). Even if they do not have any professional expertise to offer, members always have some practical experience to contribute to the group's thinking.

Does this mean that we never share our own thinking knowledge, or wisdom? No, it does not. It just means that we should do so only when we think we can add a new dimension to the group's thinking or help it renew what seems to have become an exhausted process, as this worker tries to do:

The committee had been working on a fund-raising event for some time and was struggling with making a basic decision that would affect the rest of the plan. The group talked at length, and everyone gave his or her opinion about which way we should go, but eventually we ended with a stalemate, with all of them rigid about their positions. At that point, I tried to reflect what they had been saying by telling each one, "Sounds like you're saying . . . and it sounds like you're saying . . . , so is the question . . . ?"

The worker in the next example, in contrast, simply stops the process altogether to impose his own views instead of encouraging the group to expand its own process:

One of the subgroups liked my colleague very much, while the other one hated her, and they were always arguing about it. At one session, one of the more vocal members began to talk loudly and passionately about why he hated my colleague, and I decided that the argument was fairly threatening to the quieter members, so I asked everyone to be quiet and listen to me talk about extremes of opinion. I thought if they understood the impact of their illness on the way they make judgments about people, they'd understand their feelings better.

We are always potential data resources, but we need to be sensitive to the fact that what we say and how we say it carries great weight. We need to take care that neither what we have to contribute nor how we say it drives other potential contributors underground. Furthermore, we need to consider the extent to which we may be the most logical or only qualified person in the group to respond to any issue at hand. If we are, then we do so. We do not intentionally ask group members to struggle with finding answers to questions that they cannot possibly answer.

In sum, the extent to which a group is able to recognize and use its internal resources as "experts" is likely to strengthen over time as members gain increasing respect for one another. The rule for helping a group develop this form of mutual aid as fully as possible remains essentially the same, however. "What should we do?" needs to be answered with, "What do *you* think we should do?" and "What does all this mean?" needs to be answered with, "What do *you* think it means?" before we contribute our own thinking. The more we *consistently turn all issues and questions back to the group,* the more likely it is that eventually all it will take is a raised eyebrow to hear, "Oops, I know. I need to ask the group!"

The Dialectic Process

Because groups are based on the notion that "two heads are better than one," this dynamic represents to a great extent the heart and soul of mutual aid, as it is often this dynamic (along with *mutual demand* and *individual problem solving*) that helps people think about the way they see and do things. Whenever there are two or more sides of an issue to be examined, options or alternatives to be assessed and selected, a consensus to be reached, or solutions to be sought—whenever there is cause for the expression of ideas and exploration of difference—this dynamic is set into motion. Although we want the group to be formed around a strong degree of commonality, we also want it to have some differences to help make and keep it stimulating and stimulated.

People always bring different ideas about, capacities for, experience with, and expectations of what it means to "think things through" with other people. Although the prospect of having a forum for the exchange of ideas, for stating our case, and even for trying to convert others to our position may be exciting, it is not always easy for the new group to establish its dialectic rhythm in such a way that everyone's voice or contribution to the thinking-through process is heard and appreciated. People who enjoy a good debate in the comfort of a familiar environment may be timid in a new group and reluctant to take up their rightful share of group space, while others may seem to take up just a bit too much space. Some people might worry about the quality or acceptability of their ideas, appreciating the power of this form of mutual aid in concept, but still concerned about how their real selves will be received in the group. Furthermore, because a new group's sense of community has not yet been established (except perhaps in terms of common expectations) people may be excited about the prospect of sharing needs, concerns, and goals with others, but they are still neither particularly invested nor interested in their co-members' ideas and opinions. Both the personal characteristics of members and the fact that the new group's sense of community is still tentative have impact on its ability to establish its dialectic rhythm. Establish a rhythm it must, however, if it is to make use of all of its potential resources.

There are three ways in which the worker can help the new group establish its dialectic rhythm. First, we can *help new members connect with one another,* both on a human level and around the group's purpose. By helping them make those connections, we help them identify and begin to build their common ground, which will help them accept and use whatever differences are to eventually emerge. That is, we help them become more open to having differences in the first place.

Second, to help the new group make space for its differences, we can *help all members speak up and express their ideas and feelings.* If the group does not establish the norms of acknowledging, accepting, and using differences fairly quickly, it will be difficult if not impossible for it to make any use of this dynamic, since debating only takes place as a result of differences.

Finally, to help the new group make use of its differences, we can *help members think and talk about the meaning and implications of their differences* as they keep an eye on their connections—both human (e.g., in, "Hey, we all care about each other here, right?") and work-related (e.g., "Hey, we're all working toward the same goal here, remember?").

Some groups can debate in a free-form way quite easily from the start. Often, however, some kind of structure is needed to help the new group meet this challenge. At the risk of being misunderstood as promoting more structure upon process than may be ideal from a mutual-aid point of view, some discussion of the use of structure for helping new groups exchange and debate ideas and opinions follows.

It is not always easy for new groups to enter into debate, and helping the new group adopt some kind of structure for examining and debating issues is often a useful tool for helping it develop its dialectic skills. One new group might need some hand raising, for example, while another might find round-robin interaction helpful (see Chapter 1). Structure might also take the form of activity, such as letter writing, role playing, or art. The possibilities are limitless, and the form of useful structure not only might vary across groups according to composition and purpose but it might also vary from moment to moment within the same group according it's developmental needs and capacities. Whatever form the structure takes, however, its purpose remains the same: to help the group make space for all its voices.

Even as it helps the group engage in this dynamic, it also—with an eye on helping the group move toward more free-form process—provides an opportunity for the group to discuss the *way* it talks (e.g., "Wait! We're all talking at once here. What can we do so we hear everyone?").

We can help a new group make the most of its dialectic potential in several ways by *helping it accommodate all of its voices.* We can *help it find its common ground.* We can *help it remain connected to that common ground* as it explores, attempts to make sense of, and uses its differences. We *can point out every moment in which commonalities may be drawn in spite of differences* (e.g., "Okay, there are some really strong differences of opinion here, but I think that what you all have in common, which is the desire to do better in your marriages, is stronger than the differences being expressed at the moment."). We can *help group members communicate and listen to one another* in such a way that they can feel their commonality while hearing their differences (e.g., "Wait a minute. Let's see what we agree on here first, and then let's look at our differences.").

Helping a group clarify and reach a consensus around its purpose often provides it with its first opportunity to practice its dialectic skills (e.g., "Okay it seems as if there are some differences in expectations for this group. Let's talk about them."). By *being there* (Middleman 1987) for each member as he or she expresses ideas and opinions (e.g., "I can see how you might feel that way, Joe."), we provide the group with the climate of safety it needs for this dynamic to take place in a useful way.

Generally speaking, as a group matures over time its interaction process often evolves naturally into a free-form pattern. And as members assume increasing responsibility for managing the group's affairs, they also assume increasing responsibility for returning to a more structured format for debating whenever needed (e.g., "Hey guys! We're talking all at once, and I can't hear anything anyone is saying! How about if we go one by one?") and for monitoring their own process and progress (e.g., "Boy! I've been doing all the talking here, haven't I?"). Because the group's sense of community becomes more solid (e.g., "We may have our differences, but we are still a group here, and we can still work together."), as members become better communicators and listeners and increasingly interested in what comembers have to say, they also become increasingly able to reach for and make use of their differences without feeling as if the group could fall apart. This means that it becomes increasingly less necessary for the worker to help the group structure its dialectic process or to refer it to its common ground during the expression and exploration of difference. That it is strong enough to accept and use its differences toward mutual aid simply becomes understood.

Groups have an opportunity to make use of this dynamic from their very first moments, then, as they debate issues around purpose and expectations. They become increasingly better able to make full use of it, however, as they become increasingly committed to one another, as their sense of community grows, and as their differences feel less threatening.

Discussing Taboos

Discussing taboos is a dynamic with a great deal of power—but its power can be negative as well as positive. For example, we have all probably felt at some time or other that we have said "too much too soon." When this happens in a small group—that is, when taboo issues are raised before some beginning sense of intimacy has been established—the whole group can suddenly feel awkward and uncomfortable. Sometimes, in fact, group members who find themselves in such a position feel so uncomfortable that they leave altogether, as in this case:

> At the beginning of our second meeting the women started to talk about their goals. When Janine's turn came toward the end, she got into a lot more detail than the others had. I could see the others get more and more uncomfortable— fidgety, looking embarrassed or down at their laps. The rest of them had just shared a little—more about their situations than the actual abuse. Janine went on for a few painful minutes, and when she stopped, I admit I wasn't sure what to do—the group was so quiet. So I decided to "universalize" some of what she'd said, saying, "So, it sounds like you'd like to work on. . . . That sounds like what Diana was saying." Somehow, I felt my remarks were insensitive, but the atmosphere felt so depressed I wanted to move on. When we met the next week, Janine didn't show up. I called her and left messages on the phone machine— I even wrote her a note. But I didn't hear from her.

All critiques of this worker's intervention aside, the point here is that in a new group, the worker may need to protect members from an overzealous tendency to rush into a false state of intimacy, a tendency often cultivated from simply being nervous about being in a new situation, from unrealistic expectations of membership, from having been asked (unfortunately) to do just that in previous groups.

Still, while we do not urge a new group to plunge into this dynamic of mutual aid, we do need to help it establish a norm of speaking about the normally unspeakable, since the opportunity to do that is a powerful source of mutual aid. The practice question, therefore, is how we can help the new group establish a norm of speaking about taboo issues without intruding on its early need for privacy. Do we simply hope for an opportune moment? We could, but then we might run into the kind of trouble illustrated in the previous example. Or what if the group decides to remain polite for lack of other direction? In that case, we might never encounter an opportune moment. Fortunately, there is no need to struggle too much with this question, for it is often the case that the need to speak about the normally unspeakable is exactly what propels people to groups: issues of adequacy addiction, aggression, authority, dependence, fear, guilt, loneliness, loss, performance, or victimization, to name but some. Just as a group's introductory process provides it with a forum for its first attempts at debating, it frequently also provides one for establishing a norm of discussing taboo issues, and helping the new group hash out and come to terms with its purpose can help it establish this norm by encouraging the members to share the needs, concerns, desires, and goals that have, in fact, brought them to the group. We protect the new group from becoming overly intimate, however, by being very specific about the nature of information we ask for, as the worker in a group for battered women does here:

It was our first meeting, and after we went around with names, I wanted the women to start talking about the group's purpose. To get them started, I asked them to talk a little bit about their families—who was living in the house with them and their husbands—and also to just say a few words about the abuse incident that had gotten them to leave. I knew we'd get more into it later, but I wanted the women to begin to talk about their situations and also to start to see what they had in common.

At the same time, we freely and openly give voice to the needs and desires that have propelled the members to this group, as this worker does here in order to begin to normalize the discussion of taboo issues:

I said I was glad they'd come that night, because I knew it wasn't so easy for all of them. After some chitchat about weather and such, I suggested we start getting to know one another a little—I knew them all slightly, but except for two couples, they didn't know one another. What they all had in common was that they'd lost a son or a daughter to AIDS, and even though I knew it was very painful for them to talk about, I still did the introductions around that. I asked them to take a few minutes to tell us about where they lived and who they lived with, and then I asked them to share with the group a little about the children they'd just lost—what they actually died of, when they had died, how old they were—that sort of thing.

In this case, group members have two taboo issues to deal with. The first is that their children died of AIDS, a stigma for many of them in and of itself. The second and perhaps less obvious is that they have outlived their children. By acknowledging both circumstances right away, however, the worker gives the group permission to talk about them, while asking for specific information gives the process some structure as well. In contrast, consider the following process:

The group was for kids from immigrant families having some real trouble in school. They had been here long enough to speak English—in fact, they'd taken extra classes at the center, and there were six of them in the group. They knew each other a little bit, but I didn't know them, and neither did my coleader. After we all said our names, we started to talk about why we were here together, that they were all having trouble in school and that we hoped this group could help them do better. I suggested we all tell the group a little about ourselves, but you know how kids are—no one responded, so I asked the girl next to me to start us off.

In this case, the purpose of the group is immediately acknowledged, but the request for members to tell a little about themselves does not provide nearly enough structure to direct, and hence protect, the ensuing process.

In sum, a group's introductory process (e.g., personal introductions, articulation of individual needs and goals, and general discussion and clarification of group purpose) frequently provides a logical forum for helping it establish this mutual-aid dynamic as a norm. Simply *referring to group purpose* acknowledges members' specific needs or concerns or problems. *Helping members give voice to those issues* helps them begin to speak about the normally unspeakable. And even when its content (i.e., the nature of the group's business) does not deal directly with taboo issues, if a group is expected to function as a mutual-aid system, its introductory processes (i.e., how it is going to go about that business), can be used to help set this dynamic into motion by asking members to begin to engage in real talk about real things.

As a group matures and members begin to feel they have one another's trust and common interests at heart, opportunities to discuss taboo issues can provide much positive power. First and most obviously, perhaps, the relief in having a chance to speak about the normally unspeakable, particularly when the issue holds personal meaning, is very powerful. Second, because taboo subjects are usually surrounded by myths and misconceptions, opportunities to address taboo issues in safety also provide power—educational power to separate fact from fiction. Sex-education groups for teenagers, such as the one in this next case excerpt, often provide this kind of power:

> The group was talking about birth control methods. You wouldn't believe some of the "methods" they'd heard about! If a woman jumps up and down after intercourse, then she won't get pregnant. Or if she has intercourse in a certain position, or if she douches right after sex, or if she has sex in midcycle, and on and on. No wonder they're in trouble! Once we were talking about self-image, and lots of the guys agreed they could tell if a girl's a virgin. It was the old story—if she's "bow-legged," she's not a virgin. One boy even claimed that if a girl's got hair on her upper lip, it means she's had sex. I could see that our work was cut out for us!

As time goes by, if a norm for the discussion of taboo issues is established, not only does the appreciation for opportunities to speak about the normally unspeakable grow, members' capacity to make use of this dynamic grows as well and their talk becomes more real; as real ideas, real opinions, real attitudes, and real feelings are more freely shared, and as myths and misconceptions have an opportunity to be aired, debunked, and corrected.

Although making use of this dynamic does get easier over time, even the mature group may have difficulty making full use of it. Talking about taboo issues is often so unacceptable and demanding because it requires people to talk about issues considered very personal and revealing. A group may become so satisfied with having been able to discuss one particular taboo issue that it resists moving to other related issues ("Okay, we've talked about *this.* Do we really need to get into *that* as well?"). This type of obstacle often occurs when one taboo issue normally leads to another. For instance, members of a couples group might reach a certain comfort level talking about roles or about the relationship between income and authority, but they may still feel reluctant to talk about the sexual problems they are experiencing. Or a group of people with terminal illnesses might get to a point at which members can share the devastating effects of their illness but might still have difficulty addressing the impact of their impending death.

A group's discussion may also seem to become stuck at a certain level ("Enough already! Do we really need to talk about this some more?"). This type of obstacle frequently develops when the group feels overwhelmed by the issue at hand and wants to address it only in small bites. For example, members may be willing to acknowledge their differences but may have difficulty exploring either the *source* of their differences ("Let's not open Pandora's box, here. Let's just agree to disagree.") or the *implications* of those differences ("What will happen to us if we can't agree?").

Finally, the group may have difficulty agreeing about just how deeply it wants to work at all, as in the following case:

> Toward the end of a session an argument developed between Phil, who said he wanted to "work harder, dig deeper," and Rose, who said the group was "just right" for her. The other members took Rose's side and accused Phil of wanting too much for himself. Phil got angry and defensive. He said he felt dismissed by the rest of the group and that Rose tended to be superficial. I hoped they'd work it out, but they didn't, and then the session ended. Rose didn't come back, so we didn't discuss it again.

These obstacles are often referred to as *gatekeeping* and reflect some wish in the group that the work, however defined, not move beyond its current point or level. They reflect the fact that the group is finding its work of the moment overly demanding. Although gatekeeping affects more than a group's mutual-aid potential, it absolutely affects mutual aid by preventing the full exploration of issues. At moments such as this, another mutual-aid dynamic needs to be set into motion, one that will help the group, as Phil puts it, "work harder, dig deeper." That dynamic is *mutual demand,* discussed later in this chapter.

In sum, there are two keys to helping the group make the most of its mutual-aid potential in this way as it matures over time. The first is to *help the group establish a norm of real talk* by using its introductory processes to raise the issues that bring members to the group and that are not normally discussed elsewhere (e.g., "In this group, it will be normal for us to talk about real things, and we will begin to do that by talking about the group's purpose."). The second is to *pace the group's process.* While we may need to slow the new group down (e.g., "Wait! Wait! Not so fast, here. We want to do this, but let's take it one step at a time. The better we know one another, the more we can do."), we may, as it matures, replace that kind of intervention with increased demands for work (e.g., "Come on, let's not give up on this or push it aside. What's going on, here?"). In the first instance, we help the group move toward use of this dynamic. In the second, we help it actually make use of it.

All in the Same Boat

It might seem logical to assume that when a group forms around a common cause this dynamic exists from its first moments, but in reality it takes both time and effort for the same-boat dynamic come to life. As Shulman (1999) says, the difficulty that people have in identifying their self interest with that of others poses one of the major obstacles to mutual aid. This next example offers a good case in point:

Jane, a new member, began to provoke others by suggesting that, unlike them, she was in the group by mistake. After a few sessions of that the rest of the members confronted her about it. I asked the group if it was acceptable to them that Jane remain in the group if she harbored those feelings. They reluctantly agreed, but Jane dropped out after two more sessions.

Thus, although we might assume prospective group members are in the same boat because we can imagine them together in a particular group, members of a new group do not necessarily feel as if they are in the same boat. Only when they have had opportunity to connect their hopes and desires to those of others and understand how the group's overall purpose ties their goals together will they begin to feel this dynamic.

The worker's vision of mutual aid plays an important role in helping the new group develop its same-boat quality. It is, after all, the worker who begins the planning process with a group in mind and who has a vision about how a particular group composed of particular persons can become and function as a mutual-aid system around a particular purpose. It is the worker who helps the new group begin to feel its same-boat quality by sharing his or her vision of and hope for mutual aid and by making that vision contagious ("All for one, and one for all!"). It is the worker who helps the group bring its same-boat dimension to life ("Not only can we do this, but we are doing it together."). In short, *lending a new group our vision* of mutual aid and *expressing our faith* that it can become a system of mutual aid go a long way toward helping it begin to feel its same-boat potential. But just as it is unreasonable to expect new group members to share intimate thoughts and feelings, it is unreasonable to assume that a new group will automatically feel its same-boat quality. The best we can expect is that new group members see themselves on the same ocean!

As a group matures and develops to an increasing awareness of common cause, it also has occasion to develop an increasing sense of "same-boatness." As that happens, it generally becomes less and less necessary for the worker to make common-cause connections—to point out every time one member's experience resembles another's or the extent to which the feelings or ideas expressed by one person are reminiscent of those expressed earlier by another. At the same time, however, because members become increasingly comfortable in sharing their real thoughts and feelings, they also begin to experience tugs of difference. What the group needs as it matures, therefore, is some help to keep sight of its common ground—that is, its same-boat image—as it explores and tries to make use of those differences.

There are two keys to helping group members stay in the same boat as the group matures. First, we need to *help members recognize that* the *differences* emerging are a result of their work and process *are occurring within, not outside of, their common ground* (e.g., "We may disagree about exactly what to do, but we still agree we need to do *something* here"). Second, we need to *help them recognize that the whole of their common ground is greater than the sum of their differences* (e.g., "We may not see eye to eye here, but what we have in common is stronger than our differences.").

This dynamic also has an impact on the ending group. When it comes time for a group to end, the more powerfully it has experienced its same-boat quality, the harder it often is to cope with its termination. "The higher you fly, the harder you fall," as the saying goes. In fact, it is not uncommon for groups that have felt this dynamic intensely to seem as if they are truly falling apart as they approach the end, as members react to feelings of impending loss by trying to gain some distance from and lessen their bond with the group before termination "undoes" it for them first.

What can the worker do about such a state of affairs? Often, a simple acknowledgment that this *is* the state of affairs enables the ending group to stay together until its formal ending. But there are a few other things the worker can do as well, and while they do not apply only to practice with a group having special difficulty ending, they do help particularly tightly knit groups use their mutual-aid power to negotiate that process.

Reaching for group members' strengths to help shape the process of ending (e.g., "Okay, we have four meetings left. How should we use them?") can help them feel as if they still have some control over the group's process, while reaching for their strengths to contribute to the quality of the group's ending (e.g., "Joe, you're such a good organizer. How about helping us develop a plan for next week?") can help group members to remain involved as well. *Asking group members to use their mutual-aid skills* to help one another in very specific ways, such as getting to meetings (e.g., "Phyllis, would it be helpful to get a call to remind you about group on Tuesday? Who can do that here?") can help them see what skills they have developed. *Giving the group plenty of time to reminisce* about the way its mutual-aid process and progress has developed over time (e.g., "I remember when Betty first brought that up. Everyone was surprised, but we really got into it, didn't we? And you said the process ended up being really helpful to you, too, Ray. Remember?") can help members absorb and integrate the ending of the group. Finally, *asking group members to think about and identify the new skills* (mutual-aid and other) that they can take with them (e.g., "What are some of the ways in which you think this group has helped you and will continue to help you outside the group?") can help them make the transition from past to future.

In sum, helping the ending group make use of its mutual-aid skills, helping members recall their growth process, and helping them think about how that process can and will continue after the group ends are all ways in which we help give tightly knit members hope for life after group while helping them see the group through to its end.

Mutual Support

As stated in Chapter 2, the opportunity to feel supported is often one of the major incentives for joining a group. To the extent that people look forward to spending time with others who they believe share common needs and goals, this dynamic is in some ways set into motion before the group even begins. As with the same-boat dynamic, however, mutual support does not come about automatically simply because people come together as a group. Until members have had at least some opportunity to care about one another, they will have little reason, other than in the most abstract sense, to feel this dynamic.

There are two sides to mutual support: sympathy and empathy, and although most people come by sympathy quite easily, the ability to empathize generally takes greater effort. In a new group, therefore, we need to *help members discover their common experiential ground* so that they can become sympathetic to one another (e.g., "I've been there, and I know how you feel."); and we need to *help them discover their common feeling ground,* so that they can stretch their capacity for support to include empathy as well (e.g., "I have not been there, but I've felt similarly to the way I think you feel.").

Because increased safety and comfort in the group lead to real talk, and real talk often leads to the expression of difference, there may still be moments when the members of a mature group find it difficult to feel and express mutual support, even if it becomes a strong group norm over time. This is especially true when whatever differences do emerge are significant ones. It might be easy to maintain a climate of mutual support when differences are over minor matters, when members do not feel their personal integrity is at stake, or when they believe they will suffer loss because a particular solution is adopted (such as loss of face, friendship, or power). It might also be easy when the differences do not have *value* weight (that is, if one way of being or doing is not perceived as better or more moral or proper than another). It is less easy to maintain a climate of mutual support, however, when differences are significant—that is, when they reflect important philosophical or religious differences, for example, or racial or cultural approaches to ways of doing, or even, in some cases, differences around what the group's own approach to doing should be. What the maturing group most needs, then, to keep mutual support alive as talk becomes increasingly real and differences emerge is to maintain a climate of empathy (e.g., "We may not see things the same way here or have encountered the same experiences, but we have all felt the same way") so that its common affective ground does not disappear from view even when its common experiential ground is shaky.

Once group members care about what happens to one another and can accept, even appreciate, their differences, the group often becomes the one place where they feel accepted and supported, as in this case of a group for men with AIDS:

The group had been together for about four months, and at our last session, we all went around and talked about what it had meant to us. The men all agreed that this was the one place where they hadn't felt shunned or stigmatized or where people were scared of them—that here, they'd just been able to relax and be themselves.

Mutual Demand

The "demand" component of mutual demand entails group members carrying out whatever process is necessary to tackle those personal, interpersonal, or whole-group goals that brought them to the group in the first place. Many people, particularly small-group veterans, bring with them preconceived notions about what that work should look like, and such a state of affairs can pose a problem for practice with groups from a mutual-aid point of view.

In many groups the demand for work (however "work" has been defined by the group) is unidirectional rather than mutual. That is, it is made by the worker of group members, not by group members of one another. Hence, although members of a new group might be prepared to respond to the practitioner's demands for work, they are usually less prepared to respond to those of their peers. In fact, they may respond with a "Who the hell are you?" attitude. A unidirectional approach to work is in direct contrast to what needs to happen toward establishing mutual aid, however. Members must assume some responsibility for making demands for work from one another, and all such demands, such as those to dig deeper, to stay with it and not give up, to try harder, to try again, to think it through some more, to listen

more carefully, or to communicate more sensitively must be acknowledged as legitimate.

There are three basic obstacles for a group to overcome in making
full use of this mutual-aid dynamic. The first is new members'
mindsets—and the common expectation that the right to impose demands for work belongs only to the worker (e.g., "*He* will see me
through this/help me do this."). The second is the reluctance of new
members to respond to comembers' demands for work (e.g., "Who
put *you* in charge?"). The third is the reluctance of new group members to assume the right and responsibility for making demands for
work from their peers (e.g., "Who am *I*, really, to make such a demand?"). What the new group needs most to overcome these obstacles is *education* and the *chance to practice*. On one hand, educating
the new group about the look of work from a mutual-aid point of view
helps new members contrast previous experiences with the work
norms that we have in mind and understand the relationship between
the concept of shared authority and mutual aid (e.g., "In this group,
we all have the right to make demands on and the obligation to respond to demands from one another."). On the other hand, practicing
the exchange of mutual demand helps the group develop its skills at
doing so and helps members identify their unique strengths as they
contribute to the thinking-through process.

As the group matures and members become more open to this kind
of exchange, they become better at it as well, both at initiating it (e.g.,
"I'm having some real trouble with this. What do the rest of you
think?") and at using such a process to give and take help (e.g., "I feel
like giving up. I've done everything I know how at this point. Any
ideas?").

Individual Problem Solving

Some of the issues of mutual demand relate to this dynamic as
well. Just as small-group veterans often bring old ideas and expectations about what the work aspect of membership looks like, they also
are likely to bring preconceived notions about individual problem
solving. Often, their vision is one of group members, one by one,
raising ("presenting") personal issues or concerns for feedback—
usually from the worker while others listen and learn but sometimes

from fellow members, as well, who adopt the role of assistant therapists.

The problem for mutual aid with any type of presenting format is that all too often issues raised by one member are perceived and treated by the others as strictly individual ones. In this situation, even if the discussion of one person's experience is helpful to others, whatever help takes place is only tangential, as a side effect rather than purpose of the process. It is often possible for nonpresenting members to get the point, of course, when a worker and a group member engage in a dialogue around a specific issue, but such a process is not mutual aid. Just as demands for work need to be made among group members in order to reflect mutual aid, individual problem-solving processes need to include and touch everyone in the group to reflect mutual aid. Thus, although the opportunity to listen to a problem-solving dialogue between the worker and another member and increase personal awareness through that process is often thought of as mutual aid, it is not. For any individual problem-solving process to both reflect and create mutual aid, group members must have the opportunity to actively seek, acknowledge, and talk about the relatedness of their issues.

As with mutual demand, what the new group needs most to help it make use of its mutual-aid potential in this way is to be educated about the look of individual problem solving from a mutual-aid rather than a presenting, or individualistic, point of view. The differences between these two approaches to individual problem solving are dramatic, and Chapter 6 discusses how we can help people transform apparently individual issues into useful whole-group food for thought so that mutual aid can, in fact, be maintained even as specific situations are addressed.

It is easy for a new group to fall into a presenting format, or, as Kurland and Salmon (1992) phrase it, into *casework in a group,* but there are several skills we can use to help it get a taste of and refine its own skills at individual problem solving with mutual aid in mind. We *share very specifically ways in which individual problem solving can become a vehicle for mutual aid* (e.g., "We might be looking at Sarah's specific situation, but there are some basic underlying issues that pertain to everyone in the group, I think."). We *make our expectations regarding the individual-problem-solving process clear* (e.g.,

"If we're going to give one another some real help here, we'll have to look at these issues in depth. So let's not think in terms of dividing the group's time into equal or equitable shares. Instead, let's try to make whatever so-called individual issue is at hand useful for everyone."). We *can help the group establish norms* that will promote problem solving from a mutual-aid point of view (e.g., "No, Seth, you're not taking up too much time. In fact, tell us more about what happened and how you feel so that we can try to see the issues as you do and use our own experiences to help you. We all have some of the same issues to deal with here."). And we can *help the group reach for its common ground* so that the threads of commonality that run through members' issues can become food for collective thought, even as the dialogue moves from situation to situation.

As the group develops over time and members gain a firmer grasp of their common ground, they usually become better at using individual problems as a basis for mutual rather than individual aid. We can usually stop teaching them the look of this process from a mutual-aid point of view and simply help them make personal meaning of, and take personal advantage of, each so-called individual situation that arises even as they contribute to searches for solutions. We do this by *asking them to reach into their own lives* and reflect on their own experiences in search of commonality as they listen to others describe their situations. We *ask them to share their stories and the nature of their commonalities* with the group. We *ask them to speak only about themselves and for themselves* rather than speak about or for others. We *ask them to refrain from giving one another advice.* And we *ask them to constantly reflect on the process, assess its personal meaning, and share that assessment* with the group.

Rehearsal

Rehearsal, which refers to the practicing of new ways of being and doing, involves taking risks. We cannot practice approaching another group member without taking a risk of rejection. We cannot use role play to practice how we might interact with someone outside the group without risking the possibility of being wrong or looking foolish. It is difficult for the new group to use this mutual-aid dynamic, and what it needs is an opportunity for members to get to know and trust one another, at least in some measure. Even if group members have preexisting relationships with the worker or with each other, new relationships need to be developed within the context of this group. We may have a vision of the group as a safe place to try new ways of being and doing, but to expect the members to feel safe enough to use this form of mutual aid as soon as they come together is unreasonable. It is, in fact, often easier for new members to rehearse ways of being and doing outside the group and to report the results later than it is to do it in the group.

Does this mean that if a new member communicates or listens poorly or collaborates poorly, the impact of his or her interpersonal style gets ignored or that the negative impact of ways of being and doing are left unacknowledged and unaddressed because of the group's newness? No. The group is indeed a perfect place for examining ways of being and doing, and the nature and quality of group process is always a legitimate target for intervention. It is always appropriate to ask a group to help its members adopt and practice ways that are more conducive to mutual aid, to say something such as, "Oops, I'm not sure Peter got his point across. Can we try again, Peter?" But this kind of rehearsing is unintended and takes place simply because the group members are in a group. More demanding is the kind of rehearsing that is intended, the kind that people use consciously and purposefully to develop or improve certain skills. This takes more time to develop because members need to feel a sense of safety before they will take the risks called for by intended rehearsal.

We can do a few things to help the group establish a climate of safety. We can *model risk taking from the beginning* so that members can see that making mistakes in the group will be acceptable. The more we take risks ourselves—by wondering out loud, for example, or admitting when we do not know—the more the members will follow suit. We can *encourage and help new members to also take some risks.* We can ask them to offer suggestions, for example, or encourage them to speak up (e.g., "Peter, you've been looking as if you want to say something."). We can praise whatever risk taking does occur (e.g., "I'm so glad you brought that up, Marie. I bet there are others who feel the same way you do" or "who don't understand that either" or "who are wondering about that too."). We can *encourage members to act in concert rather than in competition* (by encouraging the selection of both content and process that require cooperation, or by helping the group work toward consensus, or by selecting whole-group rather than individual activities) to help them begin to identify themselves as a community. As Middleman (1987) argues, even the use of words such as *we, us,* and *our* helps a group develop its sense of community or *groupness* and, through that groupness, a sense of safety for trying out new ways of being and doing. Finally, as the group matures, we can *become increasingly demanding* with regard to the group's use of this dynamic. We can ask group members to increasingly stretch their level of trust of one another and of the group as a whole. Although we might select an activity with the new group specifically because it does not require too much personal revelation, or because participation is not apt to create the potential for embarrassment, or even because success does not depend on a great degree of interpersonal trust, we might, with the more mature group, do just the reverse. We might suggest an activity specifically because it does require some personal revelation or because it does require that a group member place a large amount of trust in another member or in the group as a whole.

Once the group is established as a safe place to rehearse—that is, a place to freely experiment with new ways of being and doing—members often look forward to and enjoy having a place where they can both be creative and exchange help with their peers in this special way.

Strength in Numbers

A group may look powerful to the outsider, but in reality its power exists only to the extent that members feel a sense of common cause and a strong feeling of *we-ness*. All groups have the potential to flex their muscles, but it is rare that the new group has the wherewithal to do so. It may have been formed around a common cause, but its members have as yet little reason to go out of their way or out on a limb for one another. The new group's strength in numbers is still just theory, not reality, and before that strength can become a reality, members need to feel bonded to one another and to the group's purpose. They need to come to care about what happens to one another and about achieving the group's purpose. They may care very much about achieving their individual goals as they enter the group, but until members have had opportunities to clarify together the group's raison d'être and to understand how their own goals are tied to that purpose, the concept of common cause, and hence the group's strength-in-numbers potential, will remain relatively vague.

Sometimes groups are formed for the express purpose of exercising their muscle, as in the case of social-action groups, and in such groups, the idea that it takes time to develop their strength-in-numbers potential is often regarded as a moot issue. It is expected that because people joined the group precisely for its potential power, they already feel bonded by their common cause, but that is not usually the case. Even with a strong and clearly identified common bond, the manner in which the members work toward their purpose (e.g., norms, processes, relationships, and so on) will have an impact on how fully they can actualize this dynamic. If competition rather than collaboration predominates, if problem solving becomes a search for solutions to individual concerns without maintaining the search for common ground, or if members perceive their primary relationships to be with the worker rather than with one another, then the group will not necessarily actualize its strength-in-numbers potential. It may sense its potential for strength, but the extent to which members are willing to put themselves on the line for comembers or for the group will always be related to how much they have come to care about what happens to one another and to the group as a whole. A group's strength-in-numbers potential exists from the outset, therefore, but its capacity to use its strength for mutual-aid purposes develops only as the members come to care about one another, as their collective investment in the group's common cause grows, and as they come to have faith in the group's ability to achieve results.

How do we help a group actualize its strength-in-numbers potential? Basically, we encourage and help group members to develop a strong commitment to one another, to mutual aid (both in idea and in practice), and to the group's purpose. We *voice our own commitment to and faith in* the new group and in its potential for mutual aid—that we believe the group can achieve its purpose, that it can become greater than the sum of its parts, and that members will be able to develop into a system of mutual aid. We *model* what commitment actually looks like—by giving priority to attending meetings over other possible activities, for example, or by being on time, or by helping members get to meetings, or by giving consideration to timing or fees. And we *ask members directly* to make a commitment to the group—both in spirit (e.g., "You come; you commit.") and in fact (e.g., "Please be on time.").

Groups are famous for their strength-in-numbers potential, but this mutual-aid dynamic is often the slowest to develop because its actualization is so inextricably tied to a group's sense of community and commitment. Therefore, although it takes time for groups to develop all mutual-aid dynamics in depth and breadth, developing this particular one usually needs even more time. To some degree the others can be identified, experienced, and used from the beginning, but a group's strength in numbers will not be realized until it has opportunities to experience the rewards of having transformed itself from a *group* to a *Group* (Hartford, 1964), a community whose collective strength (its capacity to exercise power, in this case) is greater than the strength of its individual members.

In sum, even if members have shared their hopes and expectations with the worker or with one another before the group begins, it still takes time for them to discover and actualize the many ways in which they can give and take help. Some dynamics may unfold more quickly and more easily than others, and some may unfold in full, while others remain relatively untapped. In general, however, they unfold slowly over time as group members' belief in and trust of one another grow. The next section discusses the role of the worker in this process.

THE CHANGING ROLE OF THE WORKER

Because the norms of mutual aid are often quite different from the norms of many other groups to which the members also belong, much of the practitioner's work with the new group is devoted to teaching members the look and language of mutual aid. As the group matures and begins to feel a greater sense of community, and as it becomes more and more committed to working toward its purpose, members become increasingly able to identify the various mutual-aid opportunities. As that happens, much of our teaching repertoire can be replaced with a facilitation stance, or helping group members actually take advantage of those opportunities.

That people may know what being a good group member entails does not necessarily mean that they automatically know how to be one. As the group matures and progresses beyond its "getting to know you" stage, our focus shifts from teaching people what good membership looks like to helping them become and remain good members. We shift from helping the group clarify and agree on its purpose to *helping it take advantage of mutual-aid opportunities* for working toward that purpose. We shift from helping it identify its common ground to *helping it take advantage of the personal strengths, skills, and talents* that exist in the group. And we *shift the lion's share of responsibility for managing the group's affairs from our shoulders to those of the group.* If norms conducive to mutual aid have been established over the course of the group's development (see Chapter 4) and if the practitioner has not held too tight a rein on its affairs (see Chapter 7), a mature group is usually capable of assuming responsibility for its affairs and functioning well as a system of mutual aid.

As termination grows near, members often begin to distance themselves from one another and from the group, and as that happens, the group may begin once again to resemble the new group in some ways. Lateness or absences may increase. Group members may suddenly find themselves all talking at once. Or they may once again turn to the worker as the expert and exhibit other such new-group behaviors as they become anxious about "life without group." This kind of stepping back in no way implies that the group's venture with mutual aid has been a failure, however. It is a normal state of affairs for the ending group, as members think about moving on and attempt to make that transition. The worker's role can, to some extent, be conceptualized as remedial as the group begins to end, therefore. Reeducation tasks resume some priority. Members need to be reminded of the importance and meaning of the group's norms. They may need some help to stick with those norms, and they need to be helped to identify and retain the skills they have developed.

To the extent that we shared our vision of mutual aid with the new group, we now need to share our vision of "life after group" with the ending group and help members stabilize their gains. We begin this process by *encouraging them to identify the skills* they believe they have gained. We *ask them to identify which mutual-aid processes* helped them gain those skills. We *encourage them to identify and dis-*

cuss previous and current situations in which the group's mutual-aid process was useful to them. We *help them anticipate future situations* in which the group's experience as a mutual-aid system will be useful to them. We *help them make use of the rehearsal dynamic* through such activities as role playing or skills-focused "homework" to help them practice new ways. We *help the group as a whole reflect and reminisce* about its maturation process as a mutual-aid system. As group members share their perceptions about the kind of help that has taken place, they become able to see the ways in which mutual aid has enriched their lives as members of this group, and they become better able to see how mutual aid can enrich them in other groups and in their lives generally.

KEY POINTS OF THIS CHAPTER

1. Mutual aid is not a de facto dimension of group life. It takes time for groups to develop a sense of community and to take full advantage of their mutual-aid potential.

2. The expectation that mutual aid will occur simply as a result of people's coming together in a group inevitably leaves everyone in the group frustrated and disappointed.

3. A group's development as a mutual-aid system is incremental (i.e., it is a mutual-aid community in the making), and its capacity to act as a mutual-aid system is differential (i.e., the way in which it is able to make use of its mutual-aid potential varies according to how strongly its members feel their common ground).

4. The desire to see mutual aid established as a group norm needs to be balanced with an understanding of the group's developmental needs and capacities.

5. Only as group members get to know one another and become better able to see their common ground will they become fully open to one another as potential mutual-aid resources. And only as they become open to that possibility will they begin to actualize that potential.

6. Although it may be appropriate for people who have attained some degree of intimacy to trust one another with their personal thoughts and feelings and to take risks, either on behalf of or in

front of one another, it is equally appropriate for relative strangers to maintain some degree of privacy and distance.

7. The worker's role with the group is to bring and share his or her vision of mutual aid, to help it learn and establish the norms of mutual aid, to help members engage in mutual aid, and to help them reflect upon and assess their mutual-aid efforts.

RECOMMENDED FURTHER READING

Berman-Rossi, T. (1992). Empowering groups through understanding stages of group development. *Social Work with Groups* 15(2/3):239-255.

_____. (1993). The tasks and skills of the social worker across stages of group development. *Social Work with Groups* 16(1/2):69-82.

Brandler, S. and Roman, C. (1991). *Group Work: Skills and Strategies in Effective Interventions.* Binghamton, NY: The Haworth Press.

Breton, M. (1995). The potential for social action in groups. *Social Work with Groups* 18(2/3):5-14.

Galinsky, M. J. and Schopler, J. H. (1989). Developmental patterns in open-ended groups. *Social Work with Groups* 12(2):99-114.

Garland, J. A. and Frey, L. A. (1976). Applications of stages of group development to groups in psychiatric settings. In *Further Explorations in Group Work,* ed. S. Bernstein, pp. 1-33. Boston: Charles River Books.

Garland, J. A., Frey, L. A., Jones, H. E., and Kolodny, R. L. (1976). A model for stages of group development in social work groups. In *Explorations in Group Work,* ed. S. Bernstein, pp. 17-71. Boston: Charles River Books.

Hartford, M. (1971). *Groups in Social Work.* New York: Columbia University Press.

Mackey, R. (1980). Developmental process in growth-oriented groups. *Social Work* January:26-29.

Schiller, L. Y. (1995). Stages of developing women's groups: A relational group model. In *Group Work Practice in a Troubled Society: Problems and Opportunities,* eds. R. Kurland and R. Salmon, pp. 117-138. Binghamton, NY: The Haworth Press.

Steinberg, D. M. (1993). Some findings from a study of the impact of group work education on social work practitioners' work with groups. *Social Work with Groups* 16(3):23-39.

Toseland, R. W. and Rivas, R. E. (1995). *An Introduction to Group Work Practice.* New York: Macmillan.

Whelan, S. and McKeage, R. L. (1993). Developmental patterns in large and small groups. *Small Group Research* 24(1):60-83.

Chapter 6

Individual Problem Solving
from a Mutual-Aid Viewpoint

KEY CONCEPTS OF THIS CHAPTER

Aggregational Therapy of Individuals
Casework in a Group
Common Ground
Equal-Time Approach to Individual Problem Solving
Filled Time
Group Time
Individual Problem Solving
Individual Problems As Collective Food for Thought
Me-Too Syndrome
"Other-Directed" Group Process
Pluralistic Approach to Time
Presenting As a Problem-Solving Format
Purposeful Use of Self
Self-Reference
Self-Reflection
Squeaky-Wheel Approach to Individual Problem Solving
Time As a Dimension
Time As an Individual Resource
Whole-Group Meaning

PROLOGUE

ROSELI: Uh . . . who wants to go?
JOHN: I don't know. Do you want to go?

JULIA: I don't know. Do you want to go?

JOHN: I don't know. Do you want to go?

JULIA: I don't know. Who else wants to go? You want to go?

TINA: I don't care. Should I go?

RAOUL: You go.

TINA: You don't mind?

RAOUL: No, I don't care.

TINA: Okay . . . then . . . should I go . . .?

* * *

My time is your time, and your time is my time.

Individual problem solving is a key dynamic of mutual aid (see Chapter 2). In fact, because of their ability to bring together a variety of ideas, feelings, and perspectives, groups are particularly well suited to that task. Ironically, however, never does mutual aid seem to be in greater jeopardy than when it comes time for a group to do just that. Jeopardized by what might be characterized as a series of misunderstandings, when it comes time for a group to help its members work on issues of personal concern, mutual aid often falls by the wayside altogether as members, one after another, "go" or present their problems for practitioner feedback instead of using one another's problems to try to reach common ground.

What are these misunderstandings? First, the nature of mutual aid itself is often misunderstood as advice. Thus, the process is also often misunderstood as a series of moments in which group members, one after another, raise specific issues for feedback (e.g., "Have you thought of . . . ?" "Have you tried to . . . ?" "Why don't you just . . .?"

These two misunderstandings of mutual aid—advice and the presentation of individual issues for feedback—are fundamental ones and almost always lead to yet a third misunderstanding, one regarding the use of group time. Consider the case of this group:

WORKER: I would like to bring something up with the group. Some people have mentioned to me that there isn't always enough time for them to talk. Sometimes many people have pressing concerns, and we have only an hour and a half. I wonder if the group has ideas to deal with this problem.

GLORIA: Well, I know I talked a lot when my daughter got in trouble, so maybe the person who needs it most.

WORKER: How can we determine that?

HELEN: We could ask everyone; go around.

CLAIRE: Why don't you just pick?

WORKER: Well, I might on occasion, Claire. So, Helen mentioned going around. How so?

CLAIRE: Well, just ask who wants to talk, or each person says a little.

WORKER: Marie, what do you think about that?

MARIE: There's no way. The one who's most upset should talk.

GLORIA: Well, we'll just ask who wants to talk at the beginning.

WORKER: How will we help people who have trouble speaking up?

CLAIRE: I'm not sure. We'll ask around. I think we got a good idea, now.

HELEN: Yeah, we get the idea.

WORKER: Okay, we'll discuss it again and see how it's working out. (The next meeting begins with a few minutes of silence)

CLAIRE: [giggles] Well, who's going to talk today?

GLORIA: I'm feeling really good. I had a good week. I'd like to listen to someone.

JUNE: Well, I had some trouble with this guy at school . . . uh, is it okay for me to talk? [addressing the question to the worker]

WORKER: Ask the group.

JUNE: What do you think? Does anyone else want to talk?

HELEN: Well, I do a little, but you look really upset. I'll talk after.

MARIE: Go ahead, June. You look upset.

Does this conversation sound familiar? Well it may, for many groups end up with this kind of dilemma precisely because they misunderstand the process of mutual aid and the use of group time for individual problem solving from a mutual-aid viewpoint. They treat time as if it were an individually distributable resource, something to which some people might have access while others do not, instead of treating it as a dimension, as something to which we all have inherent and constant access. Generally speaking, however, we do not assume that we can partialize time among people. Granted, you may do one thing for fifteen minutes while I do something else; but those fifteen minutes are still available to both of us. We no more regard ourselves as entitled to only ten minutes of any given day than entertain the possibility of "giving up" part of a day to others or have discussions about which of us should have ownership of which part of the day. Yes, we may talk about wasting time or killing time or not having done anything with our time, but that is casual talk, and upon reflection, we would all undoubtedly agree that we all have access to time always, even if we use metaphors that suggest otherwise to describe our feelings about how we used it. It is their way of thinking about group time and mutual aid, then, that has cornered these members into a no-win situation, as worker and members alike operate under a collective assumption that whatever time one member is "given" is time that others will have to give up. The problem for mutual aid is that this way of thinking about time inevitably leads groups to engage in a presenting rather than mutual-aid approach to individual problem solving, as one member is given time to present his or her issues, and then another, and so on, with the only question being how much time each one should get.

But doesn't a group need to share time in some way? Isn't time sharing what being in a group is all about? Yes, it is. But there are *ways* of sharing. If time is shared in such a way that members experience only that which is devoted to their specific situation as having any significant personal value, then the group inevitably ends up in a state of *casework in a group* (Kurland and Salmon 1992), as each person awaits his or her personal allotment. As a result, much group time takes on other-directed value for much of the group. However, if time is shared in such a way that each member perceives all of the group's time as having significant personal value, then time takes on *whole-group* meaning. By providing a dimension of self-interest to all group members all the time, it provides opportunities for mutual aid.

The problem for mutual aid lies not with the concept of using groups for individual problem solving, therefore. When it comes to problem solving, two heads are inevitably better than one. It lies with the approach to that process, with the fact that when many groups try to help their members work on issues of personal concern, they so often seem to lose their mutual-aid character.

Why does this happen? Why is it that even practitioners who believe in mutual aid often still approach this process in a way that is in fact counterproductive to mutual aid? First, many people who work with groups have little or no training in that method. Second, people in the helping professions are so often mandated to partialize, partialize, partialize in order to make problem solving manageable that they end up with an *overpartialized* mindset! (If elephants are best eaten one bite at a time, perhaps individual problems are best attended to one member at a time.) Third, the concept of presenting—a process in which specific problems are presented to a group for specific solutions—has become so traditional a group process that it has simply become a norm.

The problem for mutual aid with both partializing time and presenting is that they are often too specific (i.e., individual oriented) rather than collective (i.e., group oriented). That is, they focus on and remain focused on specific situations of specific individuals rather than promote a search for collectivity, common ground, and community. In fact, when group members relate in some way and try to talk about themselves during other people's presentations, they are often treated as interlopers.

If we want groups to maintain their mutual-aid character even as they attempt to help members work on issues of personal concern, we need to think of that particular helping process not as one in which problems and feedback get serially presented but as one in which individual concerns have the potential to provide collective food for thought.

Two common approaches to individual problem solving cause workers to fall prey to *casework in a group:* the "equal time" approach and the "squeaky wheel" approach. The rest of this chapter is devoted to helping people who work with groups avoid these traps.

COMMON PROBLEM-SOLVING STRATEGIES

Should We Be Fair? Or Should We Be Relevant?

One common approach to using groups for helping people work on issues of personal concerns is that, in the interest of fairness, each person should have, as Claire put it in the earlier excerpt, the chance to "say a little" in each session. This is the equal-time approach. The other is that, in the interest of keeping practice relevant, whichever group member needs time most is the one who should get it most. This is the squeaky wheel approach. To the extent that these approaches treat time as if any of it could belong to any one particular person, they both raise problems for group work practice generally and for mutual aid more particularly. In fact, even if it were possible for people to own time, these approaches would still raise serious practice questions due to their inherently individualistic orientation to group process.

What are those problems? To begin with, no group can ever address each specific situation of each member at each session and, furthermore, do it well. Let's say that after lopping off a few minutes of start-up and wind-down time from a ninety-minute group session, we divide the balance of time equally among seven members. Each person would end up with about ten minutes to call his or her own. Can any group—no matter how skilled the practitioner—really do justice to a problem or concern of any significance in a mere ten minutes? An equal-time approach might satisfy a fairness mandate, but the price a group pays for being fair is that its process is also apt to remain fair— as in fairly superficial.

On the other hand, let's say that in the interest of relevance, we decide that whoever needs the "floor" most (i.e., time to present his or her particular situation) should be the one to get it most. This approach, too, raises some perplexing questions. How can a group assess which of its members does, in fact, need it most? Will the worker do that? If so, how? Will we test and measure degree of need in a group, for example ("Okay, Tom scored a 5; Dick scored a 6; Harry scored a 7; Harry gets our attention today.")? What happens if two people receive the same "score"? Or will we carry out an assessment of need outside of and prior to the group ("Hi, Ray. I'm calling to see who should get group time tomorrow night. . . . How are you doing this week?")? Clearly, when all is said and done, it might be easier just to let group members fight it out!

Further, what happens to those who "lose" the competition for time while the "winner" takes his or her portion? Does the group ever balance out? How can we (or they) know their time will even come in time? Does the fact that some group members need it more also mean that some need it less? If so, what happens to them? What is their role in the group to be? How are they supposed to make use of the group? Finally, what happens to members who may need it just as much as their comembers but who are less able to assert their rights to it?

Thus, although the idea of being relevant is attractive, this approach also raises a number of strategic questions for practice by promoting precisely the kind of climate that is counterproductive to mutual aid. It forces people into a state of perpetual competition, and it places the group as a whole in the impossible position of comparing the intensity and urgency of its members' needs. True, this approach has an advantage over the equal-time approach in its inherent acknowledgment that meaningful problem solving needs time. In terms of mutual aid, however, that advantage is lost because group members still ultimately perceive time that does not belong to them as belonging to someone else and thus without much significant personal value.

In sum, to the extent that both of these approaches reflect forms of *casework in a group* or, as Hartford (1978) put it, the *aggregational therapy of individuals,* they are inherently individualistic in orientation and inevitably place groups in the no-win position of pitting their desire for quality (time to explore, understand, and resolve problems) against their desire for quantity (everyone gets a chance to receive some personal attention).

What is the alternative? Is there a way for groups to maintain their mutual-aid character even as they engage in helping people work on issues of specific personal concern? Yes, there is. The alternative is to think of time as an inherently whole-group commodity rather than as an individual one capable of being partialized among people. And yes, as long as the group is formed around a clear and strong commonality, it is possible for it to maintain its mutual-aid character even as it helps members examine their specific situations. In fact, several group-specific skills (identified later on) exist to help us help groups do just that.

This discussion is not just semantic nit-picking. The ways in which we conceptualize both a group's helping process and its use of time have very real implications for practice, from pregroup planning to evaluation. If we insist on partializing time into a series of individual presenting moments, our groups will always struggle with who should go, who should get what amount of time, how to decide who gets what, and how to keep the process most fair or most useful. If, on the other hand, we decide to treat group time as a dimension, as we do in our everyday lives, then we will quickly discover that the "so much to do and so little time" dilemma so inherent in presenting or casework in a group no longer applies. Instead, we will realize that all the members of a group must inevitably make some use of group time all the time—that no amount of group time can ever really be used by one member while remaining unused by others. We will also realize that our most pressing practice question is no longer one of enough or not enough time but rather one of how to enable all group time, including that which is devoted to helping people look at specific situations, take on and maintain personal meaning for all members, and thus of collective interest all the time.

THE MUTUAL-AID APPROACH

Applying two time-related concepts from other fields can help us understand how to think about the use of group time for individual problem solving from a mutual-aid viewpoint. One concept has to do with the pluralistic nature of time. The other has to do with whether or not time feels productive, or "filled."

The pluralistic approach to time, a concept originally developed to analyze organizational function, is useful to mutual-aid practice because it helps us realize that although we often talk casually about getting or giving or giving up time, to treat time in this way is illogical (Whipp 1994). It confirms for us that as a dimension, time is inherently incapable of being manipulated in such ways, that although the manner in which time is used may vary from part to part within a system (in the case of groups, from person to person), time itself is inescapably used by all things. One can neither own time nor give it away. This reminds us that it is more accurate to think of systemic function as a reflection of simultaneous multiple activities, with all parts of any system always engaged in some kind of function, however that engagement looks, rather than think of any systemic function in terms of serial action and reaction (first one person uses group time, then another, and so on). In other words, it may be possible for time to be partialized along longitudinal lines (such as being used first in one way and then in another way), but it cannot be partialized along lateral lines (first one group member uses it, and then another uses it). It reminds us, in a nutshell, that just as in the saying "My time is your time, and your time is my time," there is always a multiple engagement of time in a group, no matter who has the floor.

The idea of filled time, on the other hand, originally developed by economic theorists, speaks to the feel of time (Owen 1991). Filled time is that which is perceived or felt as personally productive, while unfilled time is that which is perceived or felt as personally unproductive.

The idea that time can be filled or unfilled takes on special significance in terms of mutual aid because it cautions us that time can, in fact, be felt as unproductive. That is, it alerts us to the facts that group membership does not in and of itself cause people to experience time as well spent and that only when they perceive group process as personally meaningful will they be apt to feel their time has been well spent, or filled. It reminds us to think of personal situations as potential food for collective thought rather than as discrete individual property, and it confirms that even if the presenting approach to individual problem solving creates highly filled time for the presenter, it is still likely to create relatively unfilled time for other members.

Although the concept of plurality was developed to examine organizational function, and filled time was developed with analysis of economic theory in mind, they can help us understand the consequences of how we use group time. By making us aware of the fact that all group time is used in some way by all group members, a pluralistic way of thinking about time helps us realize the illogic of thinking that we can ever partialize time among people. And, by reminding us that it is possible for group process to be experienced as personally unproductive by some people even when it is perceived as productive by others, understanding time as capable of feeling filled or unfilled helps us set into motion the kind of process that can provide significant personal meaning for each group member.

A good way of giving real-world value to a discussion of differences in approach is to imagine the results of those differences. Let's compare, therefore, the look and feel of individual problem solving in a group that takes a mutual-aid approach, as conceptualized by Kurland and Salmon (1992), with the look and feel of such a task in a group that follows the commonly accepted presenting approach (Table 6.1).

TABLE 6.1. Miss X and Mr. Y: Cases in Point and Counterpoint

A Mutual-Aid Approach to Individual Problem Solving: Miss X's Group	A Presenting Approach to Individual Problem Solving: Mr. Y's Group
An individual member raises a problem, issue, or situation with which she or he is concerned.	
Miss X, a member of a group of adults in a psychiatric day-treatment program, says she had some trouble with her boss at work yesterday (at the agency's sheltered workshop site) and wants to talk about it with the group.	Mr. Y, who "got into trouble" at work yesterday (an agency-sponsored sheltered work site), would like to talk about what happened with his group.
The problem is clearly identified by the individual and the group.	
Miss X begins to describe her situation to the group. Her boss became angry because she had forgotten to do something he'd asked her to do. It wasn't really part of her job, she says, and she just "blew up" and walked out of the room. She's sure her boss is even angrier now, but she can hardly remember everything she's supposed to do. She can't be expected to add a bunch of extra stuff too! She's afraid to go back to work on Monday morning.	Mr. Y begins to describe his situation to his comembers. His boss asked him to deliver a package to an address to which he'd never been before, and that really scared him. Instead of telling his boss that, he instead told him he couldn't do it because the delivery was out of his way and his workday was almost over. His boss looked pretty mad when he left, and Mr. Y is afraid to return to work on Monday morning.
The problem is explored	
As Miss X more fully describes her version of what happened at work, her comembers try to build a picture of what really happened, what she thinks, and how she feels. They interrupt her with comments (e.g., "I don't understand what you mean when you say it's not part of the job.") and ask her questions about the situation (e.g., "What do you mean you 'blew up'?" or "What did you say your job is, exactly?") And they try to come to understand the	Mr. Y's comembers are encouraged to seek clarification from him about his situation so that they may better understand the nature of his situation and how he feels about it.
As Mr. Y more fully describes his version of what happened at work, his comembers try to build a picture of what really happened, what he thinks, and how he feels. And they interrupt him with comments (e.g., "I don't understand what you mean when you say the delivery was

way she feels by asking her to talk more about her feelings, as well (e.g., "Can you say more about how you felt when . . .?" and "How do you feel about it now?"), all for the purpose of reaching common ground (e.g., "Have I ever been in a situation like that?"), for trying to identify issues of common interest (e.g., "Have I ever been asked to do something I thought wasn't fair?") and common feelings (e.g., "How did that make me feel?")

While the demand for work is that they explore Miss X's situation in full, this demand is made for the purpose of helping the group engage in *mutual aid*. Group members are asked to listen and explore with a self-referential ear (i.e., with thought to their own lives and experiences) as well as with an ear to Miss X's actual situation.

The worker asks group members to recount situations they have experienced and dilemmas they have faced that are relevant to the problem that has been raised by Miss X.

Miss X's comembers are asked to share the connections they have made between their experiences and hers (e.g., "Has anyone else come up against this sort of thing?") and between their feelings and hers (e.g., "Can anyone recall a time when she or he felt the way Miss X feels?"). And through their storytelling, or *me-too* syndrome, the group explicitly identifies its common ground, even as it explores its differences. Some group members might recall similar situations and recapture similar feelings ("Last year I had that kind of trouble with my boss, and I got really mad, too."). Others might recall similar situations but recapture different feelings ("When I had trouble at my job, I didn't feel so angry as I did stupid and discouraged . . .")

out of your way.") and ask him questions about the situation (e.g., "How much time did you have left at work?" or "What are you afraid your boss will do on Monday?"). And they try to come to understand the way he feels by asking him to talk more about his feelings (e.g., "Can you say more about what you were so afraid of?" and "Now, how do you feel?").

In this group, members are not expected to transform Mr. Y's specific issues into generic food for thought. They are not expected to seek common ground. They are not expected to seek clarification for the purpose of understanding the specific nature of Mr. Y's situation and for the purpose of helping him resolve that situation.

Possible "solutions" to the individual's problem are identified.

Once Mr. Y's comembers think they have enough information to be of help to him, they begin to search for solutions to his situation by offering suggestions as to what he might now do (e.g., "Do you think you could approach your boss on Monday morning and . . .?" or "What if you were to call him tomorrow and . . .?").

TABLE 6.1 (continued)

and yet others might recapture similar feelings related to very different situations (e.g., "I never had a blow-up with my boss, but I did have a terrible fight with my dad once...."). The exact scenario of similarities and differences does not really matter. What matters is that group members have the opportunity to use Miss X's situation to identify a core of common issues (the difficulties and fears around meeting new expectations, for example) and the opportunity to identify those aspects of Miss X's situation that can provide them with personally interesting food for thought (coping with anger or feeling frustrated or helpless, for example, or feelings about and ways of reacting to authority or how to manage fear) and that they would find useful to explore (e.g., "How do I usually ...?" or "What happens when I ...?" or "What would happen if I were to ...?").

This particular step clearly adds a great deal of time to the overall process, since group members are asked to reach into and share their own experiential repertoires. It contributes far more than time, however, to the development of a process that feels filled for some while remaining essentially unfilled for others. It provides, in other words, a forum for experiencing mutuality and mutual aid.

Possible "solutions" to the individual's problem are identified.

Once the members of Miss X's group feel that their stories have brought them to common ground (at least affective if not experiential), they now use their personal experiences to help Miss X seek solutions to her situation. Even now, however, as they are

The worker and group members help the individual decide on a course of action or solution that she or he wants to try.

As Mr. Y variously responds to suggestions, and as courses of action take on more or less feasible shape (e.g., "Why don't we pretend it's Monday morning and play it out ...?") the individual-problem-solving process comes to a close. From Mr. Y's perspective, time has asked to think of possible solutions to Miss X's situation (e.g., "Any ideas about what Miss X might do?"), and asked to continue to reflect on those possibilities on behalf of Miss X (e.g., "What would happen, I wonder, if Miss X were to do what Mary did when she . . .?"). They are also asked to share their reactions to those possible solutions on their own behalf (e.g., "Anyone remember trying that? What happened?"). Even as they contribute to the brainstorming process on behalf of Miss X, then, by maintaining a dual focus—one eye on Miss X's situation and one eye on their own needs, desires, and goals—time continues to feel filled for them as well, as they review and share jobs well done and those not so well done.

The worker and group members help the individual decide on a course of action or solution that she or he wants to try.

When the members of Miss X's group feel that they have identified as many possible solutions as they can to help Miss X resolve her problem, they help her try various solutions on for size. Although the group's visible focus moves very specifically onto Miss X's particular situation at this point, members are still asked to engage in self-reference and reflection. Even now, they are asked to use their own experiences to provide help to Miss X (e.g., "Remember I told you about that awful fight with my fa-

been well filled. His comembers, on the other hand, may feel quite differently. True, they may have drawn upon their own experiences in order to help him think things through, and they may have engaged in some self reflection, but the purpose of this process, however, has been understood by everyone as intended to help Mr. Y address a particular situation, which means that everyone except Mr. Y has been expected to use his or her thinking power in a primarily other-directed way (in this case, directed toward Mr. Y and his situation).

These group members have used their time primarily for Mr. Y's sake, then, to help him address his particular situation. And even if in the process of doing so they have identified issues with which they too struggle, they have purposefully refrained from sharing their own stories—from entering into a *me-too* syndrome—so as not to infringe on what is collectively understood to be Mr. Y's time. But as a result, the members of this group have been denied the opportunity to create filled time for themselves or to engage in mutual aid. Consequently, only Mr. Y's time has been truly filled.

TABLE 6.1 (continued)

ther? I tried to ignore it afterward, thinking things would get back to normal. They didn't, though. Here's what happened. . .") rather than offer suggestions about what she should or should not do (e.g., "Why don't you just . . .?"). Even as the members of Miss X's group help her select a course of action, time continues to feel filled for them, as they use their own stories to contribute a variety of perspectives for view and review (e.g., "Here's what I did once when I was asked to do something scary . . .").

The worker asks all in the group what they have taken out of the discussion that has transpired.

As all of the members of Miss X's group are asked to share with the group how the process of looking at her particular situation has contributed to their own thinking, being, and doing, the process comes to a close.

Although engaging in self-reference and self-reflection during the previous part of the process has helped them identify their own needs and strengths, this part of the sharing process helps them make explicit how looking at Miss X's situation has been of specific interest and use to them as well.

The juxtaposition of these two approaches to individual problem solving demonstrates the most important differences between individual problem solving from a mutual-aid viewpoint and problem solving from a presentation viewpoint. In Miss X's group, a demand is made that members engage in self-reference and self-reflection throughout their process of looking at her problem. To the extent that we all use our own lives and experiences to try to understand others, Mr. Y's comembers may also engage in self-reflection. They are not explicitly asked to share that process with the group, however, or to engage in active self-reference, since the problem-solving time belongs very specifically to Mr. Y. The group begins and remains very much focused on his specific situation, and all exploration and examination of issues are carried out for the purpose of understanding that situation. The members of Miss X's group, on the other hand, are asked to explore her specific situation not only for the purpose of helping her but also to identify generic food for thought, a demand for work that is intended to help them connect with the process on their own behalf as well as that of Miss X.

Furthermore, the members of Miss X's group are asked to use their life experiences throughout the process as a way of being helpful. They are asked to share their own stories—what happened to them that was similar, how they handled their own situations, and how they felt about what happened—all to the end of creating a process rooted in empathy. In contrast, when Mr. Y's comembers believe they have enough details about his situation and feelings to understand his dilemma, they are free to offer suggestions about what he might do to resolve his problem without examining the issues at hand on their own behalf.

Both Miss X and Mr. Y do much of the talking in the group, since describing their situations well enough for their comembers to fully understand them requires stating, restating, explaining, elaborating, clarifying, and other forms of enlightenment. In Mr. Y's group, however, members listen as assistant therapists and thus the process becomes *casework in a group*. In Miss X's group, however, because comembers are asked to listen with a self-referential ear in search of common ground, they have the opportunity to develop a process in which they, too, have a personal investment. Even if they all cannot reach back to situations similar to that of Miss X, they can always think of situations, past or present, that have evoked similar feelings to the ones Miss X expresses. Whichever the case, as they think and talk about their own lives while listening to Miss X's situation, they have the opportunity to fill time for themselves also. As they identify their common ground and use their differences within that common ground to think about their own ways of being and doing even as they seek to help Miss X, they set the stage for mutual aid. As Miss X uses her situation to inform and enlighten that process while her comembers use their life experience to inform and enlighten it as well, they discover opportunities for mutual aid. They deepen their understanding of themselves and one another by making their self-reflection expressive through story sharing, and actualize their potential for mutual aid. The problem-solving process may have been catalyzed by a so-called individual problem, but identifying the elements of the problem that are common to all of them and exploring those elements on their own behalf as well as on behalf of Miss X has transformed what could have easily remained an individually oriented process to one of mutuality, mutual interest, and mutual aid.

The need for some manner of individual problem solving comes up in all sorts of groups. Although the overall purpose of task-oriented groups is not to help members work on individual problems, per se, the very impetus for their formation in the first place is still a belief that whatever the task is to be, it is more likely to be achieved by a task *group* than by a number of task-oriented individuals. That is, they are formed precisely because they can provide individuals with access to the thinking, help, and support of others. How to help a group's thinking-through process remain relevant and meaningful to everyone in the group as it examines the various concerns of its members, therefore, will always be a salient practice question. The next section discusses what needs to happen for any group to maintain its mutual-aid character as it engages in individual problem solving.

WHAT NEEDS TO HAPPEN
TO CATALYZE MUTUAL AID

If we expect the members of a group to be capable of transforming individual issues into food for collective thought, then they need to begin with a strong common base. The more they are in the same boat, the more they will be able to derive personal meaning from looking at other people's situations. Thus, if the needs around which we form the group are too abstract (e.g., "We all have human needs"), it will be that much more difficult for people to find their common base and to redirect the problem-solving process from being an essentially individual one to being a process with whole-group meaning. As we think about forming a group, then, it is important that we not conceptualize prospective members' needs so abstrusely as to make the reach for commonality too difficult. Further, if we expect members to share a common departure point for their work, then we need to provide them with a departure point (i.e., purpose) that is both clear and relevant. If we formulate a group purpose that is too vague (e.g., "The purpose of this group is to help you improve the quality of your life") or too loose (e.g., "The purpose of this group is to help you do whatever you want to do"), members will also have difficulty keeping the commonality of their concerns in focus. As we formulate purpose, therefore, we need to conceptualize it as being broad enough to encompass more than the goals of one individual but not so cosmic as to be without concrete meaning to actual process (see Chapter 3).

Finally, because the presenting format is such a common approach to helping people work on personal concerns, we need to prepare prospective members for what individual problem solving will look like from a mutual-aid viewpoint, so that they will know what is or is not expected from them in the group. As Alex Gitterman (1989) states, "When members are clear about what behaviors are preferred, permitted, proscribed, and prohibited, they are likely to be less anxious and more available to each other" (p. 13).

How can we do that? How can we prepare people for individual problem solving from a mutual-aid viewpoint? First, we *describe and discuss the many dynamics of mutual aid* (e.g., "There are many ways in which the members of this group will be able to help one another.") We help members prepare for the look of the process (e.g., "If someone wants help with a particular problem, for example, . . ."). And we *help them prepare for the feel of the process* by explaining that although it is sometimes annoying in our everyday lives when people respond "me too" just when we are trying to feel "special," it is this very syndrome that will single-handedly maintain a group's mutual-aid character and save it from the *casework in a group* trap. There are several ways of helping prospective group members prepare for individual problem solving from a mutual-aid viewpoint, then—for helping them, as Gitterman says, be less anxious about group process and more open to the idea that other people's situations can provide them with meaningful food for thought.

Several group-specific skills can also help us help members keep mutual aid in play even as they look at one another's specific situations. Simply including a *discussion about individual problem solving from a mutual-aid perspective* in the group's contracting process can help the group reach a collective understanding and expectation of the process to be. *Asking members to react to what is being said and done* in the group can help them search for (e.g., "So, are we all talking about how hard it is to . . .?"), think about (e.g, "So, what did you do, then, when you felt that way?"), and identify (e.g., "How does that relate exactly to what was just said, Tom?") their common ground. *Encouraging group members to share their feelings* (e.g., "Does anyone remember feeling like Ron?") can help create a climate of support in the group. *Encouraging them to identify common feelings in spite of the differences* among their stories can help them develop and maintain a climate of empathy (e.g., "Okay, Jim, so you're saying you've never had that kind of experience. . . . Have you ever felt that way though?"). *Encouraging self-referential contributions* (e.g., "Oops! Hold it, Marion. You need to talk about your own feelings and experiences, remember?") while *discouraging feedback that has purely intellectual roots* and no visible self-reference (e.g., "Uh oh! Wait a minute, Joe. Remember we agreed we wouldn't start with the words 'I think you should . . .'?") both sets and keeps in play the me-too syndrome so crucial to mutual aid. *Encouraging group members to explore one another's situations in depth* (e.g., "Okay, so maybe you feel differently, but do you see what Bill is saying—where he's coming from?") can help them understand the generic dimensions of their so-called individual concerns (e.g., "It seems to me that the common issue here is how helpless people feel when . . ."). *Letting our eyes roam in search of reactions* as group members talk together (e.g., "Sarah, you looked just now as if you really relate to what Larry just said. . . .") can help the group explicitly identify themes of common interest while giving members the freedom to express differences (e.g., "Larry, I saw those eyebrows shoot up! What are you thinking?"). *Helping everyone participate* (e.g., "So, everyone is having this kind of trouble in one way or another with their kids, right?") keeps the process whole-group meaningful all of the time. *Asking group members to assess the process as it unfolds* (e.g., "Are you saying, then, Joe, that you do not understand Greg's position?") helps them keep tabs on the look and feel of the process from their own personal perspectives. And *asking them to assess the problem-solving process as it comes to a close* (e.g., "Okay, let's take a look at what we just did.") helps the group as a whole identify very specifically and concretely the nature of the mutual aid that has just taken place and helps each member identify exactly which issues have been of particular relevance and interest (e.g., "When Judy said she felt helpless it really made me mad, and I thought, 'Why doesn't she just quit?' But then when Louise talked about her experience, I got to thinking. . . .").

KEY POINTS OF THIS CHAPTER

1. Time is a dimension and incapable of being divided among people. All group members must make some use of group time all the time.
2. To the extent that they each attempt to partialize group time along individual lines, both the equal-time and squeaky-wheel approaches to individual problem solving result in *casework in a group* (Kurland and Salmon 1992).
3. From the mutual-aid viewpoint, individual concerns are windows of opportunity for discovering common ground, for providing whole-group food for thought, and for giving all of group time whole-group meaning.
4. The presenting format for individual problem solving in a group tends to result in time being perceived by nonpresenting members as personally unproductive, or *unfilled* (Owen 1991).
5. To avoid both a unidirectional presenting format and advice giving, the mutual-aid approach to individual problem solving relies on use of self, a process that consists of self-reflection (thinking about one's own experiences) and self-reference (the sharing of one's own stories).
6. If people who work with groups remain preoccupied with dividing group time among members, they inevitably end up using

their time watching their watches instead of using it to help people discover common ground and, through that common ground,
paths to mutual aid.

RECOMMENDED FURTHER READING

Dewey, J. (1910). *How We Think.* Boston: Heath.
Hartford, M. (1978). Groups in the human services: Some facts and
    fancies. *Social Work with Groups* 1(1):1-10.
Kurland, R. and Salmon, R. (1992). Group work versus casework in a
    group: Principles and implications for teaching and practice. *So-
    cial Work with Groups* 15(4):3-14.
Somers, M. L. (1970). Problem-solving in small groups. In *Theories
    of Social Work with Groups,* eds. R. Roberts and H. Northen,
    pp. 331-367. New York: Columbia University Press.

Chapter 7

Mutual Aid and Authority

The real leader has no need to lead—he is content to point the way.

Henry Miller, *The Wisdom of the Heart*

KEY CONCEPTS OF THIS CHAPTER

Active Participation in the Helping Process
Approach to Authority
Authority
Central Authority
Commitment
Community
Consensus As a Decision-Making Method
Decentralized Authority
Democratic-Humanism (Glassman and Kates 1990)
Group Development
Having a Real Say
Laissez-Faire
Mutual-Aid Character
One of the Gang (Kurland and Salmon 1993)
Self-Determination
Voting As a Decision-Making Method
Worker As Leader
Worker As Partner

* * *

Power tends to corrupt, and absolute power corrupts absolutely.

Lord Acton, Letter to Bishop Mandell Creighton

Generally speaking, issues of authority present interesting food for thought in practice with groups. To the extent that a mutual-aid system must have the *privileges and responsibilities* of managing its own affairs, however, as Gertrude Wilson and Gladys Ryland (1949) stated it, issues of authority may be said to present essential food for thought (see, for example, Galinsky and Schopler 1977; Konopka 1983; Kurland and Salmon 1993; Lang 1986; Middleman and Wood 1990a; Newstetter 1935; Northen and Kurland 2001; Schwartz and Zalba 1971; Shulman 1999; Trecker 1955; Wilson and Ryland 1949).

Some people who work with groups conceptualize central authority as a vehicle for providing people with professional help. Hence, they take primary responsibility for shaping the group's affairs. They assume the position of be-all and end-all in the group's helping process. And when they speak of their role in a group, they speak of group "leadership" (Birnbaum et al. 1989; Galinsky and Schopler 1977; Glassman and Kates 1990; Konopka 1983; Middleman 1978; Rooney et al., 1981; Steinberg 1992; Wayne and Garland 1990).

The mutual-aid approach to working with groups has a very different point of view regarding both the raison d'être of professional authority and its use, however. It conceptualizes central authority as an obstacle to the group's helping process (Galinsky and Schopler 1977; Glassman and Kates 1990; Newstetter 1935; Trecker 1955). In contrast to exercising central authority in the service of providing professional help, it actively seeks to decentralize authority in the service of helping people help one another (Breton 1990; Coyle 1949; Glassman and Kates 1990; Kurland and Salmon 1990; Middleman and Wood 1990a; Newstetter 1935; Papell and Rothman 1980; Schwartz and Zulba 1971; Trecker 1955). When it speaks of the worker's role it speaks of *partnership* rather than leadership (Trecker 1955)—the group's end of the bargain being to make an effort to develop into and function as a mutual-aid community, and the worker's end being to contribute his or her professional knowledge, skills, and authority to help it do so.

This chapter discusses this partnership process. The theoretical basis for decentralizing authority is presented. The use of authority as a teaching tool to help the new group develop its mutual-aid potential and to help the maturing group maintain its mutual-aid character as its talk becomes increasingly real and its work increasingly demanding is discussed. The impact of voting and consensus on a group's ability to maintain a humanistic as well as democratic climate (Glassman and Kates 1990) is described. Some food for thought is offered to help the practitioner assess the impact of his or her own ways of being in a group on its ability to develop into and function as a mutual-aid system. The chapter concludes by identifying group-specific skills for sharing authority and for helping a group maintain its mutual-aid character as it exercises its own authority.

HAVING A REAL SAY AND THE GROUP'S NEED FOR IT

Maintaining central authority over the life of a group poses an obstacle to its mutual-aid development in three ways. First, it prevents members from exercising their fundamental right to self-determination, and by denying them the right to actively participate in shaping their helping process, it denies them the opportunity to keep the group's process relevant and useful from their point of view. Second, it prevents members from group building. That is, it impedes the development of a collective esprit de corps committed to the group as a mutual-aid community. Third, it prevents the group from having an ongoing forum for identifying its strengths and using those strengths to meet its needs.

The Need for Self-Determination and Active Participation in the Helping Process

Permitting a group to have a real say in what it should do (e.g., "Okay, so what should we do at this point?") and then helping its members assume as much responsibility as they can reasonably accommodate for shaping process (e.g., "So how should we go about this, then?") actualizes a group's right to self-determination. That right, in turn, helps to ensure that whatever process takes place remains both relevant and useful from its viewpoint. (See Coyle 1959; Glassman and Kates 1990; Kaiser 1958; Konopka 1983; Middleman and Wood 1990a; Newstetter 1935; Northen and Kurland 2001; Phillips 1954; Schwartz and Zalba 1971; Tropp 1978; Wilson and Ryland 1949.)

A real say can take many shapes and can be directed to all types of affairs, ranging from minor to major. Having a real say might look similar to this, for example:

> Most of the members of a group of adult Russian émigrés had difficulty understanding and speaking English. As I did not speak any Russian, the language in common became Yiddish, which everyone knew well. Nonetheless, to the tremendous annoyance of other members who could never quite keep up, two members who spoke English haltingly insisted on using English to speak together and with me. The result was that members were busily translating for one another in "asides" as other members were talking. Finally, this state of affairs became identified as a major problem for the group. At first, the problem was identified specifically as these two members' insistence on speaking in a language the others could not readily understand. They defended themselves by claiming that they wanted to use every opportunity to practice their English. After further exploration, members reidentified the problem as the difficulty in relating to one another in any coherent manner because of the language barriers. The issue for decision changed from what to do about these two annoying members to what to do about the very real language barrier. After lengthy (and chaotic!) discussion, the group decided that a refocus of purpose was appropriate and that a new component would be added to the group's original purpose. From that point on, I spoke Yiddish so that everyone understood, and the others expressed themselves as best they could in English, with one another's help.

And having a real say may be similar to this, as well:

> This was only the group's second session, and other members were visibly upset by Jerry being high. The issue for decision became whether or not Jerry should be permitted to stay at that session and further, what to do should this happen again to any one of them. After discussion, which included Jerry, it was decided by consensus, again including Jerry, that although he could remain with the group at that session, members would no longer be permitted to remain in the group in that condition.

The issues being addressed in these groups are different, yet they have something very much in common. In each case the right of membership extends far beyond the right to discuss what is going on in the group. It extends to the right to make decisions about what should or should not happen in the group. That right—the right to participate in *shaping* the group's affairs: to assess the status quo, to propose change, and to have that proposal taken seriously, is what having a real say is all about. Having a real say, therefore, does not occur in the following example:

The group had gone down to four members, which we (worker and coleader) thought was too small, so we asked the group if they wanted to take new members or terminate. They decided to terminate.

Why does this process not reflect a real say? It does not reflect a real say because the group's say is limited to selecting from a range of options that have been predetermined by the workers. The group may appear at first glance to have a real say. It might even believe that it has a real say. In reality, however, its say is very limited and has little impact. What if members feel comfortable with the group just as it is? Too bad. The right to exercise such an option has not been presented. What if a member has a different way of conceptualizing the situation or defining the problem? Too bad. Other ways of seeing the picture will never be known because they have not been requested. And the reason they have not been requested in this case is because the workers are operating from a *hidden agenda,* which never permits a real say because an outcome or range of acceptable outcomes is already in mind. This group has some say over its affairs, then, but to the extent that its members are denied the right to think about whether a problem exists, to define the nature of that problem if they do perceive one, and to decide whether they desire to change the status quo, it does not have a *real* say.

How would it look to give this group a real say? The workers would share their perceptions of the group's situation (e.g., "Here's what we see and here's our thinking."). Members would be asked to share their perceptions (e.g., "How do you see things?"). They would be encouraged to think through all possible courses of action, including maintaining the status quo (e.g., "Okay, let's look at all the possibilities here."). They would be helped to adopt a course of action compatible with both the group's internal needs and desires and those of its setting (e.g., "I hear what you're saying, Amy, but here's the problem I think we'd run into if we do it that way . . .").

A group need not have unbridled authority over its affairs to be conceptualized as a mutual-aid system. All groups need to keep an eye on the parameters within which they may and outside of which they may not operate, and much of the stuff of practice is mediating between their needs and desires and those of its setting (Schwartz 1976, 1977). But even with attention to real-world factors, a great deal of discretionary decision-making space usually exist between "anything goes" and "nothing doing." The problem for mutual aid is that the more the worker wields power over that space, the less the group can exercise its right to make that space meaningful. If a course of action is not feasible given the mission and mandates of the setting or other factors, it is a legitimate use of the worker's authority to help the members understand the issues and their implications. On the other hand, if a course of action is feasible and from the group's point of view reflects a legitimate route to mutual aid, then its right to adopt such a course of action, even if it does not represent the worker's personal preference, needs to be respected if mutual aid is to take place (Glassman and Kates 1990; Middleman and Wood 1990b).

The Need for Community and Commitment

The right to have a real say over its affairs also helps a group become and remain committed to its mutual-aid potential by creating ongoing opportunities to develop, experience, and strengthen its sense of community or *we-ness*. Beyond committing to their own helping process, people need to feel committed to the group as a community of mutual aid if they are to make the effort needed to develop it into a mutual-aid system. It is not impossible for a group to develop some sense of community and commitment to mutual aid under the rule of central authority. In fact, sometimes it is that very state of affairs that compels a group to mobilize its mutual-aid potential as it seeks to rebel against a worker who is oppressive (Breton 1989, 1990). Still, the more the group is perceived by the members as the worker's group, to which they have simply been invited, the more difficult it will be for them to make the efforts that developing a mutual-aid community requires. When the worker maintains central authority over a group's affairs, then he or she presents the people in that group with yet another obstacle to developing mutual aid! Consider the following example:

After a series of absences, Julie returned to the group just prior to the group's formal production. During the previous several weeks, the other members had been practicing intensively for their production, and Julie had missed all rehearsals. As it became apparent that Julie wished to renew her membership, several members expressed their reluctance to allow her return. They were worried about her ability to perform on such short notice, and the issue for decision became whether or not to allow Julie to reenter the group at such a late date. After a lengthy and heated discussion, which included Julie as well, one member suggested that Julie not participate in choreographed pieces but that she participate in the improvisational pieces, since they do not require such dependence on others. Everyone, including Julie, agreed that this solution was a fair one.

What would have happened here if the worker had simply made some decision on her own regarding Julie's reentry into the group—if she had not permitted, even encouraged, the group to have a real say at this moment? First, any decision she made would have almost certainly disgruntled at least one member. Second, she would have denied all of them a serendipitous opportunity to revisit and reflect on the group's meaning and mission. Her permission and help in thinking through and dealing with the issues enabled the group to reach a solution acceptable to everyone. It also provided each member an opportunity to review his or her commitment to the group as a community, to its work, and to its purpose.

In sum, the more we maintain central authority, the more difficult we make it for the members of a group to commit their efforts to building a community of mutual aid. They may commit their efforts to the group as a personal need-meeting strategy, but without the right to make a difference in the group's affairs—to have a real say in what the group should do and how it should do it—the more difficult it will be for them to commit their efforts to helping others meet their needs as well.

The Need for a Forum to Identify Strengths

Finally, having a real say in what the group should do and how it should do it enables a group to function as a mutual-aid community by helping members identify very specifically the various ways in which they can help one another or harness their strengths.

It is one thing to talk about people's strengths; it is quite another to see them in action (Northen and Kurland 2001), and having a say over group affairs provides members with that very opportunity by creating an ongoing forum through which they can identify their strengths and contrast them with those of others. Perhaps one member is highly skilled at sorting out issues. As the group attempts to make decisions that advance its purpose, those who are less competent at that can have an opportunity to see that skill in action. Perhaps one member is especially open to self-reflection while someone else has difficulty with it. One member may be gifted at planning while another tends to be haphazard. Or one member is an attentive listener while others have a hard time letting people finish their sentences. Someone may express opinions with sensitivity while others have difficulty expressing theirs without alienating their listeners. Some members are particularly good at collaborating while others tend to be competitive or individualistic.

The possibilities for exchanges of strengths are endless, but only through the interaction that occurs as a result of shaping the group's affairs can those strengths become available for use and for exchange and can the mutual-aid process move from one of imagination (what could or should be) to one of reality (what is or is not). If the worker's strengths (i.e., his or her knowledge, wisdom, imagination, creativity, experience, and expertise) dominate the group's affairs, then it will be difficult for the group to both develop a self-image and function as a mutual-aid system. Consider this situation:

> The group was angry with Judy, who came and went as she pleased. Sometimes she attended group, sometimes she didn't. One day when she came in, the rest of the group told her they thought she shouldn't stay. I expressed the feeling that I didn't think Judy should be ousted.

In this case, a moment of conflict presents a clear opportunity for group members to harness their strengths. They are expressing some real differences in terms of feelings, in terms of behavior, and in terms of expectations. But what happens? Instead of taking advantage of this opportunity to help the group reach for and use its strengths to explore its differences, the worker simply announces what she believes should happen, preempting members from exchanging perspectives, from exploring and sharing their feelings, from thinking about their needs and desires, and from using their own strengths and skills to work things out.

In short, having a real say forces a group's strengths to the surface of its process, which is precisely where they need to be if the group is to function as a mutual-aid system. A group might identify its needs under the maintenance of central authority, but it will have little opportunity to identify and cultivate its strengths to meet those needs. (See, for example, Breton 1990; Birnbaum et al. 1989; Galinsky and Schopler 1977; Kaiser 1958; Konopka 1983; Lowy 1978; Middleman and Wood 1990a,b; Papell and Rothman 1980; Schwartz and Zalba 1971; Steinberg 1992; Tropp 1978; Wilson and Ryland 1949.)

In these ways, the maintenance of central authority impedes a group's ability to fully develop its mutual-aid potential, and prevents it from exercising its right to self-determination and from ensuring the relevance and usefulness of its process. By creating a state of affairs in which the worker is viewed as the host and members essentially as guests, it impedes the group's ability to develop a self-image as a mutual-aid community. When the group is denied an ongoing forum for identifying and using its strengths, it is prevented from creating a process through which it can actually be a system of mutual aid.

To decentralize authority does not mean to abdicate all authority, however (Kurland and Salmon 1993). Groups need the worker's help to adopt and keep mutual-aid norms in play as they work toward their purpose, and teaching a group how to become a mutual-aid system and then helping it maintain its mutual-aid character as it develops are legitimate uses of authority. The next section discusses this approach to authority.

AUTHORITY AND GROUP DEVELOPMENT

The mutual-aid approach to work with groups conceptualizes professional authority as a tool for teaching and facilitating mutual aid, and its use is guided by two factors. First, it is guided by the group's developmental needs and capacities of the moment. Second, it is guided by an understanding that the capacity of a group to identify and use its own leadership potential in the service of mutual aid matures over time (Berman-Rossi 1992, 1993; Garland and Frey 1976; Garland et al. 1978, Glassman and Kates 1983, 1990, Kurland and Salmon 1993; Middleman and Wood 1990a; Schiller 1995; Schwartz 1961). The primary goal of the worker is, therefore, as Middleman and Wood (1990a) put it, to work himself or herself out of a job.

The Use of Authority in the New Group

As discussed in Chapter 5, groups need time to fully develop their capacity for mutual aid and the worker's help to learn the ways and means of mutual aid. How, specifically, do we use our authority to help the new group develop its mutual-aid potential? First, we *use it to provide a structure for talk* that will help the members identify their connections and common ground. Second, we use it to *help the group develop a purpose* that reflects the needs and desires of all of its members while remaining compatible with those of its setting. Third, we use it to *help the group adopt* norms that are conducive to mutual aid (see Chapter 4), to help it think through the ways in which it might function as a mutual-aid system, and to help it set and keep that process in motion.

Consider this first group session, as described by the worker:

> We had put this group together for teens whose parents had AIDS. At our first meeting, after I said a few words of welcome and they introduced themselves, I asked the group where they thought we should start, what they wanted to talk about. I knew it would be hard, but I wanted it to be their group.

In this case, the worker has abdicated the responsibility to use professional authority in order to help a group begin its journey as a mutual-aid system and, as a result, the group will have some real difficulty just getting off the ground. From a mutual-aid viewpoint, a new group always needs a place to start, even if tentative, and it is entitled to help in making that start, even if its direction eventually changes (see Chapter 3). Therefore, using professional authority to help the new group begin its growth process as a mutual-aid system is a legitimate and important use of authority.

The Use of Authority As the Group Matures

As the group matures, so does its capacity to function as a mutual-aid system, and as that happens the worker can exercise his or her authority less and less actively, returning to more active duty in times of crisis (Glassman and Kates 1990; Middleman and Wood 1990a), such as new "first times" (e.g., the addition of new members, or when a group begins work on a new task) or in other moments of special difficulty, such as groupthink or conflict. Here is such a state of affairs, as described by the worker:

> Once I let the group "fly" and it ended in real chaos. We'd met for several months and the group had become really dull, so we thought a newsletter would be an interesting project to liven things up a bit. They wanted to do it on a regular basis, and we agreed we could probably put one together every two months or so. But when we started to work on it, all hell broke loose! All they did was fight

and argue about every little thing—who would do what and how to do it and what was supposed to be included. They couldn't agree on anything, especially two members who kept vying for control. One kept saying, "I used to be a journalist, you know," and the other would answer with something like, "So what? Who put you in charge? This is a group effort, remember?" The rest of us would try to get a word in edgewise, but we eventually gave up. The group got smaller and smaller, and by the time I left a couple of months later, we never even produced one newsletter.

That this group is in crisis and could use the worker's help is fairly evident: everyone talks at once, no one seems to be listening to anyone else, group members are engaged in apparently constant argument, and process is dominated by competition rather than collaboration. As reflected by her admission that she cannot get a word in edgewise, the worker has abdicated legitimate authority and has become just another "one of the gang" (Kurland and Salmon 1993). Thus, the group is ultimately devastated by its process.

How might the worker have used her authority to help the group at this moment? First, members need to talk about the nature of their differences, and a legitimate use of authority would be to help them share their feelings and perspectives about what is happening in and to the group. Second, group members need to turn their differences into food for thought, so another legitimate use of authority would be to help them share and explore where each of them is coming from. Third, the group needs to rediscover its common ground, which means another legitimate use of authority would be to help it reidentify and reflect on its commonalities. Finally, the group needs to transform a moment of conflict into a window of opportunity for working toward its purpose as a mutual-aid system, so yet another legitimate use of authority would be to help members think through the possibilities and adopt a course of action with which they can all live. In brief, the group needed the worker to say something such as, "Hold on! Hold on! What's going on, here?" and to provide help as the members respond to that question.

In sum, as a group matures and becomes increasingly competent as a mutual-aid system, the worker can step back and return to active duty only when its mutual-aid character is in peril. To allow a group a real say regarding its affairs does not mean to abdicate authority altogether. A mutual-aid system has the right to the worker's use of authority to help it understand, develop, and stay in touch with its potential as it exercises its voice.

HELPING THE GROUP EXERCISE ITS SAY ALONG HUMANISTIC AS WELL AS DEMOCRATIC LINES

DECISION MAKING

With teeth
gritted,
the
group
groped
and
grappled
until they
gradually
discovered
common
ground.

To
gain a
grip
on the
grueling task
ahead,
they agreed to
grind
coffee
to be served
with
granulated sugar
in
green cups.*

---

*"Decision Making" originally appeared in *Social Work with Groups Newsletter,* December-January 1994-1995, and is used here with the permission of its author, Andrew Malekoff.

A mutual-aid system must exercise its say with the needs of all of its members in mind. The extent to which a group shapes its affairs has an impact on its mutual-aid potential, and the way it uses its authority also impacts that potential (Bernstein 1976, 1978; Galinsky and Schopler 1977; Glassman and Kates 1990; Konopka 1983; Lowy 1978; Steinberg 1992; Trecker 1955). If members treat their authority simply as a vehicle for getting things done (e.g., "Let's not waste time here. Let's put it to a vote.") rather than as an ongoing forum for thinking things through (e.g., "Let's take some time to hear from everyone here and try to reach a decision with which we all agree."), then opportunities for mutual aid will still be lost. Some needs will be met, but others will remain unmet. Some desires will be satisfied, but others will be unsatisfied. In short, some group members will be winners, others will be losers, and a climate of division and competition, rather than one of unity and collaboration, or *democratic-humanism,* as Glassman and Kates (1990) refer to it, will be fostered. Thus, in addition to the right to a real say over its affairs, a mutual-aid system must take all of its voices into account. A *democratic* climate may be established when the group has a real say, but a *humanistic* climate will be established only when that say reflects a state of consensus.

It is not difficult for a group to function along democratic lines once authority is decentralized. All it has to do is put its issues to a vote, and voting is often conceptualized as a logical and proper reflection of having a real say. Two problems are associated with voting for a mutual-aid system, however. First, voting threatens the very sense of unity and community that decentralizing authority attempts to promote by inherently creating winners and losers. Second, voting is far more goal oriented than process sensitive, far more concerned with reaching a decision than with the feelings of those affected by that decision. Although voting reflects democracy in action, it does not necessarily reflect a state of humanism.

Consensus, on the other hand, does reflect humanism in action and is, therefore, particularly compatible with mutual aid. It seeks the voices behind the show of hands to make sure that feelings about and meaning assigned to the issues are expressed. It seeks to hear all of the voices to make sure that the issues are understood from as many viewpoints as exist in the group. It also seeks to integrate the substance of those voices into its decision-making process.

In brief, consensus is particularly compatible with mutual aid because it seeks to be inclusive rather than exclusive and because it calls for skills beyond those that are necessary for voting. It calls for group members to express their feelings and ideas, to clarify their positions and to listen to those of others, to attend to their differences as well as to their commonalities, and to integrate their differences into their own use of authority. In short, it calls for members to think things through and grapple with the issues until a particular course of action reflects a *group* decision (Bernstein 1978).

In the short run, consensus may be less efficient than voting as a decision-making strategy. But because consensus forces a group to take whatever time it needs to think about the impact of its own use of authority, what it lacks in efficiency it makes up in effectiveness at keeping mutuality and mutual aid alive.

Does this mean that it is never appropriate for a mutual-aid system to put its affairs to a vote? Absolutely no. Voting may well be in order on occasion, especially when there is no strong investment by any particular party in a particular outcome. Still, it must be said that a group's sense of community will be that much more safeguarded and its mutual-aid character that much more strengthened if it agrees by consensus to decide to vote!

PROFESSIONAL REFLECTION

When all is said and done, just how real a say a group ever has over its affairs depends on how the practitioner feels about authority, and taking a moment to reflect on our own approach can help us think about our own feelings and attitudes. It can help us assess the degree to which we might share our authority while not relinquishing it altogether and the degree to which any intent we might have to share it gets translated into real action. Even if we espouse a belief in shared authority the question of whether our practice efforts and interventions promote such a state of affairs still remains.

What can we ask ourselves? To begin with, we may have stated that we wanted group members to be actively involved in shaping the group's affairs (e.g., "In this group we will decide what to do together."). But do we discover in retrospect that we tend to exercise authority on their behalf anyway, that we routinely tend to take over the decision-making process, especially with regard to issues we consider important? When the group begins to exercise some internal leadership (e.g., "What if we were to do this other thing instead?"), do we seriously entertain new possibilities? Are we more often disinclined to modify a planned agenda (e.g., "I think it would be better to do what we planned, don't you?")? Or do we often find ourselves cramming what we want to see done into the last moments of a session because it is so important, as this practitioner admits?

> Once I've got members' attention, I almost don't encourage communication so that I can give them the information I want them to have.

We may have also stated that we wanted members to be actively involved in shaping the group's process (e.g., "Okay, so then let's decide how we're going to do this."). But as we reflect on previous process, do we notice that in spite of having voiced such an expectation we always seem to have had the last word about protocol (e.g., "I see your point, but I think this way is really best for the group.")? And do our justifications for taking that last word go something like this: "Well, the group was not really capable of deciding about that issue" or "about how to do that"? Or, in contrast, do we note that we rarely contribute our ideas, even when the group is in trouble, with a rationale such as: "Well, if people are going to learn new skills, they just need to muddle through things"?

We may have also stated that we expected and wanted members to express their real selves (e.g., "In this group, everyone will have the right to express what he or she really thinks and feels."). And we may have stated that whatever differences emerge as a result of that process will be welcome, even valuable (e.g., "It will be okay, even useful, in fact, for us have moments in which we do not see eye to eye."). When we think back to such moments, however, do we notice that when members do express their real feelings and opinions we tend to take a moralistic stance, as this worker does?

> At one point, an older member accused the youngest member, who was thirteen, of acting like a baby—which of course made her giggle even more ner-

vously. I thought the older member was being cruel and suggested she try to remember what it was like to be thirteen.

Or do we put an end to the group's discussion altogether when we are uncomfortable with it, as this worker does?

Ramona often provoked other members to anger. One day the other members said they would leave if Ramona stayed. I reminded her to be more focused and not go off on ridiculous tangents.

Or do we put an end to it when we fear its direction, as these workers do?

Joyce was routinely scapegoated by the others and knew how to push all our buttons. One time she became particularly angry about something another member had done outside the group. I felt pretty angry with her, and I didn't feel comfortable about letting the conflict evolve, so in the interest of providing balance I asked them (Joyce and the other group member) to meet me in private after the meeting.

Jay was making jokes about sex, competing with me for everyone's attention. Finally I turned to him and said, "Okay, well, no one can really help you with that right now. Could we continue?"

Or perhaps we realize that we tend to go to the opposite extreme, that even if all hell breaks loose, as the practitioner put it in an earlier case example, we simply leave the group to its own devices.

Finally, we may have stated that we wanted all the voices in this group to be heard (e.g., "Everyone's contribution will be welcome here"). But as we reflect on our own ways of being and doing, do we notice that we do not always leave enough room for that to happen? Do we, in fact, do less and less talking as the group matures? Or do we, even as the group matures, seem to hear the sound of our voices more than those of others? Do group members often need to struggle simply to get a word in edgewise? Do we often assume sole responsibility for answering questions and giving information? Or do we do just the opposite, rarely contributing to the group's process, even when doing so would help it advance its thinking-through process?

Asking ourselves questions such as these can provide us with some useful insight into the extent to which our use of authority promotes mutual aid. If we find that we are more often than not the group's focus of attention, we need to back away from the spotlight and allow the group to take a greater share of the stage. On the other hand, if our presence in the group seems irrelevant, then we need to review our expectations—both of our professional role and of group process. In this case, we may not be using our legitimate authority enough to provide our share of help for advancing process (see Kurland and Salmon, 1993). The next section identifies the many group-specific skills available for helping a group assume a real say over its affairs and for helping it maintain its mutual-aid character as it conducts those affairs.

GROUP-SPECIFIC SKILLS FOR DECENTRALIZING AUTHORITY AND FOR HELPING MAINTAIN A DEMOCRATIC-HUMANISTIC CLIMATE

Several group-specific skills are available to help us share, or decentralize, authority. Simply *being sensitive to our authority* in the group, *giving careful thought to the impact of what we say and do* on a group's ability to identify its own leadership strengths, and *always being willing and prepared to offer a rationale* for whatever we say and do set the stage for shared authority. *Explaining that we both desire and expect members to share* in all decision making as it affects the group makes our intent to share authority explicit. *Encouraging and helping group members to participate* whenever decision-making moments present themselves (e.g., "Okay, we need to make a decision at this point. What should we do?") helps them establish a norm of shared authority. Continually making *statements that praise collective effort* (e.g., "I know it wasn't easy to work this out, but look what a great job we did!") helps keep that norm in play. *Modeling* our own sense of commitment: being on time, being prepared, being thoughtful before we speak, and letting members know we assign a high value to their attending group sessions helps group members become committed to the group. *Taking every occasion to link members' experiences* (e.g., "Hans, it sounds as if your thinking is similar to Joy's." or "It sounds as if you have had the kind of experience Abby was just describing a minute ago, Ann." or "So, it seems as if you too, Tony, have been in many foster homes.") helps them discover their common ground. And *making statements that recognize and praise individual contributions* to the group's thinking-through process (e.g., "That's a really interesting idea, Joe" or "I know it wasn't easy for you to talk about that, Kevin. Thanks!") connects group members to the process, encourages them to participate, and helps them assume shared responsibility for the group's process and progress. *Encouraging and helping group members to express, clarify, and elaborate* their ideas and feelings (e.g., "Inez, can you give an example about what you mean?" or "Rob, can you say more about how you feel?") and *helping them to think through the implications of their process* (e.g., "say, I hear what's being said, but what's really going to happen if we do it that way? Let's talk about that.") helps the group identify both its needs and its strengths. *Encouraging the identification and articulation* of all ideas when decisions are called for (e.g., "All right. We need to talk about next week. Any ideas?") helps the group develop its capacity for internal leadership. *Fostering role flexibility* helps group members develop good "followship" skills so that the same people are not always caught in the same roles (e.g., always the leader or always the comic relief or always following someone else). And *making note of members' skills, strengths, and talents* at every possible opportunity (e.g., "You have such a good way with words, Judy" or "That wasn't an easy job, organizing all of us, Jerry. Bravo!" or "You were great in that role-play, Frank. Nice work!") helps them develop their appreciation for the special skills, strengths, and talents that they each bring to the group's group-building process.

Finally, many group-specific skills can help us make sure a humanistic as well as democratic culture rules the group's own exercise of authority. We *help the group take into account all of its voices, including those of difference* (e.g., "Okay, we seem to have some different opinions about what to do, here. Let's hear more about each one."). We *encourage it to identify all its options,* no matter how far fetched (e.g., "What *might* we do at this point, then?"). We *help it think through the implications* of each option for each member and for the group as a whole (e.g., "What will doing it this way mean for each of us, then?"). And we *periodically check for consensus,* especially when process is lively (e.g., "Okay! Let's stop for a second and see how everyone feels at this point."). We *help people who have trouble speaking up do so* (e.g., "Jump in, Marie. Tell us what you're thinking."), and *we point out to the group when it is overlooking some of its voices* (e.g., "Hold on a second, here. I think some views have been expressed that are not being considered."). We *encourage and praise whatever group process is inclusive and promotes collaboration* (e.g., "Wow! Look what working together has done here!"). We *point out when we note exclusivity or competition* (e.g., "Uh oh! We don't seem to be on the same page here."). And we *encourage ongoing reflection throughout the group's decision-making process,* so that each member may assess its personal value and to allow the possibility of change (e.g., "Okay, let's look at how we're doing here.").

KEY POINTS OF THIS CHAPTER

1. To the extent that issues of authority generally present interesting food for thought in practice with groups, they present absolutely essential food for thought for mutual-aid practice with groups.
2. While central authority is often viewed as a vehicle for providing professional help, mutual-aid practice views the decentralization of authority as a vehicle for helping people help one another.
3. Having a real say over the group's affairs helps keep its process relevant and meaningful, helps the group develop an esprit de corps committed to mutuality, and creates a forum for mutual aid.
4. Decentralizing authority is not synonymous with laissez-faire. Central authority impedes mutual aid by placing a choke hold on group process, but laissez-faire also impedes it by not helping the group stay in touch with the parameters within which and outside of which it may operate as a mutual-aid system.
5. Generally speaking, the more mature the group, the more capable it is of actively and directly exercising its authority. Over the course of its development, then, the less the worker needs to actively and directly exercise his or her authority.
6. To maintain its mutual-aid character, a group must promote a humanistic as well as democratic climate. As a decision-making strategy, therefore, consensus is far more compatible with mu-

tual aid than voting. Where voting is inherently divisive, consensus promotes unity and community. Where voting is goal oriented, consensus is process sensitive, and where voting requires only a show of hands, consensus requires the use of thinking-through and problem-solving skills.

7. Reflecting on personal ways of being and doing in a group can help the worker assess the extent to which his or her approach allows a group to have a real say over its affairs. It can also help assess the degree to which any intent to decentralize authority has been translated into action.

RECOMMENDED FURTHER READING

Bernstein, S. (1976). Values and group work. In *Further Explorations in Group Work,* ed. S. Bernstein, pp. 145-179. Boston: Charles River Books.

_____. (1993). What happened to self-determination? *Social Work with Groups* 16(1/2):3-14.

Birnbaum, M. L., Middleman, R. R., and Huber, R. (1989). "Where social workers obtain their knowledge base in group work." Paper presented at the Annual Meeting of the National Association of Social Workers, San Francisco, October.

Breton, M. (1988). Liberation theology, group work, and the right of the poor and oppressed to participate in the life of the community. *Social Work with Groups* 12(3):5-17.

Cohen, M. B. (1994). Who wants to chair the meeting?: Group development and leadership patterns in a community action group of homeless people. *Social Work with Groups* 17(1/2):71-87.

Falck, H. (1955). Central characteristics of work with groups—a sociocultural analysis. In *Group Work Practice in a Troubled Society: Problems and Opportunities,* eds. R. Kurland and R. Salmon, pp. 63-72. Binghamton, NY: The Haworth Press.

Galinsky, M. J. and Schopler, J. H. (1977). Warning: Groups may be dangerous. *Social Work* March:89-94.

Garland, J. A. and Frey, L. A. (1976). Application of stages of group development to groups in psychiatric settings. In *Further Explora-*

tions in Group Work, ed. S. Bernstein, pp. 1-33. Boston: Charles River Books.

Garland, J. A., Jones, H. E., and Kolodny, R. L. (1978). A model for stages of development in social work groups. In *Explorations in Group Work,* ed. S. Bernstein, pp. 17-71. Hebron, CT: Practitioner's Press.

Glassman, U. and Kates, L. (1983). Authority themes and worker-group transactions: Additional dimensions to the stages of group development. *Social Work with Groups* 6(2):33-52.

————. (1990). *Group Work: The Humanistic Approach.* Newbury Park, CA: Sage.

Konopka, G. (1983). *Social Group Work.* Englewood Cliffs, NJ: Prentice-Hall.

Kurland, R., and Salmon, R. (1990). Self-determination: Its use and misuse in group work practice and social work education. In *Working from Strengths: The Essence of Group Work,* eds. D. Fike and B. Rittner, pp. 105-121. Miami Shores, FL: Center for Group Work Studies.

————. (1993). Not just one of the gang: Group workers and their role as an authority. *Social Work with Groups* 16(1/2):153-169.

Lindemann, E. C. (1980). Group work and democracy—a philosophical note. In *Perspectives on Social Group Work Practice,* ed. A. S. Alissi, pp. 77-82. New York: Free Press.

Lowy, L. (1978). Decision-making and group work. In *Explorations in Group Work,* ed. S. Bernstein, pp. 107-136. Hebron, CT: Practitioner's Press.

Middleman, R. and Rothman, B. (1988). Will the real group worker please stand up! *Social Work with Groups* 11(1/2):16-170.

Newstetter, W. (1980). Regulatory principles. In *Perspectives on Social Group Work Practice,* ed. A. Alissi, pp. 101-109. New York: The Free Press.

Rooney, R. H., Rooney, G. D., and Herbst, A. P. (1981). Continuing education and graduate training needs for group work: Results of a survey of social workers who lead groups. *Journal of Continuing Social Work Education,* Spring:11-34.

Schiller, L. Y. (1995). Stages of developing women's groups: A relational group model. In *Group Work Practice in a Troubled Society:*

Problems and Opportunities, eds. R. Kurland and R. Salmon, pp. 117-138. Binghamton, NY: The Haworth Press.

Schopler, J. H. and Galinsky, M. J. (1981). When groups go wrong. *Social Work* 26(5):424-429.

Schwartz, W. (1961). The social worker in the group. *The Social Welfare Forum,* pp. 146-171. New York: Columbia University Press.

_____. (1976). Between client and system: The mediating function. In *Theories of Social Work with Groups,* eds. R. Roberts and H. Northen, pp. 171-198. New York: Columbia University Press.

_____. (1980). On the use of groups in social work practice. In *Perspectives on Social Group Work Practice,* ed. A. Alissi, pp. 268-284. New York: The Free Press.

Steinberg, D. M. (1992). *The Impact of Group Work Education on Social Work Practitioners' Work with Groups.* New York: City University of New York.

Toseland, R., Rivas, R., and Chapman, D. (1984). An evaluation of decision-making methods in task groups. *Social Work* 29:339-347.

Trecker, H. B. (1955). *Social Group Work: Principles and Practices.* New York: Whiteside.

Wayne, J. and Garland, J. (1990). Group work education in the field: The state of the art. *Social Work with Groups* 13(2):95-109.

Chapter 8

The Role of Conflict
in a Mutual-Aid System

KEY CONCEPTS OF THIS CHAPTER

Being There for All Group Members at All Times
Common Ground
Conflict As the Expression of Difference
Conflict As a Legitimate Group Dynamic
Conflict As a Tool of Mutual Aid
Conflict As a Whole-Group Issue
Interactions Approach to Conflict

* * *

Do not use a hatchet to remove a fly from your friend's forehead.

Old Chinese Proverb

Conflict plays an important role in mutual aid (Bernstein 1965, Gitterman 1989; Glassman and Kates 1990; Papell and Rothman 1980; Shulman 1999). The discovery, expression, and exploration of commonality may be what helps people become open to one another as potential resources, but it is conflict, or the discovery, expression, and exploration of their differences, that will propel them to entertain new ways of looking at old pictures.

Conflict is often visualized as a fisticuffs situation or a heated exchange that ends in chaos. The mere idea of it tends to strike terror in the heart, and all possible resources are brought to bear on either avoiding or putting a quick stop to provocative moments. In reality, however, conflict is not in and of itself a violent state of affairs. It is merely the result of expressions of difference, and although commonality is one important facet of mutual aid, the opportunity to explore difference and entertain new ways of looking at old pictures is an equally important facet.

Mountains of contemporary professional and popular literature show that conflict resolution is very much an *idée moderne*. Mutual-aid practice is less concerned with conflict resolution per se, than with using conflict as a vehicle for exploring the meaning of differences, for encouraging expanded understanding of and appreciation for others, and for helping people develop mutual respect and empathy when confronted by irreconcilable differences.

This chapter is not a treatise on conflict resolution, therefore. Rather, it offers some keys for helping groups use conflict to move toward rather than away from mutual aid, which means that when conflict occurs (and differences do crop up in any group that values the expression of real ideas and real feelings), it needs to be treated as an opportunity for helping people think through their own ways of being as they listen to, learn about, and learn from those of others.

There are a few important keys for helping people use their differences in the service of mutual aid. The first is to conceptualize conflict as having the potential of being useful, even helpful, and to approach conflict responsively rather than reactively.

The second key is two sided. One side is to accept conflict as a normal consequence of group life. The other is to help the group accept conflict and treat it as a legitimate tool for mutual aid. Helping the group adopt an attitude that conflict is expected and acceptable is important if we want it to establish and maintain a climate in which members feel free to express their real feelings and ideas.

Third, since the mutual-aid approach is a psychosocial rather than an individual-defect approach to working with people (see Chapter 1), we need to treat conflict as a result of difference rather than as a symptom of individual fault. This will encourage group members to search for understanding and maintain a climate of support when differences emerge rather than judge and find fault.

The fourth key is to refrain from trying to resolve conflict alone, to stop ourselves from trying to make things better for the group by smoothing things over (e.g.,, "Let's not fight, folks. It won't get us anywhere, will it?" or "Let's not argue here; we have so much to do.") or by suggesting that members do not mean what they are saying (e.g., "Come on, Selma, you know you don't really mean that!").

When we stop people from expressing their real feelings, ideas, and viewpoints, we deny them opportunities to examine their positions, explore the meaning of their differences, and help one another think about, learn about, and learn from their differences.

The fifth key is to engage the entire group in the examination and exploration of the issues when conflict does occur. If its strengths are to be used in the service of mutual aid, then the strengths of each member need to be called on to deal with each situation. Otherwise we negate the reason for having a group in the first place.

The sixth key is to *be there* for all group members at all times (Middleman 1987). This does not mean that we remain neutral about positions taken in the group; in fact, we often feel more aligned with one feeling state, attitude, viewpoint, or philosophy than we do with another. Nor does it mean that we never express our own feelings or challenge points of view. In fact, if we want to help people learn from one another, helping them think about their ways of being is part and parcel of the task. Being there means that we make sure everyone who wishes to be heard has that opportunity without being subjected to overly harsh criticism, chiding, or contempt from others. It means that we help the group give all of its members a chance to express themselves in safety. In addition, it means that when we express our own feelings or positions, we do so in a way that does not alienate those with whom we disagree or threaten the group's sense of unity and community.

The seventh key is to help the group keep sight of its common ground. Being involved in conflict situations is not easy, even when real talk is valued. As differences arise, therefore, it is essential that group members be helped to remember commonalities as they examine and explore the meaning of those differences.

Each of these seven keys is discussed in greater detail in the next section.

KEYS TO USING CONFLICT FOR MUTUAL AID

Key #1: Conflict Can Be Helpful

Variety is the spice of life.

Not all groups are structured with mutual aid in mind, but when people are invited to contribute their strengths and skills to group process, those strengths and skills become the building blocks for mutual aid (Breton 1990). As time goes by and members feel increasingly comfortable in exercising those strengths and skills, however, differences of all kinds inevitably arise. Even when groups are formed around a common cause, people bring some differences with them, ranging from the philosophical . . .

to the mundane . . .

(*Source:* Sketches are by, and courtesy of, Michel Moyse.)

Whatever a group's mission or composition, it is unrealistic to think that it can be composed of people who have no differences whatsoever, even if they should choose to sweep their differences under the rug. Thus, the mutual-aid approach to working with groups proposes that when a moment of conflict does occur—be it among group members or between the worker and one or more members—it shall be exploited to the group's advantage. This means that whenever conflict occurs, we acknowledge it as a legitimate dimension of group life and help members examine and explore it so that they increase rather than decrease their understanding. In fact, when differences exist, we actually encourage their expression so that members can have an opportunity to think about their ways of being and contrast them with those of others. By helping them do this, we also help them assess the impact of their ways and entertain new possibilities. Thus, we help the group accept difference. We help it examine ways in which diversity might enhance the quality of its existence, and we help the group explore ways in which difference might enrich the personal lives of its members.

Does this mean that when all is said and done, conflict is still a negative state of affairs but one we need to "make the best of" since it is unavoidable? No; in fact, quite the contrary. Conflict is neither a negative state of affairs nor even a setback in the group's affairs when it creates opportunities for people to engage in self-analysis, to teach others, to learn from others, to discover new common ground, or even to respect irreconcilable differences. From a mutual-aid viewpoint, it is a positive and potentially useful state of affairs, valued for its capacity to stimulate thinking. Exploring the meaning and impact of culture, religion, or ethnicity, for example, may have a very real impact on people's lives and expectations and can help people develop a greater understanding of and empathy for other viewpoints even as it gives them the chance to review their own. At the same time, conflict is not an *inherently* useful state of affairs. If a lack of respect for difference exists in the first place, it is likely to take a destructive course (Konopka 1983). However, if the right to differ is respected and appreciated, conflict can create rich opportunities for reflecting, learning, and changing (Bernstein 1965).

Must a group experience conflict in order to experience mutual aid? No. As Chapter 2 discusses, mutual aid has many dynamics, some of which may be experienced more often than others or in greater intensity than others, and some of which may not be experienced at all. The introduction and appreciation of diversity will always enrich a group, therefore, but it is not essential that groups experience conflict in order to be conceptualized as mutual-aid systems. It is never appropriate to purposefully escalate situations for the sake of creating conflict, but in regard to mutual-aid, it is always appropriate to encourage and help a group explore whatever differences do emerge in the service of better understanding and appreciation.

As with the case of authority, the greatest barrier to helping groups make use of conflict is often the worker's own attitude (Bernstein 1965; Galinsky and Schopler 1977; Glassman and Kates 1990; Konopka 1983). Generally speaking, people are socialized to fear and avoid conflict, to think that harmony constructs and that conflict destructs. Thus, it is not uncommon for conflict in a group to be conceptualized as an unwelcome visitor rather than as a legitimate expression of difference related in some way (even if unclearly so at first glance) to the group's affairs (Steinberg 1992). Treating conflict as such, however, creates obstacles to mutual aid.

First, group members become reluctant to express their real ideas and feelings, fearing that the expression of what makes them individual and unique will make them less valuable in the eyes of the comembers. As a result, the group misses opportunities to discover its strengths and skills. Second, unexpressed feelings tend to resurface later, while their existence haunts or wreaks havoc in the group in the meantime. Power struggles over seemingly minor issues may erupt, impeding the group's ability to work. Cliques may form, endangering the group's sense of community. Absenteeism rates may rise, threatening morale as well as endangering the sense of community. People may even drop out of the group altogether, threatening its very existence.

Conflict does not always destroy, then, and harmony is not always useful. Conflict may appear destructive at first glance by bringing a degree of disorder to a situation, but by shaking up the status quo, that disorder can create a highly constructive state of affairs when it propels people to greater heights of insight and sensitivity. If we treat conflict as taboo, either by sweeping differences under the rug or by avoiding them in the first place, we create some very real barriers to mutual aid by giving the group a mixed message about the value of authentic expression.

Key #2: Expect Conflict to Happen and Help the Group Accept It

If differences in group life are expected, and if helping group members explore the roots of conflict is key to mutual-aid practice, then a request for "order" when differences do emerge is a counterproductive intervention. Rather, members need to be helped to accept their differences as a natural consequence of group life (e.g., "Naturally and fortunately, we bring differences as well as commonalities with us to this group."), and they need to be helped to explore the meaning and impact of those differences on them as individuals and on the group as a whole (e.g., "Okay, let's look at these differences, where they come from, and what they mean to us."). We do not have to embrace conflict with open arms (e.g., "Okay, let's have a good fight!"). We can, however, embrace the belief that people's differences always present interesting food for thought.

Exploring and resolving differences is very important work in group. Thus, helping the members of a group accept and make use of their differences is often the most important work that we as group workers will ever do. What can we do to help make differences acceptable? How can we help people make use of their differences? First, we can help group members release their negative feelings, as the worker does in this excerpt:

> I said, "What's happening here?" They said that it was "no big deal," of course, and wanted to move on. I wouldn't let it go, though. I kept insisting that we talk about what had just happened. We did, but it was hard and slow for them—you know teens, they just wanted to let it go, but I didn't.

Then, we can encourage the group to fully explore its differences, as this worker does:

> The group members claimed they didn't really care, so I said to everyone, "There's a lot more to this than meets the eye, I think. This isn't in any way resolved," and continued to try to get them to talk. We spent the whole hour at it.

And finally, we can help the group keep talking until all of the salient issues have been identified and discussed, as this worker tries to do:

> After some time, the issue that was bothering them was revealed. This all happened at the end of the meeting, though, so we couldn't really talk about any of it in depth. At the end of group I said, "We have a conflict here in the group, and we can't just forget about it. We need to talk about it again next time."

Simply by encouraging their expression and exploration, we help make differences acceptable and useful, and we confirm that when we said we wanted people to express what they really think and what they really feel in the group, we really meant it. If we do not make it acceptable (e.g., "Let's not fight, folks." or "Hey you two, let's talk about this after group." or "Come on, Henry, you know you don't really mean that."), the group's mutual-aid potential will suffer because real positions will be driven underground, real feelings will fester, and the group will be yet another exercise in civility, providing few occasions to look at old pictures in new ways.

Key #3: Treat Conflict As a Result of Difference, Not Fault

The mutual-aid approach to group work takes its cue for intervening in conflict from interaction theory (Schwartz and Zalba 1971; Shulman 1999), in which conflict is seen not as a consequence of individual defect (e.g., "It's John's fault.") but as a consequence of differences brought to life by some aspect of group interaction, as this worker's intervention reflects:

> I said something like, "There's something going on here that I think we all need to talk about."

From this perspective, conflict reflects a momentary poor fit between or among the ways in which people are feeling, thinking, or seeing a particular picture or approaching a particular task, or the clash that results from some difference in needs, desires, goals, or expectations.

When we conceptualize conflict in terms of individual fault rather than interpersonal difference, we create two very specific problems for mutual aid. First, when members feel their ways of thinking or doing are conceptualized as faulty, the climate of the group becomes unsafe for real talk about real things. As Glassman and Kates (1990) state, the group loses its humanistic dimension. Second, it usually leads to some form of *casework in a group* (Kurland and Salmon 1992) as members devote their energy to analyzing what is "faulty," or "fixing" one another instead of trying to develop a collective understanding of and empathy for different positions.

In contrast, conceptualizing conflict as a result of difference means that it is the nature of members' differences that becomes the target for intervention, never their persons. Here, for example, is how it might look to personalize the source of conflict and target a group member as an object of intervention:

> Betty just couldn't sit still in group and participate appropriately. One day, one of the other members finally challenged her about it. I told Betty that if she was going to continue behaving in such a hyperactive way, she shouldn't return to the next group.

How is conflict personalized in this example? Very simply: the worker focuses on Betty's behavior and only Betty's behavior rather than what seems to be happening between Betty and her comembers. Conceptualizing the conflict as an interpersonal issue, on the other hand, would prompt a very different intervention. The worker would ask the group to talk about what seems to be happening (e.g., "It seems to me that we're having a problem, here. What's going on?") and encourage anyone and everyone to respond and begin a dialogue about what is, in fact, going on. As a result of the worker's intervention, however, Betty does not return to the next meeting, and one of the raisons d'être of groups—to help people look at, think about, and perhaps change their behavior—is completely negated. This next worker also conceptualizes conflict as an individual fault and thus personifies her intervention:

> I said to Gary, "Your opinion is only one. Others, too, have good sense. Do you notice that others are not responding positively to you?" Others chimed in, and Gary left the room.

How might this worker have intervened if she thought of conflict as a result of difference instead of someone's fault? She, too, would have asked the group to examine and explore its differences (e.g., "Okay, there are many strongly felt opinions here. Let's talk about them.") rather than focus on the position or behavior of only one person.

In the following case, the worker manages to depersonalize conflict. Instead of focusing specifically on one or another person, she asks the group as a whole to get involved:

> I stopped everything and asked the group what was going on. At first, no one said much, but I waited. Then I asked again, and they started to talk.

In sum, a key to making conflict useful for mutual-aid purposes is to conceptualize conflict as the expression of difference rather than attack any one particular way of thinking, being, or doing. Keeping the group climate "fault-finding free" will keep it safe for real talk and open to acknowledging and using its differences.

Key #4: Don't "Take Over" When Conflict Occurs

If a group's differences are to be useful, then members need to talk about what is being said or done in the group. They need to talk about the conflict at hand. They need to talk about the issues that are provoking the conflict. They need to talk about how and why they believe their feelings or attitudes differ. They need to talk about the meaning and impact of their differences on the group. Finally, they need to talk about the impact of their differences on their personal lives. When conflict occurs and we take over, then we effectively deprive people of all of these opportunities.

What are some ways in which we might take over? Here is one way:

> Finally, one day I asked Frank to take time out or just sit quietly, at which point he became quite angry. I escorted him out of the room, warned him that his behavior was unacceptable, and referred him to his caseworker.

And here is another:

> Jay got really angry at another member who had offended him just before we started. I tried to get them to talk, but Jay just displaced his anger on me. So I told him, "Okay, if you're angry, you don't have to stay; we can talk about it later." He did stay, but he was silent for the rest of the meeting, and then we talked about it after.

What should have happened instead in these groups? Essentially, some demand for work from everyone in the group should have been made. The workers should have encouraged and helped the members talk about what was happening in and to the group and helped them deal with their differences, as this worker tries to do:

> An argument developed among three members about the "right" way to do something. I stayed quiet, because even though they were passionate about their positions, they were tolerating other points of view. . . . I also tried to get the others to participate by asking what they thought. It was slow going, but we did continue to talk about it.

Conceptualizing conflict as a whole-group issue, then, the exploration of which everyone has a stake in, is an important key for dealing with conflict from a mutual-aid viewpoint. The temptation to take over needs to be resisted so that the group might have an opportunity to tap into its own resources for identifying the issues and working things out. If we take over, our message is, even if inadvertent, that we do not believe the members are capable of mutual aid.

Key #5: Engage Everyone in the Group

If conflict is a whole-group issue, as noted above, then everyone in the group—not just the overtly involved parties—needs to be engaged in its examination and exploration. Regardless of who is doing the talking at the moment of conflict or who is angry with whom, if only the overtly involved individuals are asked or permitted to participate in examining their differences, then, once again, we will be doing *casework in a group* by placing some members on standby while attending to others, as this worker does:

> During one session, two members became very angry with each other. I stood up and shouted, "STOP!" Then I told one member to leave the room and come back when he had calmed down, and I said to the other one, "Go sit on the sofa! Now!" We took a five-minute break, and when we came back together, I had one member sit at one end of this long table in the room and the other one sit at the opposite end. Then I asked them to please, calmly, talk about their differences. The other members listened.

Instead, everyone in the group needs to be encouraged to take part in the examination and exploration of whatever differences are confronting the group, as this worker tries to do:

> One member was particularly provocative. She was very competitive, made nasty asides, cruel comments, and generally bul-

> lied the group. In one session, Debbie told me how angry she was about something this other member had done in school. Others said they knew about it too. So I asked them, "All right, what's going on here? What's happening?" They said, "Oh, nothing, we don't want to talk about it here." I asked them if the problem involved the group, and a few of them answered, "Well, some of us." So then I said, "Well, then, let's use the group to resolve it."

And as this worker also tries to do:

> The argument escalated to the point at which the challenger shouted something like: "Who died and left you boss?!" They shouted a little more, while the others were pretty cowed. Finally, when a stalemate became clear, I said, "Let's slow down. . . . What's really going on?" The two started to argue again, so I turned to the others and asked, "Where is everybody, anyway?"

Sometimes when feelings are so strong that group members seem incapable of hearing one another, a moratorium of some kind seems in order. Even this decision needs to be a whole-group process, however, so that we do not appear to be sweeping the group's difficulties under the rug, and so that the group may take responsibility for and make plans for revisiting the issues.

Key #6: "Be There" for Everyone

When differences emerge in a group, it is not all that unusual for practitioners to agree more with one person than with another or to feel more closely connected to one feeling state than to another. Expressing such an alignment before all others have had an opportunity to express and explore their own viewpoints, however, usually creates division just when the group most needs its sense of community. Actively *being there* for all members at all times by refraining from taking sides in times of conflict is another important key to helping groups use conflict for purposes of mutual aid.

It is often tempting to take sides when differences are expressed in a group, particularly when someone reflects our own point of view, but mutual aid requires that we need to resist doing so for two reasons. First, taking sides is divisive and threatens whatever group-building progress is taking place. Second, if it appears that we identify with some members and not with others, their trust in us will be diminished, and they will become concerned about our ability to be there for them in the future.

How might taking sides look in practice? The following is an example:

> Greg said that sometimes he had hallucinations. Frank refused to believe him. Frank said that Greg couldn't possibly [have hallucinations], not with his diagnosis. They argued for some time and ended with some rather angry words. I knew Frank was right, but I didn't say anything while they were arguing. Finally, I stopped them and told Greg that Frank was right and then asked if I should bring the diagnostic manual to the next meeting to prove it. The issue was dropped.

In this example, it may be true that one member is correct and another is incorrect. Saying so is perfectly acceptable if the issue is actually one of diagnosis (as if the parties were therapy students responsible for filling out diagnostic charts, for example). However, that is not the issue. The issue is taking members seriously. Greg's experience (which is, by definition, subjective) is not given the consideration it deserves. It is discounted by Frank, as well as the worker, who adds insult to injury by offering to "prove" to Greg that his perceptions are invalid. It is likely that Greg did not leave this meeting feeling valued or supported.

Here is another example of taking sides:

> Bernice tended to remain aloof, often implying to the other members that she was different from them in some very significant ways. At one session they confronted Bernice about her airs. One member told her, "You don't connect to people!" I allowed the confrontation, but she couldn't handle it. Eventually, Bernice became too anxious and left the group.

In this case, the worker clearly sides with the group against Bernice by referring to her ability to "handle" the confrontation, which reflects a nonempathic position. Without a doubt, Bernice was on her own during the conflict.

Being there for all group members at all times, on the other hand, can be found in this example:

> I could see George was really furious with Jack. They were arguing, and I heard George say he was going to leave, so I said, "Look, George, you're really upset with Jack, and he needs to know why. You're both important to this group; you can't just get mad and leave. So do you think you can sit here now and talk to us and then hear what Jack and the rest of us have to say?"

Another example of being there for all members::

> Eventually, they ended with a stalemate, with everyone being rigid about their positions. At that point, I tried to reflect what they had been saying by telling each one, "Sounds like you're saying . . . and it sounds like you're saying . . . , so is the question . . . ?"

Does the mandate to refrain from aligning with one or another member or subgroup mean that we can never express our own position? No. It simply means that if we have an opinion to express, we need to do it in such a way that we are not experienced as accepting of some members and rejecting of others. It means that although we express our ideas and feelings with candor, we balance that candor with the same kind of sensitivity and respect that we ask of the group by being clear about where we are coming from and by allowing, even helping, members to argue their cases with us, and by being open to difference so that we do not drive as-yet unexpressed viewpoints underground.

Key #7: Help the Group Keep Sight of Its Common Ground

To the extent that it signifies the presence of real talk, stimulates self-reflection, and provides new ways of looking at old pictures, conflict is integral to mutual aid. But conceptualizing conflict as a valuable tool of mutual aid does not make dealing with it a simple matter. Usual ways of being and doing are often comfortable, incentives for maintaining the status quo are often strong, new ways of looking at old pictures are often alien, and feelings are often passionate. The final key for helping a group use conflict to move toward rather than away from mutual aid, then, is to help people keep sight of what they have in common, what it is that keeps them together, and what is in it for them to try to understand their differences. General common ground needs to be identified and solidified (e.g., "Okay, we all seem to want to do something special for that occasion."). Specific commonalities need to be identified (e.g., "It sounds as if you're saying that you disagree with Judy's approach, Joe, but that you agree that her son needs some kind of limit setting. . . ."). The group's purpose needs to be used as a constant reference point for helping members see that what they have in common is stronger than the sum of their differences (e.g., "Okay, we have lots of ideas about how to proceed here. Let's think back to our purpose. . . .").

GROUP-SPECIFIC SKILLS FOR HELPING A GROUP USE CONFLICT

In helping a group look at its differences, we have at our disposal a powerful tool for helping it discover the path to mutual aid. Simply *acknowledging that differences will emerge in the group we have in mind* (e.g., "We are bound to have some differences here, and that will be okay.") begins to set the stage for the use of differences by acknowledging that differences are to be expected and accepted. *Encouraging open and free communication* (e.g., "Okay, so let's talk about this."), *helping members express their ideas and feelings* (e.g., "Let's hear how everyone feels about this."), and *reaching for and accepting discrepant perceptions* (e.g., "So, Joe, you seem to see things in a very different way. . . . Can you say more?") are all skills that convey our faith in the group's ability to deal with whatever differences arise. *Helping members express themselves* in ways that others can hear them provides a structure for disabling harsh criticism while confirming our intent and desire to help the group make its differences useful. We can help them do this in two ways. We can *tone down overly loud messages* (e.g., "Wait a second, Lucille. It's clear you have some very strong feelings here. Can you tell us less about what you think Sam is doing and more about how you feel?"), and we can *amplify those that are too subtle* (e.g., "Hold it. I think some feelings have been expressed here that the group isn't picking up. . . . Sal, can you repeat what you just said?"). *Asking members to stick with difficult moments* (e.g., "Yes, okay, we clearly have a strong difference of opinion here, but let's not just give up. Let's keep talking.") helps them analyze the roots of their conflict. *Asking them to explore the meaning and impact of their differences on the group* (e.g., "So, what do you think this means for us as a group, then ?") helps them make use of conflict. And finally, *being there for all members at all times* (e.g., "Okay, Phyllis sees it one way and Gladys sees it another. That's okay.") helps the group maintain a climate of goodwill as it looks at its differences.

KEY POINTS OF THIS CHAPTER

1. Helping people understand the roots and meaning of their differences is one of the things that groups do best and it is integral to mutual aid. Stunting conflict, therefore, deprives a group of one of its greatest strengths.
2. The outcome of a conflict situation may be less important than the ability of people to deal with difference in a more mature way (Bernstein 1976). Thus, the primary goal of mutual-aid practice with groups is not conflict resolution per se, but to provide opportunities for people to think about actions and interactions, to think about their impact, to entertain the possibility of adopting new ways of being and doing, and to gain a deeper and fuller appreciation for diversity.
3. Conflict is an expected, even useful, dimension of group life, and people need to be encouraged and helped to accept it as such.
4. If conflict is to be used for mutual-aid purposes, it needs to be treated as a result of interpersonal difference rather than a symptom of individual fault.
5. Any attempts by the worker to take charge or to smooth things over when conflict occurs deprives group members of opportunities for mutual aid by preventing them from looking at, thinking about, and learning from their differences.
6. Calling the whole group to action in times of conflict expresses the worker's faith that it has the strengths and skills to deal with

its differences and provides an opportunity for members to use their differences for learning, growing, and changing.

7. Taking sides or being perceived as taking sides in times of conflict creates a climate counterproductive to mutual aid. It is divisive and stunts the expression of real opinions, real attitudes, and real feelings.

8. Helping the group stay in touch with its common ground even as it examines and explores its differences helps it accept and integrate those differences.

RECOMMENDED FURTHER READING

Bernstein, S. (1965). Conflict and group work. In *Explorations in Group Work,* ed. S. Bernstein, pp. 72-106. Boston: Boston University School of Social Work.

Galinsky, M. J. and Schopler, J. H. (1977). Warning: Groups may be dangerous. *Social Work* 22(2):89-94.

Garland, J. A. and Kolodny, R. L. (1976). Characteristics and resolution of scapegoating. In *Further Explorations in Group Work,* ed. S. Bernstein, pp. 51-74. Boston: Charles River Books.

Glassman, U. and Kates, L. (1990). *Group Work: The Humanistic Approach.* Newbury Park, CA: Sage.

Konopka, G. (1983). *Social Group Work.* Englewood Cliffs, NJ: Prentice-Hall.

Middleman, R. and Wood, G. G. (1990). From social group work to social work with groups. *Social Work with Groups* 13(3):3-20.

Northen, H. and Kurland, R. (2001). *Social Work with Groups.* New York: Columbia University Press.

Papell, C. and Rothman, B. (1980). Relating the mainstream model of social work with groups to group psychotherapy and the structured group approach. *Social Work with Groups* 3(2):5-23.

Schwartz, W. (1977). Social group work: The interactions approach. In *Encyclopedia of Social Work,* ed. J. B. Turner, 2(16), pp. 1328-1338. New York: National Association of Social Workers.

Schwartz, W. and Zalba, S. (1971). *The Practice of Group Work.* New York: Columbia University Press.

Shulman, L. (1967). Scapegoats, group workers, and pre-emptive intervention. *Social Work* 12(2):37-43.

_____. (1999). *The Skills of Helping Individuals and Groups*. Itasca, IL: E. Peacock.

Steinberg, D. M. (1994). "A study of social work practitioners' responses to conflict in the small group: What's happening out there?" Paper presented at the Sixteenth Annual Symposium of the Association for the Advancement of Social Work with Groups, Hartford, Connecticut, October.

VARIATIONS ON A THEME

Wisdom lies neither in fixity nor in change, but in the dialectic between the two.

Octavio Piaz, Mexican Poet
The London Times, 1989

Although Clara Kaiser's (1958) argument that mutual-aid practice is more a question of how we approach our work than one of setting or population is still true today, little did she probably imagine the current state of practice: the number of groups that come together in one-time encounters, for example, or whose members must try to find meaningful interaction with frequently changing faces, or multi-family groups with twenty or more participants. However, such groups are common today, from the offices of private practitioners who often "insert" new members into recently-vacated seats of so-called ongoing groups, to the meeting rooms of agencies under pressure to cut costs, to large-scale enterprises of all kinds. Thus, although Kaiser's argument that practice is an issue of mind-set still holds true, it is also true that groups are increasingly taking on significantly different shapes from that of the small, closed system on which many fundamental practice principles are based.

It has been stated throughout this book that mutual aid is a logical characteristic of group life. It has also been noted, however, that mutual aid is neither automatic nor inherent, that we neither become engaged with nor feel like helping one another simply because we find ourselves in the same place at the same time. Experience tells us that obstacles to mutual aid exist in all groups and that its potential unfolds only as we begin to see common ground with others, as we find concrete ways to help and be helped, and as we start to see how investing in someone else's welfare can synergistically advance our own (see Chapter 5). In other words, it tells us that mutual aid needs a visible basis for development, collective desire, and time to learn the ropes.

Thus, an important key to helping a group reach beyond its obstacles to mutual aid is to be sensitive to the time and place of our expectations—to temper what we want to see happen (i.e., our vision) with respect for the impact of time on people's desire and capacity for mutuality (see Chapter 5). In the next four chapters, the concept of time and place takes on a further dimension. Used as a framework to examine *extraordinary* obstacles to mutual aid (obstacles that exist *in addition to* those routinely faced, as outlined in Chapter 1), time and place refers to special contextual obstacles—obstacles that exist because of the group's unique characteristics, and which present, therefore, special or *extraordinary* consideration.

Exactly what are those extraordinary obstacles? To begin with, single-session and short-term groups do not have time for the natural evolution of process. As in early silent films, in which action is speeded up, they are played out, so to speak, in "unreal" time. In fact, the single-session group is so speeded up that, developmentally speaking, its first meeting is also its last! Furthermore, its purpose is generally predetermined, leaving both little time and little room for members' input. Aside from developing a vision that is engaging enough to draw people to a one-time encounter, then, and having to rather quickly help translate vision into working reality, we need to constantly view and review the relevance of purpose as we see it. Compared to the single-session group, the short-term group has a luxurious amount of time in which to carry out its work. However, expectations of what it might, can, and should do are often unrealistic. Given that the group has some time, therefore, and quite a bit of leeway (at least theoretically) in shaping its purpose, it needs structure to help it organize its time most effectively—so that it is not still struggling with its raison d'être on the fourth of eight meetings, for example. Open-ended groups, composed of constantly changing faces, can find it particularly difficult to develop enough we-ness to take advantage of their full mutual-aid potential. Finally, it can be difficult to maintain a *humanistic* as well as *democratic* climate (Glassman and Kates 1990) in groups with 15, 20, 50, and even larger membership, whose very nature provides possibilities of anonymity. The general characteristics of these four group types, then, are significantly different from the small and closed long-term system, which presents us with an ideal type for practice. In the ideal, members have time to get to know one another and to take advantage of naturally unfolding opportunities for mutual aid. They are neither frustrated by constant changes in the community nor overwhelmed by large numbers that make it difficult for the full expression of all voices.

Thus, a major implication for practice with these groups is the need to provide them with more structure (Mondros and Berman-Rossi 1991) than is generally prescribed for long-term practice with small, closed systems (see Chapters 1 and 7). In this case, structure refers to the active use of professional authority and active direction in and of the group's process; and at the risk of being misunderstood as proposing more central authority than intended, the idea of taking a back seat in group governance or, as Middleman and Wood (1990) put it, of working ourselves out of a job, may not apply quite as readily or easily as most social group workers would like.

As noted in Chapter 7, having authority over its affairs is central to a group's ability to develop collective commitment to both purpose and process. Finding and cultivating ways for groups to shape their destinies, therefore, is central to all mutual-aid practice. Conversations about what to do and how to do it help the group identify its needs and strengths, highlight ways that members can help one another, and provide opportunities for that to happen. However, as stated previously, not only do these four group types present us with *generic* obstacles, their characteristics present us with some special challenges, requiring us to take an especially active role in setting the stage for and developing the possibility of a meaningful mutual-aid experience.

To provide structure does not mean to be authoritarian, however. It does not mean to take and keep center stage in the group or to be the be-all and end-all of the helping process. Rather, it means to actively use our legitimate authority to help set the stage (e.g., active and careful pregroup planning and contact to engage all significant parties) and to maintain conditions that will best promote and maintain people's capacity to help each other (e.g., setting aside a few minutes at the beginning and end of each meeting to introduce, assess, and review; preselecting content options for the group's review; determining whether the group can resolve conflict at this time or if it needs a moratorium; taking purposeful risks to promote real talk; or, in contrast, preventing premature disclosure). Do we not always do that in mutual-aid practice? Do we not always strive to create conditions for whatever potential exists among a given group of people at a given time? Of course we do. We exercise authority throughout all forms of practice, and the why of it remains constant: always to the end of helping people help one another. However, the when, how, and especially how much varies according to many factors, such as practice setting, purpose of group, special characteristics of members, and, finally, special characteristics of the group itself. Thus, knowing that time limits impinge in a very real way on capacity, we emphasize our authority to actively help the time-limited group develop into an effective and meaningful experience. In open-ended practice, we emphasize our authority to help each *groupe du jour* develop both horizontal and vertical ties. When working with very large groups, we use it primarily to make sure that a safe climate for real talk is established and maintained. In brief, we provide structure, use our authority, and engage in active leadership not to the end of imposing our agenda, but to help each group reach beyond its extraordinary obstacles to an agenda that is meaningful and to help it discover and develop its unique mutual-aid rhythm for carrying out that agenda.

Second, identifying a purpose that encompasses all of the members' goals is an important formative task of all groups with mutual aid in mind. Group purpose helps members understand why they are together, why they are talking or doing as they are at any given moment, and whether or not the group is doing what it is supposed to be doing. The purposes of single-session groups are usually predetermined, however, whereas short-term groups often struggle with purposes that are unrealistic; open-ended groups may confront changing needs and desires or variations in commitment to their standing purpose as members come and go; and very large groups, whose potential for mutual aid is expanded through the use of small working groups, require attention to purpose at more than one level. In one way or other, therefore, purpose requires further thinking through in working with each of these group types.

Third, none of these group types can rely as easily or strongly as the small classic system on the development of affective ties to develop a sense of community. Composed of work ties and affective ties among members, common ground is essential to an identity as a community. Work ties identify possibilities for mutual aid by highlighting similar needs and concerns that bind these people at this time, while affective ties, which are the personal bonds that develop, cultivate the desire to help and be helped. A question for practice with these four group types, therefore, is how to help them cultivate a sense of community that is both capable of and receptive to mutual aid. In single-session and short-term groups the task of cultivating affective ties is clearly constrained by time, and in open-ended groups, the community is constantly changing. Although the very large group may have a strong work base from which to draw common ground, it is unlikely to promote strong affective ties, except perhaps in subgroups. In each of these groups, therefore, we need to give extraordinary attention to the discovery, identification, and solidification of work ties so that members can develop rather quickly some sense of connectedness.

Fourth, all of these group types struggle in one way or another with establishing a climate of safety for real talk. Safety speaks to (1) the freedom that members feel to express what they really think and feel without fear of overly harsh criticism; (2) the opportunity they have to raise and discuss topics that are taboo in other settings without fear of reprisal; and (3) the chance to examine, explore, and experiment with new ways of being, doing, or thinking without fear of ridicule.

For mutual aid to happen real talk must happen. No amount of chit-chat beyond that which identifies the coatrack or bathroom is likely to catalyze meaningful mutual aid; asking for conversation to move beyond the superficial is always appropriate, therefore. Nonetheless, whatever demands we make for risk taking, such as personal story sharing (see Chapter 6), need to be in sync with time and place. If, therefore, the group's affective ties are not particularly strong, as may well be the case in these four systems, even as we reach for and promote real talk, we need to recognize and accept that its depth and breadth may be uneven among members, that it may remain primarily intellectual, that self-disclosure may remain tentative, and that some topics, even if they are pertinent, will remain only partially explored. Of course, whenever we reach for real talk we entertain the possibility of difference and even conflict. As discussed in Chapter 8, the exploration of difference can provide an opportunity for self-reflection, change, and growth. However, as also noted, the shakier a group's sense of community, the more difficult it may be for members to withstand conflict and to make use of their differences in a personally useful way. In working with these four group types, therefore, it is particularly important to have a plan in place for helping people see the value of difference, for helping them use difference when it is expressed, and for dealing with conflict should it occur.

Finally, the mutual-aid potential in each of these groups is enhanced by a bit of "jumpstarting." As people experience the benefits of mutual aid, both as givers and takers of help, they become increasingly willing to make the personal commitments and interpersonal efforts that are required to keep such a process going. The characteristics of these four systems do not necessarily either readily or easily lend themselves to the actualization of the full mutual-aid potential of their members, however. Little time is available for the natural unfolding of opportunities in time-limited groups. Connections and commitment may vary among the members of the open-ended group. Although some dynamics may lend themselves to *the more the merrier* rule, such as *strength in numbers,* many dynamics are better promoted in small groups. In working with these four groups, therefore, we often need to either scout out and even create opportunities for members to help one another, even if some of those opportunities require a proverbial stretch; and thus, with each of these group types we need to be very active in setting and keeping mutual aid in motion.

In sum, time-limited, open-ended, and very large groups have more in common than we may think at first glance. In one way or another they all require a great deal of pregroup planning, preparation, and organization to help set the stage for mutual aid. In one way or another purpose needs special consideration. They all need special emphasis on work ties to help them develop a sense of we-ness. They all benefit from active leadership to promote and maintain governance that consistently reflects a *democratic-humanistic* climate (Glassman and Kates 1990). They all benefit from an explicit structure for making constructive use of difference, and, finally, from their capacity to actually function as a mutual-aid system that is helped along by some "jumpstarting."

The next four chapters examine this common ground in greater detail. Each chapter opens with an introduction to the general nature of the group type. Special time-and-place issues are then described and discussed. Implications for practice are offered, including the use of group-specific skills for helping each group overcome its particular obstacles. Admittedly, there is some overlap in the last two sections of each chapter. It is unavoidable, however, precisely because the groups have so much common ground. For example, we focus our community-building efforts in each of these group types primarily on the discovery of work ties because they are immediately accessible; thus, each section on implications for practice and skills reflects that similarity. Because each context is different, however, the overlap has been left in place to try to provide a picture of approach to practice that is as holistic as possible in each case.

Chapter 9

Mutual-Aid Practice
with Single-Session Groups

KEY CONCEPTS OF THIS CHAPTER

Affective Ties
Authority
Conflict
Difference
Real Talk
Relevance of Group Purpose
Single-Session
Stage Setting
Structure
Taste of Mutual Aid
Time and Place
Vision
Work Ties

* * *

I do desire we be better strangers.

William Shakespeare, *As You Like It*

By definition, a single-session group is a group whose first meeting is also its last. Although it might be composed of many members or go on for several hours and thus share some characteristics of a very-large group or a longer-term group, for purposes of examining implications for practice it has been conceptualized here as a closed "smallish" system (three to eight members) that meets for a brief rather than long or marathon amount of time (one to three hours).

Single-session groups are often used to provide information (such as psychoeducation for family members of recently hospitalized persons, job preparation, or volunteer orientation), support for dealing with a particular issue or concern (such as pre- or postoperative or predischarge groups) or for medically related crisis management (such as hospital waiting-room groups). At their best, single-session groups offer a rich and powerful psychosocial source of support for crisis or transition, both in the here-and-now and indirectly as future support. As one woman who had attended a group of this type for postoperative breast-cancer patients put it,

> I didn't really want to go; I was depressed and nervous, going to leave the hospital the next day and basically wanted to see my own doctor, not sit around with other people I didn't know. Anyway, one of my nurses kept trying to talk me into it, so I thought, "Well, I can always leave if I want to." It was a lot better than I thought. There were four other women who had had surgery and were being discharged the next day. . . . A nurse and a social worker led the group, and we all got a chance to compare notes, get some questions answered; maybe the best part was that we gave each other our phone numbers. One of the women and I really connected, but I think I could have called any of them if I had wanted to.

In this example the group provides support for the transition from the hospital back home, provides concrete information, and helps members to make meaning of that information. In other words, it serves as a direct here-and-now forum for mutual aid. At the same time, as soon as members exchange telephone numbers and offer to "be there" for one another when they are back home, it provides a serendipitous extension and elaboration of their mutual-aid potential.

As this example and practice experience also reveals, however, people have to make a rather large leap of faith in the capacity of a single encounter with strangers to provide them with a relevant and meaningful experience. After all, the encounter is truly brief; and in some settings, such as hospitals or nursing facilities for the elderly, for example, people are likely to be preoccupied with their own needs and concerns and not likely to know one another very well (at least as members of this group) or the practitioner (at least in this context).

Thus, it is crucial that we approach single-session practice with a vision. It is crucial that we believe in its potential for mutual aid and that we have specific ideas about the ways in which the people in the group we have in mind can help each other meet their needs. Further, it is essential that we are able to articulate that vision to others and make it contagious to anyone who will be directly touched by the encounter (e.g., potential members) or who has the power to turn the vision into reality (as in the case of the nurse in the above example who took the time to engage postoperative patients into the group).

So, what kind of mutual aid can single-session groups realistically provide? In fact, they can give people an opportunity to see that others are in the same boat, to vent their frustrations, to share concerns and anxieties, to hear about how others cope with problems or manage special situations or circumstances, and even to think about new ways of being and doing. They can offer an opportunity to participate in a strength-centered rather than problem-centered experience, one in which personal and interpersonal skills and strengths, such as good leadership abilities, are requested, valued, and even emphasized. In other words, to some extent they can offer everything longer-term groups can offer, only not *as much*. Consider this group for terminally ill persons undergoing palliative care:

TODD: Some nurses just don't know how to give a needle. They jab you and poke you until they get it right.

JERRY: You need to tell the nurse that you want the specialist, you know, the nurse who only does intravenous. She knows how to put the needle in where in belongs.

TODD: I hear what you're saying, man; but how realistic is that? Do you think I'll get special privileges when there are twenty other people on the floor wanting the same thing?

JERRY: No, but why should you suffer just because she doesn't know how to do her job right?

TODD: I worked it out another way. There's this one nurse, I call her "the Sword," because she comes into my room holding that damn needle like it's a sword. One day she poked me so hard that I screamed at her to get out of my room. But you know, later on I thought about what I did and said to myself, "That's not right." So the next time she came in I told her that I would never yell at her again, and she said she was sorry for upsetting me. Now she's gentle, and I have no problem with her. She apologizes when it hurts, and I thank her when it doesn't.

JERRY: Okay, I hear you. You made your point. (Kosoff 2002, pp.13-14)

The mutual aid in this single encounter is very powerful. The group provides members with a forum for venting their frustrations. Common ground is identified. Sympathy is expressed, and problem solving takes place. Todd has an opportunity to be heard; and Jerry has a brand new problem-solving approach, one that is much more likely to work than the one he was using previously. In just a few moments, then, both men have a chance to help and be helped in a real, immediate, and meaningful way. All this occurs in a single session.

At the very least, a single-session group can provide people a taste of mutual aid to take away with them. Perhaps they will have gained a greater appreciation for the potential of small-group membership. Perhaps they will take with them new ideas about group process in general or mutual aid, more specifically. Perhaps they will take a positive norm or two into other groups to which they belong, or perhaps they will reconsider their views of leadership. Although we may not have such outcomes as our primary goal, as experiential by-products of a single-session encounter, they are not insignificant achievements.

TIME AND PLACE ISSUES
OF THE SINGLE-SESSION GROUP

The most obvious time and place consideration for single-session practice is that the single-session group has a very limited time span in which to engage its members, identify common ground, teach them the ropes of mutual aid, to establish a culture of trust and safety for talking about things of real meaning, and harness its strengths. In a nutshell, it has little time to actually translate whatever vision of mutual aid we might have into a workable and working reality.

It is not difficult to imagine developing a sense of community, camaraderie, and mutuality with others over time, but we usually do not feel safe and connected at the first meeting of new group. Yet, a single-session is exactly that—the first meeting of a group that will have no further meetings. In addition, people join groups with varying ideas about, definitions of, capacity for, and ways of understanding mutual aid. They have had different group experiences, the nature of which influences their feelings about and approach to our invitation. People do not necessarily feel like helping one another simply because they find themselves in the same place at the same time, and even if they do they may still find it challenging to accommodate some of the norms we have in mind, such as the use of self-reference instead of advice. Even when people are committed to self-help, they may not be committed to helping others; and although this may be the case in other types of groups as well, of course, the single-session system has little time to overcome that obstacle and to cultivate both desire and capacity.

The second major time and place consideration is that the purpose of a single-session group is usually predetermined. As noted in Chapter 3, the hashing out, clarification, and refinement of group purpose serves a number of functions. It gives a group authority over its most fundamental affair. It helps to identify and cultivate common ground. It begins to establish norms of participation, investment, and commitment. In addition to identifying the group's particular needs, having a predetermined purpose helps the group identify the strengths upon which it might draw to help meet those needs. A predetermined purpose, therefore, always creates the possibility that as conceived, it is not even relevant for these people at this moment.

To be sensitive to time and place in single-session practice, then, is to accept that we may need to double our efforts to engage people into the group we have in mind, to remain vigilant about the relevance of purpose as preconceived, and to accept that the group may, to some extent, share some resemblance with the long-term system in its beginning stage (see Chapter 5). Clearly, some groups may cohere rapidly, as the above example of the men's group illustrates, and other variables, such as the group's purpose, may allow people to express themselves freely right away. Generally speaking, however, people are likely to approach new membership with some trepidation, even as they hope for a rewarding experience.

To attend to time and place in working with the single-session group, therefore, is to balance our desire for mutual aid with respect for people's right to privacy; to accept that some feelings, attitudes, or stories may remain unshared or explored; and to actively use our authority to make sure process remains immediately relevant, and to solicit whatever resources, human and otherwise, are needed to make that happen, as illustrated in the following example:

> The ICU staff, at first wary of the intrusion, became ardent sup-porters of the relatives' group. In the session described, seven people from two very different ethnic backgrounds gained strength from each other and benefitted most of all from the mu-tual instillation of hope . . . [and] the group [became] beneficial to the ICU staff because it intervenes with patients' families to allow them to be more available to their critically ill relatives in ways that foster health and recovery or smooth the course of ter-minal illness. (Holmes-Garrett 1989, pp. 155-156)

To attend to time and place once the single-session group begins is to provide enough structure for members to immediately experience the group as a safe place to be themselves, to quickly discover their common ground, and to experience some rewards of mutual aid even as they learn some of its basic norms.

IMPLICATIONS FOR PRACTICE

So, how can we help people who come together just once become open to one another as potential sources of help? First, we exercise our authority as actively as necessary to set the stage for the group's success. That is, we engage all those who will be touched in some way into our vision to make sure that the encounter will be relevant and useful. We focus primarily on helping members discover their work ties in order to develop a basis for helping. We temper our desire for real talk with respect for the fact that the group is composed of people who are and are likely to remain, at least through the group meeting, relative strangers. We immediately refer to the value of dif-ference and have a plan for dealing with conflict that includes the possibility of extra-group time with any one or more members. We go beyond the concept of seizing opportunities for mutual aid as they oc-cur to purposefully creating them as soon as the group begins.

Setting the Stage

We begin to set the stage for mutual aid in the single-session group when we *educate, prepare, and engage everyone who will be touched by the group we have in mind.* Clearly this means we try to engage potential or prospective members; but it may also mean we need to engage significant others—both theirs and ours (e.g., their other service providers or our colleagues) and both personal and professional (e.g., their family members or work supervisors) depending on the group's purpose, setting, and particular characteristics (such as age or cognitive ability of members). We try to meet with all parties in person for an in-person dialogue. If we cannot, perhaps we can have some telephone contact or, at the very least, some written contact, such as a letter of invitation or brochure that describes the purpose, content, and norms of the group we have in mind. Although a waiting-room group, for example, is unlikely to provide much opportunity for pregroup contact, a volunteer-job orientation may be scheduled long enough ahead of time for some kind of preliminary and preparatory contact.

Regardless of the kind or amount of contact available to use, we use it as a vehicle to *express the value of mutual aid in the group as we see it.* We *identify the needs that we believe the group can meet* (e.g., "Here are some of the concerns that people have brought to this group in the past."). We *talk about the look and feel of helping as a strength-centered process* (e.g., "I hope that this group will be a place where people will feel free to share ideas and brainstorm solutions together as well as express their needs and goals."). We *focus on the kind of common ground that people in the group can expect* (e.g., "You are all in the same boat here, waiting for a loved one to come out of surgery. . . ."). We *offer examples of how members of such a group have helped one another in the past* (e.g., "This is always a very difficult time for family members, but I've noticed that a chance to be with others who are also in this situation can help by just being together and having a chance to talk about your concerns."). And we *introduce mutual aid as we know it* (e.g., "I have some ideas about how to help, but so do you, and I hope that in this group you'll share yours as well."). In short, we use our authority to reach out to and engage all those who can make or break the group's success.

Sometimes, especially when they are in crisis, people see the request to take on a helping role as a waste of precious time—time during which they should be receiving our "expert" help. Even as we help prospective members understand the rights, roles, and responsibilities in a mutual-aid system, therefore, we also *help them see*

what's in it for them to participate as helpers. The better we can articulate the value of helping, the more we will create interest, investment, and commitment.

Keeping Purpose Relevant

We make sure the purpose of the single-session group is relevant
by *routinely visiting and revisiting its formally-stated purpose.* And
we *constantly assess whether the purpose as it currently stands is still
in sync with current needs and goals.* Yes, the Tuesday morning
group has taken place each week for a year. But is it still appropriate,
or even logical, to prepare for and conduct next Tuesday morning in
the same way? Perhaps it is, but perhaps it isn't. Perhaps a review of
the last few meetings or of the characteristics of potential membership suggests a rethinking or change altogether. We help to maintain
relevance during the meeting by *creating some "wiggle room" for
members to share some manner and degree of authority.* Consider the
following example of a hospital intensive-care unit waiting-room
group:

> The purpose of this group was to provide support and informa-
> tion for the relatives. . . . All families in the waiting room, no
> matter what their ethnicity or the patient's prognosis, were deal-
> ing with the same crisis, a critically ill family member, and the
> same institution, the hospital. . . . At the beginning of each
> "meeting" the goal of the leader was to make a group from the
> assembled visitors as quickly as possible, to encourage the ver-
> balization of fears, anxieties, and concerns and to provide emo-
> tional support. . . . She then mentioned a range of concrete
> problems (visiting hours, getting information from staff, loca-
> tion of the coffee shop) and suggested that families might have
> some other worries as well. The nature of these worries was in-
> tentionally left vague in order to elicit members' own associa-
> tions. . . . The need to verbalize fears and reminisce about
> patients' healthier days were common to all group members. . . .
> Doubts about staff competence and fears about approaching the
> doctors with questions surfaced frequently. . . . Members also
> exchanged their experiences with social service agencies and
> gave tips about home health care. Their allegiance grew from

intra-family to intra-group to extra-group in the time span of a single session. (Holmes-Garrett 1989, pp. 150-151)

Even within the scope of a predetermined purpose, therefore, we can always find some room to involve single-session group members in shaping content or process.

Group Building

It is usually more realistic to reach for work ties than affective ties in single-session group building. Both kinds of ties help to develop a sense of community (see Chapter 3), but there is no doubt that work ties can be more easily identified and thus immediately cultivated, while affective ties evolve over time. The discovery of common needs and goals may not motivate people's desire to engage in mutual aid as powerfully as do affective ties, but they are still valuable tools for revealing a basis for helping. Although we cannot force people to care about one another, therefore, we can always help them identify the commonality of needs and goals that bring them together at this time.

We begin to reach for work ties when we *help prospective members anticipate their common ground* (e.g., "You and the others will all share the same questions and have the same concerns as you begin this new work."). We *design the content of in-group introductions to explicitly highlight the ways in which members' needs and goals coincide.* In fact, we might *deliberately intervene during that process to clarify or affirm work ties* (e.g., "So before we move on, Joe, let me just clarify . . . Are you saying that, like Alice, your major concerns are about. . .?"). We *invite members to assume some ownership of the process* (e.g., "What are some of the commonalities as you see them so far?"). We *actively and directly point out common ground when we note it* rather than assume it is evident to others.

Promoting Real Talk

Just as it is essential that the group's purpose be in sync with its needs, expectations of real talk (see Chapters 4 and 5), both in terms of what and how much, need to be in sync with the nature of members' relationships. In effect, single-session groups are one-time collisions with strangers. At the same time, since real talk is essential to mutual aid, we *use pregroup education and preparation to help set the stage for authentic expression* when the group begins (e.g., "This group is a place where people can share their questions and concerns in a safe and supportive way."). We *think through ahead of time the kinds of risk taking that may be necessary* to develop clear parameters for self-disclosure for the group to meet its purpose. We *take some risks ourselves* to help the group expand the breadth or depth of its talk. We *pay attention to sessional processes* (Birnbaum and Cichetti 2000) in recognition that even single-session groups pass through developmental stages (see Chapter 5). For example, we formulate stage-based parameters for process (e.g., "Let's start with a bit of time for introductions; and also, let me just note that we'll need a little time to wrap up, too. I'll watch the clock."). Even as we reach for real talk, we *use a dual focus to help protect members from premature disclosure or from straying into territory that the group cannot reasonably accommodate given its time limits.*

Dealing with Difference and Conflict

Once we invite authentic expression, of course, we need to expect the possibility if not the probability of conflict. We need a plan for dealing with it and, paradoxically enough, the plan begins with immediate reference to difference (unlike in long-term practice, in which we are more likely to focus our early efforts on reaching for commonality and deal with differences as they emerge). Thus, as we think about the group we have in mind, we *anticipate some of the areas in which there are likely to be difference.* As the group begins, even as we reach for common ground, we *make explicit reference to the fact that differences as well as commonalities exist in this group.* We *highlight some of those differences in order to open the door for their expression.* And we *share examples of how some of the group's differences can enhance its ability to help.* Perhaps different ways of coping or problem-solving approaches would be particularly helpful or perhaps exploring different cultural perspectives would be helpful.

Meanwhile, we *make frequent observations that universalize feelings and help the group see its differences within its common ground* (e.g., "Joe's specific concern is different from Mary's; but you all want to do well on the test, and I think it could be really helpful to hear about different ways of preparing.").

Of course, it is always possible that, as with the polite tea-time group, the single-session group acknowledges its differences but does not explore them in depth, particularly if doing so would not clearly advance its helping process. On the other hand, if differences do lead to conflict, we need to have a concrete plan in place for dealing with it. In contrast to longer-term groups, for example, deciding to revisit the issues at a future meeting may not be possible, even if everyone is willing; nor might extending this meeting be possible. Therefore, if conflict does occur in the single-session group, we *provide clear structure* (e.g., "Okay, let's try to hear from everyone here.") and *exercise active leadership* (e.g., "Let's hear more from Joe to try to understand where his thinking comes from.") for deciding how to deal with it (e.g., "I don't think we can resolve this here." or "I think we need to listen to one another more closely here."). (See Chapters 5 and 8.) In other words, we do not necessarily avoid or squelch conflict, but neither do we simply give over the full reins for dealing with it to the group as a good "learning" experience if we know that time constraints will not permit us to do justice to the meaning of the issues at hand.

Finally, we *build some time into our schedules for extra-group contact* should there not be enough time to meaningfully address the group's differences in the meeting. Such an offer needs to be neither extended nor perceived as a form punishment (as if "staying after" school), however, but as an attempt to help beyond the reasonable scope of the group, to "be there" for all members. Perhaps most important of all is that we explain our intent and our actions—how much we think the group can or cannot and should or should not explore the issues and why or why not, so that everyone has a common understanding of what the next steps are and why.

Setting and Keeping Mutual Aid in Motion

As a mutual-aid system, the single-session must to some extent learn to fly by the proverbial seat of its pants—which is all the more reason the practitioner needs to make opportunities for giving and taking help immediate and plentiful and, even further, to help members recognize the many aspects of that process so that they can be creative in their initiation of it. In brief, catalyzing mutual aid in the single-session group requires more than carpe diem. It needs to seize and even create moments in which the group can identify and harness its members' skills and strengths. For example, *if we are able to have pre-group contact, we already begin to get a sense of how and what prospective members will be able to contribute to the group.* One person seems to have a great sense of humor, for example, while another has a great deal of group experience, another has a warm smile, and yet another seems to have excellent analytic skills. If we cannot meet with prospective members, we *might be able to get a sense of them from significant others,* such as friends, family members, other staff, teachers, and so on. Once the group begins, we *structure the content of introductions so that members are required to interact or connect to one another in some way* (e.g., "As we go around, I think it would be helpful if you could each identify how much you share in the concerns that have already been expressed."). From the very beginning we *ask questions or make observations that explicitly identify the skills* (e.g., "It sounds as if you've had quite a bit of volunteer experience in this kind of setting.") *or strengths* (e.g., "It sounds as if you've had to manage home care for a long time.") *that members bring to the group.*

Some skills and strengths, such as good expressive and listening skills, a sense of humor, or a friendly demeanor are quickly evident. Others, however, such as the ability to focus or debate or problem solve are not always so obvious. Therefore, rather than assume it is evident to everyone else, whenever we believe we see mutual aid in action we point it out; and we praise all efforts to help, even if awkward, and regardless of outcome.

KEY POINTS OF THIS CHAPTER

1. At best, single-session groups can offer a rich and powerful psychosocial source of support for crisis or transition. At the very least, they can offer a taste of mutual aid, perhaps in the form of a new appreciation for small-group participation, of mutual aid, a new group norm or two to take to other groups, or a new view of leadership.
2. The two principal time and place considerations for single-session practice are (1) lack of time to cultivate common ground, establish a culture of safety, and identify group members' skills

and strengths and (2) a predetermined group purpose, which leaves the group with little or no say over its most fundamental affair.

3. To be sensitive to time and place in single-session mutual-aid practice is to accept that we may need to double our efforts to engage members and that the group may resemble a long-term system in its beginning stage (see Chapter 5).

4. To attend to time and place in single-session mutual-aid practice is to balance our desire for mutual aid with an acceptance that some stories may remain unshared, to actively use our authority to keep the group's purpose relevant, and to provide a structure that creates opportunities for members to experience immediate reward.

5. In order to help the single-session group develop and function as a mutual-aid system, we need to have a vision. That is, we need to believe that it is in fact possible for meaningful mutual aid to occur in a brief encounter. We need to have some specific ideas about how these people at this time can do that. We also need to be able to articulate that vision to others, both potential or prospective members and all significant others.

6. It is more realistic to group build through work ties than affective ties in single-session mutual-aid practice. Work ties may not be as powerful as affective ties in motivating the desire to help, but they do provide a solid base from which to develop ways of helping.

7. Although it is reasonable to ask any mutual-aid system to engage in real talk, the real talk of a single-session group may remain somewhat reserved, not unlike that of the longer-term group in its "getting to know you" stage.

8. Approach to mutual-aid practice with the single-session group needs to contain a well-developed plan for dealing with conflict, including early statements about the role and value of difference and building in extra-group time should it be needed as a way of "being there" for all members.

9. We need to purposefully and immediately create moments in which the single-session group can identify its skills and strengths and experience success as a mutual-aid system.

RECOMMENDED FURTHER READING

Birnbaum, M. and Cicchetti, A. (2000). The power of purposeful sessional endings in each group encounter. *Social Work with Groups* 23(3): 37-52.

Ebenstein, H. (1998). Single-session groups: Issues for social workers. *Social Work with Groups* 21(1/2): 49-60.

Holmes-Garrett, C. (1989). The crisis of the forgotten family: A single-session group in the ICU waiting room. *Social Work with Groups* 12(4): 141-157.

Jagendorf, J. and Malekoff, A. (2000). Groups-on-the-go: Spontaneously formed mutual-aid groups for adolescents in distress. *Social Work with Groups* 22(4): 15-32.

Chapter 10

Mutual-Aid Practice
with Short-Term Groups

KEY CONCEPTS OF THIS CHAPTER

Advocacy
Affective Ties
Authority
Education
Group Governance
Mediation
Realistic Group Purpose
Short Term
Time and Place

* * *

If I had more time I would have written you a shorter letter.

Mark Twain

Definitions of short term vary across areas of professional expertise and work settings, even across regions, cultures, and generations.
In some settings a group that meets six times is considered short term,
and in others twenty meetings may be considered short term. Here,
the short-term group is being conceptualized as a small, closed system that meets from about two to twelve times. Clearly, the issues and
implications presented in this chapter will apply somewhat differen-
tially according to a group's actual time line. Mutual-aid practice
with a group that meets twice will probably need many of the same
considerations as single-session practice, whereas working with a

short-term closed system over ten or twelve sessions may well take on some of the look and feel of working with a longer-term group, such as taking a backseat in several group-governance functions (see Chapter 5).

As Garland (1992) states, it has been well documented that short-term groups can offer much, such as "support and stabilization in times of crisis, focused education around the acquisition of social skills, aiding stage transitions and enabling mobilization for collective work and social action" (p. 1). And as Northen and Kurland (2001) more recently elaborate:

> [S]hort-term groups . . . can be quite effective in meeting numerous needs and purposes that are more circumscribed in nature . . . to prepare their participants for a new role or situation, for example, becoming a nursing home resident, entering a new school; to provide education, particularly when the focus in on presenting a limited amount of content within an atmosphere that makes possible some expression of feelings and ideas and some modification of attitudes and behavior, for example, becoming a foster parent, understanding the needs of an adolescent child, undergoing a particular medical procedure; to help people cope with personal or family crises, for example, a child's suspension from school, the illness of a parent or sibling [as well as] for diagnostic purposes by a worker, especially with children, to clarify through direct observation the ways in which problems of children are manifested in social situations. (p. 139)

TIME AND PLACE ISSUES OF THE SHORT-TERM GROUP

As stated in the previous chapter, an important pregroup planning task of single-session practice is to constantly reassess relevance of group purpose (either of the kind of group that has been taking place with different members over time or of a new one we have in mind) so that once the group begins there is a very clear and pertinent frame of reference for its mutual-aid process. Although relevance is obviously a consideration in short-term practice as well, the short-term group does not necessarily (or normally) begin with as specifically predetermined a purpose as the single-session group. It has, at least theoretically, a great deal of input into its purpose, and one of its early tasks is to hash out a purpose that embraces the members' individual goals. However, by definition the short-term group does not have all that much time to play around with ideas and possibilities—which means, simply put, that we need to be and help others to be realistic in deciding what this group will be about. Obvious? Perhaps. Easy to do? Not always in today's climate of organizational downsizing and economics-based mandates in which much social work practice is taking place.

Compressed into an artificially and frequently arbitrary time "crunch" that often has ridiculous expectations (such as curing problems we know to be chronic and in need of long-term attention in eight sessions) we can often find ourselves not only neglecting important planning and preparation tasks but aggrandizing or glamorizing a short-term group's formal statement of purpose for fear that anything less than the spectacular will be devalued or disallowed altogether by those who watch and judge our work. After all, if the problem is not, in fact, resolved in those eight sessions, the implications are bad all the way around: either our practice is somehow deficient (in which case professional "incompetence" is duly noted by those who developed the mandates in the first place) or the governing systems and policies need major change. As one practitioner recently stated,

> I feel caught in between all of the insurance craziness and my professional values. I mean, I have some experience in this field, and I think I know what my clients need better than [some external governing system] that doesn't deal with them on a day-to-day basis. In fact, they're not even in the field. . . . So just as I begin to feel like we're developing a working relationship, it's over! It's so artificial . . . I feel like I'm losing my professional integrity. I'm told, "You can have X number of sessions for this, X number for that." But there's no rhyme nor reason, just bottom lines.

Developing a purpose for a short-term group that is realistic as well as relevant can be particularly challenging, therefore, as we try to meet the many psychosocial needs we see within the constraints of short-term-care mandates and policies. In the end, however, if expectations of capacity are out of sync with reality, all other expectations will end up spectacularly out of sync with reality as well.

Thus, to be sensitive to time and place in short-term practice is to develop a vision of the possible—a vision that is realistic to the lifeline of the group as well as meaningful to its heart. This is a task for all groups, of course, but the short-term group must come to grips with selecting rather quickly—*and* being satisfied with—the choice to work on what is likely to be only one of many possibilities. To attend to time and place in short-term practice, therefore, is to formulate and help the group maintain reasonable goals regarding both nature of mutual aid to take place (the ways in which members can help one another) and degree of mutual aid to take place (how much they can do so), a task that demands a great deal of planning and, as with single-session work, more structure and active direction than is generally prescribed for long-term work. At the same time, however, to attend to time and place in short-term practice is to emphasize whatever is in the glass, metaphorically speaking, over what is not. Our mind-set is always passed on to members; and if we begin the group with a "so little time, so much to do" or "what could be but isn't" attitude, members will find it that much more difficult to identify, appreciate, and catalyze whatever mutual-aid potential they do in fact have (Kaiser 1958).

Finally, to be sensitive to time and place in short-term practice is to recognize that there may be a need for systemic change—some kind of intervention to help expectations of what we can and should do be more realistic. Thus, attending to time and place may also mean that we initiate organizational or social action in order to mediate between unreasonable mandates and real possibilities—to advocate for the possible, in other words—a role that is not new to social group work (Breton 1995; Schwartz 1969, 1976).

A lovely and lively example of exactly this kind of action can be found in an article by Andrew Malekoff (1999), "Pink Soap and Stall Doors," in which he describes how the worker of the Young Men's Club, a group for high school boys at a New York-area alternative high school, helps members progress from using the group as a place to vent their frustrations with bathroom conditions to using its strength in numbers to demand systemic change. Their worker could easily have simply empathized with the boys over the degrading conditions while she tried to help them understand the policies that had removed the bathroom stall doors in the first place, such as issues of safety, sanitation, and so on. Instead, she sees the potential for systemic change. She suggests that the group make a list of their concerns and present them to the administration, which they do; and a few weeks later changes are made. Although this example does not reflect in particular a systemic intervention due to the unrealistic nature of a group purpose, it does illustrate the willingness to take on the role of mediation, which attending to time and place in short-term work may sometimes require.

IMPLICATIONS FOR PRACTICE

How can we help the short-term group realize its mutual-aid potential while still remaining sensitive to its particular time-and-place issues? First, we help it adopt a realistic purpose, which may include intervention in the environment in which the group operates. We provide structure and active leadership to help it organize its time effectively. Because we have the time to cultivate affective ties we do so, but we touch most immediately on work ties to help members quickly discover common ground. We temper the desire for real talk with recognition that there are some doors through which the short-term group may not pass, even in the service of mutual aid. We develop a plan for dealing with conflict that includes the possibility of compromise. We seek and exploit possibilities for mutual aid in an attempt to help the group experience some early success.

A Realistic Purpose

Identifying a purpose that is collectively helpful and agreeable is an important formative task of all groups with mutual aid in mind (see Chapter 3). Discussions of purpose legitimately crop up now and again over the life of any group, of course, as new needs are identified, or goals achieved, or perhaps as some members leave and others enter. However, although the short-term group has some time for hashing out its purpose, it does not have all that much time to brainstorm. If it is still discussing its purpose on the third or fourth of eight meetings, therefore, the issue may be one of relevance, but it might also be that as stated, implied, or understood the group's purpose is simply unattainable and thus provides more obstacles than options in focusing and advancing the work.

So, how can we honor the short-term group's right to select a purpose that is meaningful without taking up so much of its total time that there is little left over for actually working toward that purpose? First, we *use any and all possible pregroup contact to help potential or prospective members focus in on some of their needs* that mutual aid might meet. We *bring to the first meeting a range of realistic options for the group's review* (e.g., "Let's review the common goals toward which we might work."). We *help members cull from that list the most appealing options that might be best met in the time frame available* (e.g., "Okay, so we have this list of goals we're interested in and seven more meetings. What do you think we should do?"). We *help them identify the relationship between the group's overall purpose and their individual goals* (e.g., "Now that we've agreed that the purpose of this group is to help everyone here do better in school, let's talk about how the group might do that for each member.").

By giving the short-term group a kind of "quick and dirty" look at some ways of meeting its needs and of translating vision into action we bring vision to life; we provide a framework for considering, organizing, and advancing its raison d'être. We also help prevent it from using its precious time to wander the land of Oz.

Structure and Direction

Short-term groups usually need more structure and active direction than is generally prescribed by major social group work theories, particularly those at the foundation of work with classic, closed, and stable long-term groups (see Chapter 1). Thus, the idea of working ourselves *out of a (leadership) job* (Middleman and Wood 1990a) may not apply quite as readily or easily to short-term practice as it does to long-term work or as much as most group workers would like. This is not to imply that an authoritarian stance is justified in mutual-aid practice. It is not. A democratic climate is essential to mutual aid, and rare is the occasion when a group cannot in some way share authority over something. However, precisely because the short-term group does have some time to shape its affairs but not all that much leisure to play around with possibilities, we actively use our authority to help it use its time productively and to govern its time in ways that reflect a *humanistic* as well as *democratic* (Glassman and Kates 1990) climate. As Urania Glassman (1996) states it, "For effective teaching about democratic process, mutual aid, and belonging, the worker has to help the members to not use the pressure of time as an excuse for by-passing the development of a democratic system" (p. 3).

Thus, long before the group begins, we *talk with potential members and others who are responsible for or invested in the group's outcome* (Kurland 1978). We identify some of the ways in which these people at this time in this setting might come together in mutual aid. We begin to identify realistic possibilities for translating visions of mutual aid into action. Perhaps the group should be used as a forum for sharing information or for networking, or perhaps it should be used as an adjunct to a form of education that takes place outside the group—as a place to give and take support for making meaning of that education, for example. Perhaps it can be a place for focused problem solving. Whatever the group's purpose, *an orientation package* that describes the norms of mutual aid *can help prepare members for the look and feel of the group we have in mind.*

We *come to the first meeting prepared to discuss what is feasible, able to explain why, and armed with suggestions as to what the group might and can do.* As we discuss what is and is not possible, we *offer suggestions for how some needs that cannot be met through the group might be met in other ways.* We *present some examples of possible content for the group's review* and *help it think through its options and priorities.* Will members sit and talk? If so, why? If not, why not? Could they engage in certain activities? If so, how would those activities advance their mutual-aid process? Should they develop a formal plan, or should the content of one meeting serve as the basis for content in the next? Even if all of our ideas are discarded in favor of another direction, providing a concrete reference point for beginning this particular problem-solving process will help the short-term group to organize its time and focus its task.

As noted earlier in this book, some groups have the capacity to experience a wide range of mutual-aid dynamics, while others experience only a few dynamics or some intensely and others not at all. Just as a range of need exists, so exists a range of potential; and although we might well develop our capacity to help and be helped more fully over sixteen meetings than six, the framework for measuring potential (through the development of a relevant yet realistic purpose) and for measuring success (through ongoing assessment of work) is still real-world context and reason, not infinite possibility. Thus, although we may have the same general *manner* of expectations regarding mutual aid in short-term practice as in long-term work, we cannot have the same *degree* of expectations. That is, like the single-session group, the short-term group may move into similar work territory but do so with less depth or intensity. An *early discussion of process expectations* (such as the kinds of norms that will enhance its mutual-aid process), therefore, and of *progress expectations* (such as the relationship between mutual aid and their ability to meet their goals in the time frame available) *will help the short-term group develop a structure for deciding what to do and how to do it.* In sum, any and all time we devote to helping a short-term group organize its time is time well spent.

Group Building

Practice with the short-term group includes the cultivation of both work ties and affective ties. In fact, it is important to help the short-term group stay in sight of its affective common ground so that even if members cannot come to fully relate to one another's experiences in their time together (e.g., "I've been there; I know how it is."), they can at least maintain a climate of empathy (e.g., "I've not been there, exactly; but I have felt the way I think you feel.").

At the same time, an immediate and purposeful reach for work ties helps to "jumpstart" a sense of community or *we-ness* in the short-term group. Thus, as in single-session practice, we *set up the content of introductions to highlight the commonality of members' needs and goals. We use discussions of purpose as a natural venue for identifying, clarifying, and solidifying work ties. We ask questions and make statements from the group's very first moments that are intended to help members reach for that which binds them together.* And as the group matures, we *select specific verbal or nonverbal activities that require increasing trust and personal disclosure.*

Promoting Real Talk

If mutual aid is to happen, real talk about real things must also happen. No amount of superficial chitchat beyond that which helps members find the coatrack or bathroom, for example, is likely to catalyze meaningful mutual aid except haphazardly. Since real talk requires feeling some degree of safety, however, which usually takes time to cultivate, short-term practice needs to remain sensitive to just how much safety the group can realistically muster. The question is not whether real talk can take place, of course, but what kind and how much. For instance, self-reflection and self-reference toward the establishment of an empathic "me-too" climate rather than an intellectual one of "you should" requires more risk taking than giving of advice, but it is absolutely imperative to mutual aid (see Chapter 6). Risking the judgment of others can be difficult under the best of circumstances, but it is even more demanding in a group that has not yet developed a strong sense of we-ness. Certainly, over eight or so meetings people can get to know one another a bit, trust one another to some degree, and engage in real talk about real things, and through that process be of help to themselves and one another. However, as they take the chances involved in real talk before they feel fully safe to do so, it is important that members experience us as "being there" for them regardless of outcome, which we do by praising all risk taking.

To some extent, the walk and talk of the short-term group may well resemble the walk and talk of the long-term group in its "getting to know you" stage; and if practice is to remain sensitive to time and place, there are some doors through which the short-term group should not be expected to pass. Serving a group with more than it can reasonably chew will create more harm than help by making demands for intimacy that are simply out of sync with its capacity. Clearly, it is always appropriate to encourage real talk; and only by *making early and direct statements to the effect that risk taking will be assigned a higher value than not risking at all will the group understand the value of authenticity in its context* (e.g., "If we're to achieve our goals here, it will be important for us to say what we really think and feel."). *Praising all of the risk taking that does occur, regardless of results,* will go a long way in helping members take increasingly sophisticated risks. *Sharing examples of the kind of talk we have in mind as the group begins (or even with prospective mem-*

bers) can provide a useful reference point as members make decisions about what to say, when, and why.

Dealing with Difference and Conflict

Although integration and consensus are ideals of mutual-aid practice (see Chapter 8) we may need to accept compromise over consensus in short-term practice as a legitimate way of reaching some decisions or resolving conflict. Further, it may be that on occasion the best that the members of a short-term group can do is to respectfully agree to disagree. Neither compromise nor the agreement to disagree should be automatically conceptualized as process failures, however, because working toward consensus, a laborious process, may require time that this group simply does not have.

What needs to happen, therefore, is some *early reference to the fact that differences always arise when people engage in real talk* (e.g., "One of the things we need to expect is that if we share real feelings, attitudes, opinions, and life experiences we may well see things differently."). We *frame expression and exploration of difference as a legitimate tool of helping* to encourage real thoughts and feelings when they exist (e.g., "It's okay that we have some differences. In fact, different ways of seeing or thinking can really help us help each other sometimes."). We *initiate some discussion about how the group will make decisions* (e.g., "Here are a few options that I see for how we can make decisions here."). We *identify different kinds of communication patterns the group might adopt for exploring difference* (such as hand raising, talking in turn, or allowing interaction to be free flowing); and regardless of how it chooses to examine its differences, we *help it adopt a structure that allows all the members who wish to speak, speak.* We *help members examine and understand the implications of choices or solutions they entertain* (e.g., "If we vote, for example, we may end up with some of you feeling good about the outcome and some feeling bad. . . . How will we handle that?"). *If conflict arises, we help the group focus its collective energy on the following:*

1. *Identifying and understanding the implications of compromise* on its sense of we-ness and ability to work toward and achieve its purpose; that is, asking and answering such questions as,

What will it mean for us as a group if we compromise in this case? What will it mean if we decide by voting? Will we still be able to work together? Will we still want to help each other? Will we still feel a sense of community?

2. *Finding ways to integrate those implications into its future process;* that is, asking and answering such questions as, Can we use the *nature* of our differences in any helpful way? If so, what exactly can we learn from one another? If we aren't finding these differences helpful, why not? What can we learn from the way we are making decisions here about the way we *deal with or manage* differences generally?

3. *Giving all of its feelings a voice;* that is, on making sure that everyone in the group is heard.

4. *Reaching a state of affairs that is acceptable, if not ideal, to everyone involved;* that is, on coming to a final collective sentiment that what brought members together in this group is still stronger than the sum of their differences, that what brought them together is strong enough to keep them together as a group, and that their sense of we-ness remains strong enough to continue collaboration.

Setting and Keeping Mutual Aid in Motion

In contrast to its long-term counterpart, the short-term group has little time to await spontaneous combustion of ideas and possibilities for mutual aid among its members. Thus, not only do we need to be alert to every possible opportunity for identifying and harnessing the group's strengths, we need to actively scout them out. As in single-session practice, we need to help members engage in and commit to the process by providing early success.

We begin to set mutual aid in motion in short-term practice by *providing prospective members,* either in person (as in pregroup interviews, outreach, or recruitment efforts) or through written materials (such as brochures) with some *education about the dynamics of mutual aid and norms of the group we have in mind.*

Once the group begins, we use what we know about each member to *offer the new group examples of specific ways we think members can help one another* (e.g., "I know, Gina, that you've been through this before and will have some ideas for helping those who are going through it for the first time." or "Judy, I know you speak both English and Spanish very well and hope you'll help us if we need it here." or "Kevin, I know you've done a lot of research into the support systems around here, and it will be great if you share what you know with the group.").

We *initiate an early conversation about why we believe mutual aid will not only help them meet their goals but do so better than other types of group process,* such as casework in a group (Kurland and Salmon 1992). For example, we explain the differences in approach, process, tone, and outcome between advice giving and story sharing. We *initiate an early conversation about fundamental norms of mutual aid,* such as decentralized authority. For example, members may be prepared to respond to demands for work from the practitioner, as is the norm in many helping groups, but less prepared to engage in *mutual demand,* a central norm of mutual aid. And we *provide early opportunities for members to show and share their strengths* through such venues as introductions, discussions of purpose, establishing a contract, and early problem solving around content and process.

Finally, if we expect members to interact and collaborate with one another as they work to meet their goals, what may seem obvious bears restating. The short-term group needs to be small enough for members to rise to the challenge of helping one another without always feeling that in addition to that challenge they have to fight one another for space. Although they might not find their process exceptionally stimulating, a group of three should be able to create enough space for full and meaningful interaction even in one or two sessions. It may be more difficult, on the other hand, for everyone in a group of ten to leave a second meeting feeling as if he or she both took from and gave to the group in a personally relevant and useful way.

KEY POINTS OF THIS CHAPTER

1. Short-term groups have a variety of suitable purposes, from education to general support for normative life issues to focused crisis intervention.
2. To be sensitive to time and place in short-term mutual-aid practice is to adopt a vision of its possibilities that is realistic to its lifeline as well as meaningful to its purpose.

3. Attending to time and place in short-term practice mutual-aid practice involves formulating and maintaining reasonable goals how members can help one another and how much they can realistically do so. It means providing more structure and active direction than is generally prescribed for long-term work. It means emphasizing in and for the group whatever is in the glass, metaphorically speaking, over what is not. It may also mean intervening in the system if its expectations of short-term work are unreasonable.

4. Because the short-term group has some time to shape its affairs but not all that much leisure to play around with possibilities, we actively use our authority to help it use its time productively and engage in self-governance in ways that consistently create and reflect a *humanistic* as well as *democratic* (Glassman and Kates 1990) climate.

5. Both work ties and affective ties can be cultivated in short-term work. An immediate reach for work ties helps to "jumpstart" the group's sense of community, while increasingly reaching for affective ties as the group progresses helps develop empathy.

6. Short-term practice needs to remain sensitive to just how much safety the group can realistically muster. Certainly, over eight or so meetings people can get to know one another a bit, trust one another to some degree, and engage in real talk about real things and, through that process, be of help to themselves and one another. However, to some extent the walk and talk of the short-term group may well resemble that of the long-term group in its "getting to know you" stage.

7. If practice is to remain sensitive to time and place, there are some doors through which the short-term group should not be expected to pass.

8. Integration and consensus are ideals of mutual-aid practice. However, we may need to accept compromise over consensus in short-term practice as a legitimate way of reaching some decisions or resolving conflict. Further, it may be that on occasion the best that people can do is to respectfully agree to disagree. Neither compromise nor the agreement to disagree should be automatically conceptualized as process failures, however, be-

cause working toward consensus may require time that the group simply does not have.

9. The short-term group has little time to await and then exploit naturally unfolding opportunities for mutual aid. Thus, we need to be on the alert for opportunities, actively scout them out, and help members commit to the process by giving them some early success.

RECOMMENDED FURTHER READING

Breton, M. (1995). The potential for social action in groups. *Social Work with Group* 18(2/3): 5-14.

Glassman, U. (1996). "Approach to humanistic group work and short-term designs." Paper presented at the Annual Symposium of the Association for the Advancement of Social Work with Groups. Ann Arbor, Michigan, October.

Malekoff. A. (1999). Pink soap and stall doors. *Families in Society,* May/June: 219-220.

Schwartz, W. (1976). Between client and system: The mediating function. In *Theories of Social Work with Groups,* eds. R. Roberts and H. Northen, pp. 44-66. New York: Columbia University Press.

_____. (1969). Private troubles and public issues: One job or two? *The Social Welfare Forum,* pp. 22-43. New York: Columbia University Press.

Chapter 11

Mutual-Aid Practice
with Open-Ended Groups

KEY CONCEPTS OF THIS CHAPTER

Dual Focus
Equal Ground
Goodness of Fit
Groupe du Jour
Horizontal Common Ground
Inclusion
Vertical Common Ground
Visibility and Value
Whole-Group Common Ground

* * *

If we are always arriving and departing, it is
also true that we are eternally anchored. One's
destination is never a place but rather a new way
of looking at things.

Henry Miller, *The Oranges of the Millennium*

Open-ended groups can be found in a variety of settings and
formed to meet a variety of needs. Because of turnover, patient or
family support groups in inpatient medical or psychiatric settings or
postdischarge outpatient groups, for example, are frequently open
ended. Residential treatment groups are often open ended as resi-
dents come and go. Many psychoeducational groups with cyclically
planned agendas are open ended, inviting members to enter and leave

the group as they feel they have received "enough." Mandated juvenile-justice groups may be open ended as members enter and leave that system. Bereavement groups, hospice groups, and support groups for people with chronic illness or their care givers are frequently open ended, for example, as are abstinence-support groups, school groups, and groups in other settings where attendance is more changeable than stable.

The open-ended group has been conceptualized by some in the group-work literature as ranging in characteristic from a series of discrete meetings to one closely resembling a closed group with only occasional changes in membership (Galinsky and Schopler 1989; Schopler and Galinsky 1984). For this discussion, it has been conceptualized somewhere in between the two—as a series of group meetings to which people come and go over time but with enough encounters among the various members that at least some of the members develop a degree of familiarity with one another. Implications for practice as outlined in the following section, therefore, are based on the assumption that each *groupe du jour* is composed of some members who already know one another and some who do not; some who have attended the previous meeting and some who are returning after an absence; some who will return to the next or future meetings, and some who will not.

TIME AND PLACE ISSUES
OF THE OPEN-ENDED GROUP

One major time and place issue in the open-ended group is that personal pregroup contact is often not possible, simply because it is not known who will be in attendance until people actually arrive at the meeting. If it is, of course, then we have a logical forum for helping prospective members determine the goodness of fit between their goals and the group's purpose. More often than not, however, the only kind of contact we might have is through publicity and outreach materials, which means that these must clearly state the group's purpose and guidelines for membership.

It is disconcerting to feel as if we are in the wrong place at the wrong time. Even with a goal of inclusion, as with a "COCA" (come one come all) group (Northen and Kurland 2001, p. 156), purpose and membership expectations need to be defined and stated clearly enough to permit people to judge the fit between their needs and those the group claims to meet. At the same time, it is possible that some aspects of the open-ended group, such as preferences of content or patterns of interaction, and perhaps even its very raison d'être, will change over time. Thus, practice needs to be flexible enough to entertain and even perhaps embrace a new direction as people come and go and needs change.

Another time and place issue in the open-ended group is that, because it is composed of constantly changing faces, it can be difficult to create and maintain a sense of community. Naturally, the infusion of new blood into a group can have positive effects, but a challenge for practice is to refrain from labeling new blood as "good" blood and so-called old blood as "bad." That is, neither do we want to place undue burden on the shoulders of new members ("Oh boy! I'm really going to be on the spot here.") or make older members feel inadequate or incomplete ("Look, Bob, the worker's practically drooling over the newcomer! What are we, chicken liver?"). In fact, at no cost do we want to see "halo and horns" scenarios develop, which can only lead to role lock and further division in an already tenuous community. How might such scenarios play out? In one such scenario, older members feel they have the right to disagree whereas new members or those who do not attend regularly do not (e.g., "Who the hell are you?" You just got here and already you're making trouble!" or "You've missed some meetings, you know. You can't just come back and take over!"). In another, new members would have primary responsibility for keeping the group stimulated (e.g., "We've heard plenty from you, John! Let's hear from the new guys."). In yet another, the value of what members have to say would be directly related to attendance or longevity (e.g., "Be quiet, Simon! I'd like to hear what the new guys think." or "What do *you* know, Ted? You just got here!").

Admittedly, these examples are caricatured; but they serve to make the point that if rights and responsibilities are not universal in the open-ended group, the resulting climate moves it away from rather than toward mutual aid. Older or core members may well hold a certain status in this type of group simply by virtue of longevity and may even earn it as well, when they help a new member enter the group, for example. However, to the degree that status is assigned to either longevity or attendance, it cannot dictate rights, responsibility, or value.

Furthermore, although there may be time for people to develop affective ties in the open-ended group, they may do so primarily within each of their neighborhoods, as it were, but not cross over from one to the other as readily. In order to help integrate these two groups, then, we need to once again focus our early attention to helping develop whole-group common ground from whatever work ties can be made quickly evident.

Developing and maintaining a climate of safety for authentic expression may be a time and place issue for the group as well, and the group's capacity for real talk may dance back and forth as members come and go. At some time or other, we have probably all been the "new kid on the block" or heard so-called "in" jokes we do not understand and can empathize with many of the feelings and questions of new members in open-ended groups. The new members may worry about being accepted and fitting in, and existing members may worry about judgment from new sources and about having their boat rocked in yet another different and difficult way.

Difference, the paradoxical status quo as new members infuse new blood, is also a time and place issue for the open-ended group. It is a norm in this group type, but difference is not necessarily more easily accommodated here than in other groups. In fact, to the degree that strength of community is related to how well members know and care about one another, difference in general and conflict in particular can be especially threatening because people have, at least theoretically, the freedom to come and go as they please. The very fact that people may choose whether to return after a meeting in which conflict has taken place, therefore, can make negative dynamics such as scapegoating all too easy. Furthermore, although absence of the person or persons involved in the conflict may be at first a relief to those who return, they must inevitably begin to worry about the consequences of expressing difference. The norm of harmony starts to take hold, and room for talk that includes difference decreases.

Finally, although the open-ended group has ongoing opportunities to identify and harness strengths, the most obvious of those—entries and exits—appear to be neither well understood nor routinely used as such. For example, asking old timers to mentor newcomers not only helps to strengthen connections between the two groups but provides a chance for old timers to review their contributions to the group's helping process and to share their strengths. As Galinsky and Schopler (1985) note,

> old members need to express feelings related to loss, envy, abandonment, or pride in other accomplishments, to facilitate reintegration as they proceed with their work together. Even when members are only in the group for a brief period, there should be an opportunity to reflect on the experience and to evaluate its impact. (p. 76)

Thus, to be sensitive to time and place in open-ended practice is to recognize and respect the impact of constantly changing faces on both the group's capacity for and desire to engage in mutual aid. This system may well have ongoing opportunities for mutual aid, but it can also be fraught with problems of cohesion and developmental challenges due to entries and exits. Thus, to attend to time and place means to reach for the unique mutual-aid potential of each *groupe du jour* while keeping the connections between each explicit—that is, to reach for and identify both vertical common ground (the ties that bind past, present, and future meetings) and horizontal common ground (the ties that bind these people at this time). It is to equalize expectations of real talk from everyone in each *groupe du jour,* to refrain from placing undue burden for stimulation on the shoulders of new members, and to reconfirm the role and value of difference every time a new member attends. In addition, it is to recognize that the group's development process, which often has the look of a "two-step-forward, one-step-back" dance, has an impact on the depth and breadth of its mutual-aid potential at any given time.

IMPLICATIONS FOR PRACTICE

We have several skills available for helping the open-ended group develop its potential for mutual aid. To begin with, we make sure that all publicity and promotional materials are specific enough to help prospective members appropriately determine the goodness of fit between their goals and the group's standing purpose. At the same time, we remain open to a change in purpose should new needs and goals become identified. We deemphasize variance between each *groupe du jour* and, even further, between old timers and new arrivals. We maintain a dual focus to give each and every member a tangible presence. We equalize expectations of risk taking and present rights and responsibilities as communal. We initiate a conversation about the value of difference every time a new member is present and provide structure for dealing with conflict that includes the possibility of extra-group contact. We help each *groupe du jour* identify the skills and strengths of that particular encounter and ask it to build on its past helping process as well. We also make explicit in each encounter the threads that tie its helping process to those of the past and future.

Setting the Stage

To set the stage for mutual aid in open-ended practice we *make a clear statement of group purpose in all of our outreach, publicity, and promotional materials.* We also help to set the stage when we *present specific guidelines for membership* (who would find this group helpful, the kind of common ground that members can anticipate, and so on) so that interested persons can judge the goodness of fit between their goals and that purpose. We *describe very clearly the nature of the group* (the fact that faces and numbers may shift at each meeting, the duration of each meeting and so on) and *some of major implications of participation* (what it means to join in a strength-centered group experience, some of the basic norms and expectations of such a process, and so on).

Group Purpose

To maintain relevance of purpose in open-ended practice, not only do we visit and revisit it on a regular basis as we do with any group, we *visit it every time a new member attends.* Even if the conversation is a brief one, it helps to clarify expectations—to make sure that people find themselves in the right place at the right time—and identify new needs or goals as members come and go. We *ask the members of each* groupe du jour *to evaluate the degree to which mutual aid has helped them work toward their goals during the meeting* (e.g., the ideas, words of wisdom, or stories that have been exchanged or problem solving that has taken place). As we ask the group to prepare for the next meeting, we *ask members to think about the ways in which the group can continue to help them meet their goals.* In other words, as they continue to think through their needs, desires, and goals, how can the group's collective skills and strengths further their process?

Group Building: Integrating the Neighborhoods

Helping the open-ended group develop and maintain affective ties may not be a special challenge if it has some stability and is not, in effect, a series of single-session groups. However, it is likely that affective ties develop more strongly among frequent or regular attenders than among them and newcomers, unless, of course, they are invited to join by a current member. At each meeting, therefore, we *emphasize commonality by deemphasizing variance* (e.g., "Some of you have been here before, and some of you are new to the group; so let's take a moment to find out what brings us all together today."). In particular, we reach for work ties—for the common needs and concerns that bring members to this group. We promote personal connections across the old and new neighborhoods, as it were, by *having in place some kind of formal entrance ritual.* For example, we ask older members of each *groupe du jour* to help orient newcomers—perhaps even to help prepare, sponsor, or to mentor them (during, before, or in-between groups, for example). We promote whole-group we-ness by *asking for introductions from every participant every single time a new member is present* (e.g., "Some of you know one another already, but let's all go around so that those of us here today begin together."). We *structure the content of introductions to highlight the needs and desires that bring everyone to the group* generally and more specifically, to this particular *groupe du jour.* We *ask older members to talk about established group norms* (e.g., "Let's talk a bit about the way we've collaborated in the past."). We *invite whole-group discussion to determine and clarify expectations of this encounter,* helping members to work out any differences or discrepancies in understanding and to work toward consensus as one group.

Oddly enough, we also develop groupness by giving each member a tangible, individual presence. We do this by *maintaining a dual focus throughout each meeting.* The more members feel that their individual city is recognized and valued (and thus their absence is likely to be noted and regretted), the more connected and committed they will feel to one another and to the process and progress of the group as a whole. Furthermore, whether or not they return to another meeting, our message will have been that the individual participation in and contribution to group process of each and every person is noticed, rather than conveying "you're here today, gone tomorrow; so what?" and that their presence is integral to the group as a community.

Finally, to solidify horizontal common ground (the ties that bind members to one another at this time) we *initiate a conversation at the end of each meeting to ask members to identify if, when, how, and how much their interaction was helpful* (e.g., "Let's take a few minutes and talk about what went well today, what was particularly helpful, what you might like to see more of, etc."). To identify vertical common ground (that which binds each *groupe du jour* to the next), we *ask members to reflect upon how the group might continue to help them* (e.g., "So, do you have some ideas for next time?"). Sometimes referred to as a "sessional ending" (Birnbaum and Cicchetti 2000) wrap-up time at the end of each meeting serves as a transition between this encounter and the next, recognizes the value of individual contributions, and promises personal recognition at the next meeting.

Kindling and Rekindling Real Talk

The primary way of kindling and rekindling real talk in the open-ended group is by equalizing expectations of everyone—by asking that each member contribute to as well as take from the group. When we speak about the value of and our desire for real talk, therefore, we *speak about equal rights and communal responsibility* (e.g., "In this group, everyone has the right to participate in and contribute to what we do and how we do it. . . ."); and we *ask for equal risk taking in the group* (e.g., ". . . and I invite each and every one of you to speak up as you think you have something to say and hope you'll feel comfortable enough to do so."). Thus, we structure the content of introductions to reach for similar kinds of disclosure from everyone, for example, whether they have attended the group before. Asking newcomers to share some of the needs and concerns that bring them to this meeting may set into motion a norm of risk taking, but a norm of mutuality is not promoted unless the same demand is made from old timers as well. (Sometimes, repeated introductions can become a kind of an "in" joke among people who attend regularly or at least frequently, and although repetition can certainly be acknowledged with humor, it is still better for members to introduce themselves over and over again one hundred times than to have even one meeting where even one person does not know anything about the others.)

In addition to introductions, we *build into the end of each meeting some goodbye time* to acknowledge the presence and unique value of each individual, as noted earlier (e.g., "This has been a great meeting; you've all been so helpful to one another; there's been a great exchange of ideas and collaboration. Thank you."); to promise the value of humanism at the next meeting (e.g., "I look forward to your being here next time if you can."); and to form with those who return an alliance of responsibility for maintaining that *humanistic* (Glassman and Kates 1990) quality (e.g., "For those of you who return, I'll look to you to help new people know what we're about and feel comfortable, okay?").

Dealing with Difference and Conflict

As with any group, we begin to help the open-ended group deal with difference and use conflict to its mutual-aid advantage by *clarifying the value of difference as a helping tool* (e.g., "I'd like for us to briefly review some of the ways we do things here, especially how we usually make decisions and what happens when we disagree about something. . . . And if anyone has any reactions or thoughts as we do that, I hope you'll share them."). Although this is something we do in all groups, we *initiate a conversation about difference every single time a new member attends* (e.g., "Kim and Grant are new here today, so I think it's important that we talk a bit about how some of the differences we bring to the group have been helpful.").

To continue the metaphor used earlier, we *help each* groupe du jour *welcome new blood* (e.g., "It's wonderful to welcome you here tonight.") and *recognize the value of old blood* (e.g., "It's wonderful to welcome you back."). We *reiterate the importance of certain group norms in times of difference,* such as goodwill, listening with an open mind, and respect. In fact, helping the open-ended group cultivate these norms cannot be stressed enough, because conflict can feel threatening even when cohesion is high and common ground solid. If and when membership is not very stable, therefore, and when members have the freedom to come and go (and thus dismiss their differences), there is an even greater chance for conflict to close rather than open avenues to mutual aid.

Finally, we *help the* groupe du jour *adopt and agree to a structure for dealing with conflict.* Whatever structure is adopted, its ultimate goal is to help the group process its differences in a way that invites the continuation of real talk and problem solving rather than dismissal. Adjunctively, we *build in the possibility for extra-group contact for anyone who wishes it.* As always, conflict is conceptualized as whole-group food for thought and is ideally dealt with in and by the whole group (see Chapter 8). However, due to the nature of the open-ended group, building in even a little extra-group contact as an adjunct to group process can help preempt the possibility that members will simply decide to stay away from the next meeting out of anger, anxiety, or fear.

Setting and Keeping Mutual Aid in Motion

To the extent that it has ongoing opportunities to have a say over its affairs, the open-ended group also has access to its collective skills and strengths and, thus, ongoing opportunities to discover and harness its mutual-aid potential. Even open-ended groups experience stages of development (see Chapter 5), however, and visit and revisit some degree of beginnings and endings as members come and go, and middles as each *groupe du jour* engages in its work. Both the look and feel of their mutual aid may change along with changes in community, therefore.

So, what can we do to help carry mutual aid forward from group to group to group? We *build in some time at the beginning of each meeting to identify the needs, strengths, or skills that are present in this encounter* (e.g., "I see some of you have been here before, but some of you have not; so let's take a little time to all get onto the same page.").

To help make explicit the thread that ties the current meeting to those of the past, we *take the role of group historian* (e.g., "Let me take the role of historian for a few moments and talk a bit about where the group's been up to now. Anyone else who remembers or remembers differently, please jump in."). As we *invite new members to share the nature of their goals* (e.g., "So, Ted, what brings you here tonight?" or "So, Raya, what do you hope to get out of the group?") we *also invite examples of how older members have been helped* (e.g., "In addition to a few words about what brings you here, would those of you who've been here before share an example or two of how the group has been helpful to you?"). We *set aside time at the end of each meeting to evaluate both the quality and the quantity of mutual aid that has taken place* (e.g., "I'm going to set aside fifteen minutes at the end of this meeting to wrap things up—to ask you to evaluate how we did as a group today, what was helpful, what might have been different, etc."). We *ask members to reflect upon their goals for the next meeting* (e.g., "It would also be really helpful if you'd say a few words about what you'd like to see happen in the next meeting."). In other words, the ending process of each *groupe du jour* sets the stage for continuity of mutual-aid potential even as it provides an opportunity for evaluation and closure for those who do not return.

KEY POINTS OF THIS CHAPTER

1. Open-ended groups can be found in a variety of settings and to meet a variety of needs, especially where stability of membership is not possible.

2. Specific guidelines for membership in outreach and publicity materials help those who may be interested in the group determine the goodness of fit between their goals and the group's ongoing purpose.

3. The purpose of the open-ended group may be visited and revisited as members come and go; and helping each *groupe du jour* discover its work within that purpose needs to be balanced with an eye to the possibility of modifying or changing the group's purpose to meet new needs.

4. We deemphasize variance within each *groupe du jour* by emphasizing work ties and by using entrance and exit rituals, discussions of purpose, introductions, examples of past help and contributions, and expectations of the current encounter to highlight those ties.

5. Maintaining a dual focus throughout each meeting of the open-ended group is particularly important as a way of giving each member, old or new, a sense of personal value.

6. If rights and responsibilities are not universal in the open-ended group, the resulting climate will move members away from rather than toward mutual aid. Furthermore, to the degree that status is assigned to either longevity or attendance, it cannot dictate rights, responsibility, or value.

7. Affective ties may well develop in the open-ended group but may be cultivated primarily within subgroups (as among those who already know one another, for example) and not cross over as readily from the older to newer members (or vice versa).

8. The capacity for real talk in the open-ended group may dance back and forth as members come and go.

9. Although difference is a paradoxical status quo in the open-ended group, to the extent that strength of community is related to how well members care about one another, conflict can be particularly threatening to this system, which by its very nature constantly reshapes itself.

10. The open-ended group has ongoing opportunities to identify and harness strengths—the most obvious but apparently least understood of which are entries and exits.

11. To be sensitive to time and place in open-ended practice is to recognize and respect the impact of constantly changing faces on both capacity and desire to engage in mutual aid.

12. Attending to time and place in mutual-aid practice with the open-ended group means to harness the unique potential of each *groupe du jour* while reaching for vertical as well as horizontal common ground, to equalize expectations of real talk from everyone in each meeting, to reconfirm the role and value of difference every time a new member attends, and to accept that capacity for mutual aid changes along with ongoing changes in community.

RECOMMENDED FURTHER READING

Birnbaum, M. and Cicchetti, A. (2000). The power of purposeful sessional endings in each group encounter. *Social Work with Groups* 23(3):37-52.

Galinsky, M. and Schopler, J. (1985). Patterns of entry and exit in open-ended groups. *Social Work with Groups* 8(2):67-80.

Schopler, J. and Galinsky, M. (1984). Meeting practice needs: Conceptualizing the open-ended group. *Social Work with Groups* 7(2): 3-22.

Shapiro, B. (1990). The social work group as social microcosm: "Frames of reference" revisited. *Social Work with Groups* 13(2): 5-22.

Chapter 12

Mutual-Aid Practice
with Very Large Groups

KEY CONCEPTS OF THIS CHAPTER

Dual Focus
Hourglass Approach
Intergroup
Intragroup
Parallel Process
Purposeful Use of Process
Subgroup
Whole-Group
Whole-Groupness

* * *

Ideal conversation must be an exchange of thought and not, as many of those who worry most about their shortcomings believe, an eloquent exhibition of wit or oratory.

Emily Post

Managed care, increasing caseloads, waiting lists, and so-called efficiency-based approaches to the use of time are creating large groups in a number of settings today. What constitutes a very large group? There is no absolute definition. The professional literature generally conceptualizes small-group practice as working with a membership of three to ten, with some preference for a core group that is large enough to prevent ongoing dyad work by default if a member or two are not present (as in a core of five or six members) and yet small enough for every member's voice to be heard on a regular basis. Although there are no set parameters, then, the very large group has been loosely conceptualized for this discussion as large enough to divide into at least three or four (but perhaps even more) small working groups, such as a total membership of about twenty or more (as is often the case in residential floor meetings or multifamily groups or social-action groups). Depending on setting, group purpose, characteristics of members, and other variables, such as overall group lifeline and how well members already know one another, one group of fifteen may share many of the time and place issues of the very large group as described in the following discussion, of course, and another less so.

Very large groups are being used to provide education and support for transitions, such as school-based or community-based language-education or other acculturation groups for new immigrants. Agency-based treatment to families in need through the use of multifamily groups are very popular today. Psychoeducation is being provided through large groups to help families of patients about to be discharged or to provide concrete assistance to victims of large-scale trauma or their families or to help organize everyday life, as in residential floor meetings. Large socialization groups are being used to reach such populations as the isolated elderly or disabled, to provide glimpses into current events in residential settings, or to offer a chance for special-needs children to improve their social skills. Finally, large political and social-action coalitions are formed in a variety of different settings to seek and promote organizational, community, and large-scale social change.

Although *the more the merrier* rule applies well to some mutual-aid dynamics, such as sharing data, universality, and exercising strength in numbers, very large groups do not usually lend themselves to such dynamics as in-depth personal problem solving, rehearsing new ways of being or doing, or to other kinds of risk taking around much of which the helping process takes place. They do not tend to be intimate enough in ambience or provide much opportunity for each and every member to give and take from the process in as full a manner as is possible in smaller groups. Exceptions notwithstanding, then, a good rule of thumb to integrate into mutual-aid practice is that the larger the numbers, the more difficult it is for people to risk exposing the full range of their ideas, feelings, and stories. We can help the large group to discover, catalyze, and harness its whole-group potential through some purposeful use of small-group process. Northen and Kurland (2001) state it this way:

> As the size of the group increases, each member has a larger number of relationships to maintain. Each member not only has more other members to interact with but also responds to the dyadic and triadic relationships that have developed. . . . More communication tends to be directed toward the worker rather than toward other members and to the group rather than to specific members. The larger the group, the greater the anonymity of the members and the greater the difficulty in achieving true consensus in decision making. (p. 137)

Of course, many variables dictate the quality of a group experience (leadership, relevance of purpose, freedom to participate in and take advantage of what the group offers, and so on), and in some cases the value of the experience in toto may be as great in a large group as in a small one. Nonetheless, as discussed below, size of membership has an impact on a group's ability to discover and harness all of its strengths.

TIME AND PLACE ISSUES
OF THE VERY LARGE GROUP

As just noted, the larger the group the more difficult it is to accommodate all of its voices. It is common in very large groups for some members to do much talking while others do little to none or, from the other side of the coin, for conversations to remain at a somewhat superficial level so that all voices get a chance to be heard, for speakers to be interrupted, or for side conversations to take place, especially in times of difference. In fact, Mullender and Ward (1991) suggest that, "[a] larger group may need more than two workers [to] ensure that it remains empowering for all [and] workers need to be attentive to group process at a level of concentration which fewer workers might find it hard to maintain" (p. 131).

It can also be difficult for the very large group to promote a *humanistic* as well as *democratic* climate (Glassman and Kates 1990)—that is, a forum for safe self-reflection and self-reference, free expression of difference, respectful listening, and other forms of risk taking through which people help one another. Engaging in-depth analysis of issues and problems, making and meeting mutual demands for work, and other norms of mutual aid can be challenging under the best of circumstances. To try them out amid large numbers, therefore, can be particularly daunting. Anyone who has ever been in a class of twenty plus (either as student or teacher) or invited to share personal information in front of relatively unknown others knows only too well the dilemma of balancing desire to commit and contribute with fear of exposure, criticism, or ridicule. As one member of a thirty-plus member group said at evaluation time:

> I'm so glad we broke out into smaller groups, because I was feeling nervous about talking in front of everyone. There are some people here who know so much more than I do. . . . What do I know compared to them!? I felt much more comfortable working with our group of five.

Of course, we all have probably participated in process that disproves the rule and watched as some people stand in front of large audiences with no apparent qualms about speaking up loudly and passionately or attacking the positions of others. Such blustery exchanges are not what mutual-aid practice seeks to catalyze, however; just the opposite. It seeks to dig far beyond the rhetorical, beyond "speechifying," and beyond "pre-canned" expressions to a thoughtful exchange of ideas, feelings, and experiences in the hope that interaction and collaboration will offer its participants personal meaning and utility. Even when purpose is strong (as in a social-action group) or its common ground obvious (as in a tenants' association), it can be difficult for members of the very large group to form tight-enough connections to realize their full potential. It is easy for members to get "lost in the crowd," to give up, to leave the group altogether, and—most unfortunately of all—to leave it unnoticed.

To be sensitive to time and place in mutual-aid practice with the very large group, therefore, is to recognize that size has an impact on the look and feel of process in general and on the helping process, more specifically. Of course, if we have no expectations of member-to-member interaction (as in lectures, for example) then group size may be of little concern. But if we expect members to interact, to share their real feelings and ideas, and to engage in honest and open reflection and analysis as they collaborate toward a common purpose, then we need to give the kind of ongoing consideration to the nature of risk taking our expectations demand. As a result, attending to time and place in working with the very large group means to plan, develop, and structure its content and process toward maximum visibility, voice, and give-and take opportunities for each member.

IMPLICATIONS FOR PRACTICE

What can we do to help the very large group realize its full mutual-aid potential? For one, we can use small groups to foster connection and through those connections help the group establish greater safety for real talk about real things. Small groups provide faster and easier access to personal common ground, or *affective* ties, than do large groups. They provide more opportunities for intimacy and they offer more opportunities for members to make themselves heard.

At the same time, true to the adage that every solution leads to another problem, the use of small groups in large-group practice presents its own set of challenges. Small groups can help to overcome many of the time and place issues of the very large group, but in order for them to not become splinter groups with strong intragroup but little whole-group commitment, we need to help them stay explicitly connected to one another. Therefore, we use small groups to develop a model for the kind of process we desire to catalyze in the large group—a parallel process—that extends and expands the large group's potential. We do not, however, want them to develop intragroup connections *at the expense of* whole-group connection. What has transpired in each small group (either content or process or both, depending on the purpose of the conversation) must eventually be shared as whole-group food for thought. If not, we risk developing the very opposite climate than we desire: small-group loyalty but large-group division.

Setting the Stage: An Hourglass Approach

Catalyzing mutual aid in the very large group requires a kind of "hourglass" approach. The broadest level of attention goes to setting the stage for mutual aid at the whole-group level. Thus, *all beginning actions,* such as introductions (members to one another, members to group purpose, group to content and process, and so on), contracting (what members will do together and how they will do it, issues of confidentiality, and so on), and preparation (presenting the nature of the work of the moment, articulating expectations, giving instructions, and so on) are *directed to the whole group.* In other words, whenever the group is at a point of beginning—whether it be the very beginning of its lifetime or a new stage or session or new work—we think, emphasize, and reach for whole-groupness.

Our next level of attention is narrower, such as the slender middle section of the hourglass, as we go about helping the group advance its work, however defined. If the dynamics we seek lend themselves to *the more the merrier* rule, we catalyze whole-group interaction and collaboration. If we seek to initiate dynamics that require more time, space, visibility, and opportunity for personal interaction than the whole group can accommodate at the moment, then we develop and catalyze small-group process.

Finally, *we return our focus to the broad level at all endings* in order to promote whole-group integration of process and progress—to help members end in a common space regardless of where the details of their work took them during the meeting (e.g., "Let's come back together to wrap things up."). We *ask for whole-group assessment of the experience* (e.g., "I'd appreciate some feedback from you about our process here today."). And we *use each whole-group ending to reset the stage for future potential* (e.g., "Okay, so let's talk a little about next time.").

On Purpose

Attention to purpose is an ongoing task in catalyzing mutual aid in the very large group. As with all practice, of course (see Chapter 3), we help members adopt a purpose that is collectively meaningful and agreeable and invite ongoing evaluation. In addition, however, and not unlike the consideration we give to the use of activity, we *con-*

sider the purpose of selecting large-group or small-group process whenever we entertain either option (why either one would enhance members' capacity to help one another at this moment; how it would do so, specifically; and how the purpose of initiating either level of interaction would tie into overall purpose). We *make the purpose of using either large-group or small-group process explicit to members.* The point here is not to suggest that small groups be used to "manage" large numbers so much as to recommend the *purposeful* use of either large or small-group process, depending on the mutual-aid dynamics we seek to catalyze at any given moment, and to suggest that small groups can, in effect, often help the large group deepen its members' capacity to give and take help.

Purposeful use of process includes a content-related decision (e.g., "I think small groups will give you an opportunity to share your early experiences in greater depth than we can as a large group." or "Let's break up into small groups, each take a piece of this task, and come back together in twenty minutes."). It also includes a process-related decision (e.g., "I think we'll be able to work better if we do some of it in small groups.").

Group Building

To help build whole-group community in working with very large groups, we *always initiate discussion and clarification of purpose and contract* at the whole-group level. We *make statements to the whole group about its work ties* even as we use small groups to reduce anonymity, increase contact and connection, and help the development of affective ties. We *plan, promote, and maintain intergroup connection* to help prevent small groups from becoming "floating islands." For example, we make explicit how all the subgroups are working toward one goal, even or especially when they have different tasks. To maintain whole-group ownership over the group's affairs we *develop a structure for small groups to interact with one another* (e.g., asking each to act as audience for the others' report). Finally, we *ask for whole-group view and review of process at all endings* and *make direct and explicit reference to whatever intergroup collaboration that has taken place.*

Promoting Real Talk

We promote real talk in the very large group by *differentiating between the dynamics of mutual aid that are well suited to the more the merrier rule and those that require more safety and intimacy than the large group can realistically provide at any given moment.* For example, the large group may be a good venue for some kinds of brainstorming and problem solving but not others. We *use stages of group development as a framework for making decisions about how much and what kind of real talk to reach for.* And we *increase our expectations of and demands for whole-group real talk as the group matures* (see Chapter 5), using small-group process as a confidence-building tool. We *model risk taking by sharing some of our own thoughts and feelings* with the large group and *expressing gratitude when members follow suit.* We *ask small groups to interact in collective form* so that individual views are safely reflected in or represented by the group (e.g., "Some of us think . . ." or "This is what we did . . ."). As members become increasingly comfortable expressing what they think and feel in small groups, and as those groups increasingly interact, individual members will become increasingly confident to express what they think and feel to the group as a whole.

Dealing with Difference and Conflict

We begin to help the large group deal with conflict by *anticipating some of the differences that might arise among these people* (behavioral, descriptive, situational, or experiential differences). We *identify some of the ways in which exploring difference will enhance members' ability to help one another and the group to achieve its purpose.* As the group begins we *highlight the needs and goals that members have in common,* but because it may be easy for members of a large group to ignore what they disapprove of or dislike, we *make early reference to the value of difference.* We also *make direct statements about the value of difference when conflict occurs* so that members are not tempted to withdraw from interaction or simply stay away from the next meeting.

Setting and Keeping Mutual Aid in Motion

We have three types of opportunities to catalyze mutual aid in very large groups. We can ask members to help one another as members of the large group. We can ask them to work in small groups. And we can ask for intergroup mutual aid by asking small groups to interact with one another. Each venue provides a different kind of opportunity for members to give and take. Following the hourglass approach, which begins and ends work broadly with attention to the "narrow" (detail) in the middle, we *begin by initiating whole-group interaction and collaboration* by asking members to talk about their needs and goals and to contract as a whole group around structure, content, and process. As members talk together we *identify some of the common ground that is evident.* We also *promote whole-group interaction whenever we seek to expand the breadth of the group's work* (when we think difference would be stimulating, for example, or when identifying a wide range of possibilities for action). We *promote small-group process when we seek to help the group reach for greater depth in its work*—for example, to help members move into new or deeper work territory, refine their individual problem-solving skills, or increase their capacity for expression, empathy, debating, listening, and using difference. At the same time, we *ask small groups to connect on a regular basis* in order to help each group enhance the capacity of the others and thus contribute to whole-group progress. Through ongoing collective self-reflection of (e.g., "In our group, we thought about . . .") and reference to their own stories (e.g., "We came up with the four following commonalities . . .") each group system provides a safe venue for members to learn the more challenging "ropes" of mutual aid and to hone their skills. As their confidence builds, they become increasingly able and willing to make increasingly sophisticated contributions to the overall group process.

The central question here is why seek mutual aid at any one level of degree of intensity at any given moment and why? That is, what kind of mutual aid are we looking for? What makes our expectations at a particular level realistic at this time? How would these dynamics enhance whole-group potential? Why would they do so better at one level than another? Thus, we *think through how we see the large group as a mutual-aid system and make that vision explicit to the group* (e.g., "You all bring ideas and experiences to the group that I hope you'll share with one another as we go along."). We also *think through how we see small groups as enhancing that process and make that explicit as well* (e.g., "On occasion we'll use small groups to discuss and explore things in greater depth than we can as a large group."). Finally, we *make explicit the differences in our expectations regarding purpose and process between the two* (e.g., "Working together as one group will bring some breadth to our work, whereas working in small groups will help us dig into some of that work more deeply."). That is, we constantly think through which dynamics of mutual aid lend themselves to one or other format and determine how each type of interaction pattern can advance or enhance whole-group potential.

KEY POINTS OF THIS CHAPTER

1. Very large groups are being used increasingly to provide a range of services, such as education, treatment, support, socialization, and social action.
2. Although *the more the merrier* rule applies well to some mutual-aid dynamics, very large groups do not usually lend themselves to such dynamics as in-depth personal problem solving, rehearsing new ways of being or doing, or to other kinds of risk taking, around much of which the helping process takes place.
3. Although many variables dictate the quality of a group experience, size of membership has an impact on a group's ability to discover and harness all of its strengths.
4. Generally speaking, the larger the group the more difficult it is for all of its voices to be heard. It can also be difficult for the very large group to maintain a *humanistic* as well as *democratic* climate (Glassman and Kates 1990).
5. Even when a group's purpose is strong or its common ground obvious, it can be difficult for members of the very large group to form tight-enough connections to realize their full potential. It is easy for members to get "lost in the crowd," to give up, to leave the group altogether, and—most unfortunately of all—to leave it unnoticed.

6. To be sensitive to time and place in mutual-aid practice with the very large group is to recognize the impact of size on the look and feel of process in general and on the helping process, more specifically. Attending to time and place means to plan, develop, and structure content and process toward maximum visibility, voice, and give-and take opportunities for each member.

7. The use of small-group process within the large group can help it realize its full mutual-aid potential by fostering closer connection than is possible in large numbers, promoting intimacy, and providing more space for personal expression than time may permit in the large group.

8. In order to prevent small-group commitment without large-group connection, we make opportunities for small subgroups to stay explicitly connected to one another.

9. Catalyzing mutual aid in the very large group takes an "hourglass" approach, with the broadest level of attention given to setting the stage at the beginning, with the middle, or narrower, level to helping deepen the group's work, and with a return to the broad level of intervention at all endings.

10. In large-group practice, we constantly assess the selection of large-group or small-group process in terms of how it will enhance whole-group potential for mutual aid; and we make the purpose of using either one explicit to members. Purposeful use of process includes a content-related decision and process-related decision.

11. To help build whole-group community in working with very large groups, we always initiate discussion and clarification of purpose and contract at the whole-group level. We plan, promote, and maintain intergroup connection. Whenever we use small-group process we provide opportunities for the small groups to interact with one another. And we ask for whole-group process at all endings.

12. We promote real talk in the very large group by differentiating between the dynamics of mutual aid that are well suited to *the more the merrier* rule and those that require more safety and intimacy than the large group can realistically provide at any given moment, using group development as a framework for

making decisions about how much and what kind of real talk to reach for.

13. We help the large group deal with conflict by making the value of difference explicit even as we highlight the group's common ground, and by providing a structure for the full and safe expression of differences.

14. We have three types of opportunities to catalyze mutual aid in very large groups. We can ask members to help one another as members of the large group. We can ask them to work in small groups. We can set up intergroup mutual aid by asking small groups to interact with one another. Each venue provides a different kind of opportunity for members to give and take.

RECOMMENDED FURTHER READING

Mondros, J. and Berman-Rossi, T. (1991). The relevance of stages of group development theory to community organization practice. *Social Work with Groups* 14(3/4):125-151.

Mordock, J. (1996). The road to survival revisited: Organizational adaptation to the managed care environment. *Child Welfare* 75(3):195-218.

Mullender, A. and Ward, D. (1991). Empowerment through social action group work: The "self-directed" approach. *Social Work with Groups* 14(3/4):125-139.

Schwartzben, S. (1989). The 10th floor family support group: A descriptive model of the use of a multi-family group in a home for the aged. *Social Work with Groups* 12(1):41-54.

Chapter 13

Conclusion

KEY CONCEPTS OF THIS CHAPTER

A Consumer-Oriented Approach to Evaluation
Evaluating Practice Efforts
Mutual Aid As Process
Mutual Aid As Result

* * *

The mutual-aid approach to evaluation is consumer oriented. If the raison d'être of mutual-aid practice is to help people help one another, then they have the right to evaluate the extent to which it has or has not happened. This does not preclude professional evaluation, but just as helping a group develop into a mutual-aid system is a joint venture, evaluating its success as such is also a joint venture.

Since mutual aid is both a process (through help-exchanging dynamics) and a result (the help that is received as a result of those dynamics), the mutual-aid approach to evaluation is two-pronged, attending to both how process reflects mutual aid in action and how members feel they were helped as a result of that process. Clearly, process and result are closely connected. When we think about authority, for example, it is difficult to reflect on the extent to which a group assumed authority over its affairs without reflecting on its exercise of that authority, and vice versa. Still, to keep the discussion as simple as possible (since there are so many factors [i.e., process, result, and practice efforts] to consider in the assessment of a group as a mutual-aid system, and since assessment needs to take place from so many points of view at once [i.e., the worker, individual members, and the group as a whole]), process and result have been treated as separate issues here.

The next section presents an evaluation chart that reflects the gestalt of evaluation from a mutual-aid viewpoint, and the subsequent section identifies group-specific skills for carrying out the process.

ALL THINGS CONSIDERED

Evaluating a group from a mutual-aid viewpoint is both simple and complex. To the extent that everyone involved has the right and obligation to evaluate the group's process and progress, it is simple. To the extent that several factors need to be taken into account from several points of view, however, it is complex. Rather than attempt to integrate all of the factors through a long and unwieldy narrative, therefore, the evaluation process is presented in chart form (see Table 13.1).

There are two ways to use the chart. Reading horizontally gives a picture of the evaluation protocol with regard to each specific mutual-aid dynamic (see Chapter 2) as follows: Column 1 identifies the dynamic; Column 2 identifies its associated goal; Column 3 asks how much the group engaged in that particular dynamic; Column 4 asks about the extent to which members were helped as a result of that dynamic; and Column 5 poses some practice-related questions. Therefore, reading across the rows helps evaluate the extent to which the group made use of any given dynamic. For example, Row 1 identifies data sharing. Its associated goal, that the group function as a marketplace of information, is identified in Column 2 of that row. Column 3 of Row 1 asks about data sharing as a process (e.g., "To what extent did information sharing take place in the group?"). Column 4 of Row 1 asks about data-sharing results (e.g., "How was the sharing of information helpful?"). And Column 5 of Row 1 asks about the nature of practice efforts (e.g., "To what extent were questions routinely turned back to the group?").

Reading vertically gives a full picture of each of the levels of thought required for evaluation. Column 1 identifies all of the mutual-aid dynamics a group might use. Column 2 identifies the major mutual-aid goals of a group. Column 3 poses the key questions about

TABLE 13.1. A Chart for Evaluating the Group As a Mutual-Aid System

The Dynamics	Goals	Mutual Aid As Process	Mutual Aid As Result	Practice
Data Sharing	The group will function as a marketplace for the exchange of information and ideas.	Did group members share information and ideas? When? What was the nature of the information?	Was any of the information shared of particular use? How so?	Were members encouraged to see one another as sources of information? How so, exactly? To what extent were questions routinely turned back to the group? Were questions ever answered directly? When? Why?
Dialectic Process	The group will be a forum for debating ideas and viewpoints.	Were differences expressed? Did members debate issues? Can any specific debates be recalled? Did everyone participate?	Was anything gained from debates? Can members articulate ways in which they made meaning and use of the debates, especially with regard to differences that were expressed? Did they learn new skills in and from this process? What are they? Have they been put to use? How so?	Was the exchange of ideas and views encouraged? Were members helped to examine and explore their differences? Were they helped to make meaning of their differences? How so? Was everyone encouraged to participate?

TABLE 13.1 (continued)

Discussing Taboos	The group will be a place for real talk about real issues.	Did members engage in real talk? What was the nature of that talk? Did they ask all of the questions that were on their minds?	Was the opportunity to engage in real talk helpful/useful to members? In what ways?	What was said or done to help the group be perceived as a place of real talk about real issues? What wa said or done to help members actually talk and ask about what was on their minds?
All in the Same Boat	The group will feel a strong sense of community and common ground.	Did the group develop a sense of community? Can members recall when their sense of we-ness began to develop? Can they recall moments in which they most keenly felt connected?	Were members comforted by being in the same boat as others? Can they describe in what ways, specifically?	What was said or done in particular to help members discover their common ground?
Mutual Support	The group's climate will be one of sympathy and empathy.	Did members offer one another sympathy? Did they offer one another empathy? Can they recall specific moments in which they offered or received support?	Did members feel the group's support? How so? In what ways were they able to actively use the group's support?	Were members helped to be sympathetic to one another? How so? Were they helped to be empathetic to one another? How so?

Mutual Demand	The group will be a place of work, however defined by its purpose.	Did the group work toward its purpose? Did members work toward their individual goals? Did they help one another identify the work to be done? Did they help one another carry out that work?	What was the nature of the work that took place? Was the group's purpose achieved? Were individual goals achieved? Is there work left to be done? What is the nature of that work?	Were members helped to discover their work connections? How so? How was their sense of commitment to the group nurtured? What was said or done to help the group achieve its purpose? What was said or done to help the group help its members work toward their individual goals?
Individual Problem Solving	The group will be a forum for resolving issues of personal concern.	Did members raise issues of personal concern? Can specific moments in which they did so be recalled? Were individual concerns used to identify themes of common interest? Did members engage in use of self and storytelling?	Was the group's collective thinking-through process helpful for addressing personal situations? Which ones?	Was members' use of self actively encouraged? How so? Was advice-giving actively discouraged? In what way? Was story-telling encouraged? How so?

TABLE 13.1 *(continued)*

Rehearsal	The group will be a stage for rehearsing new ways of being, thinking, or doing.	Did members use the group to try out new ways of being and doing? Can they identify specific instances in which the group was used for this purpose?	Did members adopt new ways of being or doing? Which ones?	Were members encouraged to try new ways of being and doing in the group? How so? Were they helped to try new ways in the group? Were they encouraged to try new skills outside of the group as well?
Strength in Numbers	The group will be a source of strength and courage.	Were members encouraged or invigorated by being in the group? Can they recall any moments in which they particularly felt the group's power in this way?	Was the group experienced as particularly powerful by members? In which way, exactly, and how was that power useful or helpful?	Were members encouraged to conceptualize the group as a source of strength and power? How so? Were they helped to take advantage of the group's strength-in-numbers potential? How so, exactly?

the group's mutual-aid process (e.g., "To what extent did group process reflect mutual aid in action?"). Column 4 poses key questions about its results (e.g., "What was the nature of help that people received as a result of participating in the group?"). Column 5 poses key questions regarding practice efforts that took place to help the group actualize its mutual-aid potential.

GROUP-SPECIFIC SKILLS FOR HELPING A GROUP EVALUATE ITS MUTUAL-AID DEVELOPMENT

Many group-specific skills can assist the practitioner in helping a group evaluate its development and success as a mutual-aid system. For example, we *can help the group reflect on its process at all times and the meaning of its process for each member personally,* both in and out of the group. We can *encourage group members to express their feelings about what is being said and done in the group* (e.g., "So, how does everyone feel about what just happened, then?"). We can *encourage them to identify process that was particularly helpful* (e.g., "Does anyone feel as if looking at Tom's situation has been of help to him or her as well?") and *help them articulate exactly how that process was helpful* ("Tell us how."). We can *encourage members to speak up when they feel group process is not as meaningful or relevant as it might be* (e.g., "So are you saying, Marian, that looking at Tom's situation is not helpful for you?"), and we *can encourage them to articulate what is missing from their perspective* (e.g., "Okay, then, help us understand what's missing from your point of view."). We can routinely *scan the group for reactions to what is being said or done* to help make sure that everyone who wishes to share his or her assessment of the process at hand has the chance to do so (e.g., "I see you nodding your head, Jim. What's your thinking?"). We can *encourage group members to make note of moments in which they believe one or another dynamic is taking or has taken place.* We can *encourage them to identify moments in which they believe they learned new skills.* We can *help them articulate how those new skills have been helpful.* We can *help them reflect on the ways in which they believe they have been helpful to others.* We can *help members identify the extent to which being in the group helped them achieve their individ-*

ual goals. We can *help them identify areas or skills that they would like to continue to work on.* We can *ask them to assess the extent to which they believe the group reached its purpose.* We can *encourage them to reflect on and address their own contributions to meeting the group's purpose.* We can *encourage and help members to reflect on the group-building process* (e.g., by asking them to reflect on their common ground and on the way in which the group has responded) to expressions of difference and conflict. We can *help the group reflect on the ways in which it has exercised leadership and authority over its affairs.* We can *ask members to identify specific instances in which that leadership was of particular value to the group.* We can *ask them to articulate how that leadership reflected humanistic as well as democratic values.* Finally, we can *encourage group members to give us feedback about our practice efforts,* and *ask them to identify and evaluate the effects or results of those efforts from their points of view.*

In addition to helping members increase their evaluative capacity by sharpening their powers of observation, sensitizing them to the look and feel of group process, and helping them articulate their feelings and opinions to their comembers, these skills will also help ensure that group process remains relevant and meaningful from everyone's point of view.

END NOTE

As discussed in Chapter 1, it is not necessary that every dynamic of mutual aid be experienced for a group to think of itself as a mutual-aid system, nor is it necessary that the dynamics be experienced in great intensity. Some groups engage in certain dynamics while others do not, and some groups feel certain dynamics very poignantly while others do not. The factors that most dictate the look of mutual aid in a group are the capacity of its members to interact with peers, the nature of the group's purpose, and the worker's skill in helping catalyze its mutual-aid potential. The evaluation chart is not intended to be a checklist from which quantitative tallies are to be made or to represent the only or last word in evaluating a group's mutual-aid character. Rather, it provides a starting point for reflecting and discussing, much like a staff provides a starting point for making music. It is the personal characteristics of the group itself—the personalities of the members, their unique needs and strengths, the nature of the group's purpose, the challenges it has overcome in its group-building process, the specific nature of the help that has taken place, and the skill of the practitioner—that will provide the most meaningful food for thought.

KEY POINTS OF THIS CHAPTER

1. The right and responsibility to evaluate the group as a mutual-aid system belongs to all of the participants, worker and members alike.
2. Mutual aid is evaluated at two levels: the extent to which the group's process reflected mutual aid in action, and the extent to which members feel they were helped as a result of that process.
3. There are two ways to approach evaluation. One way is to evaluate each of the dynamics of mutual aid from several angles. The other is to evaluate mutual aid first as a group process and then as a result.
4. Not all groups experience all mutual-aid dynamics or experience them at the same intensity. What will most dictate the look of mutual aid in a group is the capacity of its members to interact with peers, the nature of the group's purpose, and the worker's skill in helping catalyze whatever mutual-aid potential it has.

RECOMMENDED FURTHER READING

Glassman, U. and Kates, L. (1990). *Group Work: A Humanistic Approach.* Newbury Park, CA: Sage.

Hartford, M. (1964). Frame of reference for social group work. *Working Papers Toward a Frame of Reference for Social Group Work,* pp. 4-10. New York: National Association of Social Workers.

Kurland, R. and Salmon, R. (1996). Making joyful noise: Presenting, promoting, and portraying group work to and for the profession. In *Social Group Work Today and Tomorrow: Moving from Theory to Advanced Training and Practice,* eds. B. Stempler and M. Glass, pp. 19-32. Binghamton, NY: The Haworth Press.

Middleman, R. and Wood, G. (1990). From social group work to social work with groups. *Social Work with Groups* 13(3):3-20.

Shulman, L. (1996). Social work with groups: Paradigm shifts for the 1990s. In *Social Group Work Today and Tomorrow: Moving from Theory to Advanced Training and Practice,* eds. B. Stempler and M. Glass, pp. 1-16. Binghamton, NY: The Haworth Press.

Bibliography

Alissi, A. S., ed. (1980). *Perspectives on Social Group Work Practice.* New York: Free Press.

Anderson, J. D. (1986). Integrating research and practice in social work with groups. *Social Work with Groups* 9(3):111-124.

Berman-Rossi, T. (1990). *The Collected Writings of William Schwartz.* Itasca, IL: Peacock.

_____. (1992). Empowering groups through understanding stages of group development. *Social Work with Groups* 15(2/3):239-255.

_____. (1993). The tasks and skills of the social worker across stages of group development. *Social Work with Groups* 16(112):69-82.

Berman-Rossi, T. and Cohen, M. B. (1988). Group development and shared decision making with homeless mentally ill women. *Social Work with Groups* 11(4):63-78.

Bernstein, S. (1965). Conflict and group work. In *Explorations in Group Work,* ed. S. Bernstein, pp. 72-106. Boston: Boston University School of Social Work.

_____. (1976). Values and group work. In *Further Explorations in Group Work,* ed. S. Bernstein, pp. 145-179. Boston: Charles River Books.

_____. (1993). What happened to self-determination? *Social Work with Groups* 16(1/2):3-14.

Bertcher, H. (1978). Guidelines for the group worker's use of modeling. *Social Work with Groups* 1(3):235-246.

Bertcher, H. and Maple, F. (1996). *Creating Groups.* Newbury Park, CA: Sage.

Birnbaum, M. L. and Cicchetti, A. (2000). The power of purposeful sessional endings in each group encounter. *Social Work with Groups* 23(3):37-52.

Birnbaum, M. L., Middleman, R. R., and Huber, R. (1989). "Where social workers obtain their knowledge base in group work." Paper presented at the Annual Meeting of the National Association of Social Workers, San Francisco, October.

Boer, A. and Lantz, J. (1974). Adolescent group therapy membership selection. *Clinical Social Work Journal* 2(3):172-181.

Bostwick, G. J. Jr. (1987). "Where's Mary?" A review of the group treatment dropout literature. *Social Work with Groups* 10(3):117-132.

Brandler, S. and Roman, C. (1991). *Group Work: Skills and Strategies in Effective Interventions.* Binghamton, NY: The Haworth Press.

Breton, M. (1988). The need for mutual-aid groups in a drop-in center for homeless women: The sistering case. *Social Work with Groups* 11(4):47-61.

_____. (1989). Liberation theology, group work, and the right of the poor and oppressed to participate in the life of the community. *Social Work with Groups* 12(3):5-17.

_____. (1990). Learning from social group work traditions. *Social Work with Groups* 13(3):21-34.

_____. (1995). The potential for social action in groups. *Social Work with Groups* 18(2/3):5-14.

Briar, S. (1966). Family services. In *Five Fields of Social Service: Reviews of Research,* ed. H. S. Maas. New York: National Association of Social Workers.

_____. (1971). Social case work and social group work: Historical foundations. In *Encyclopedia of Social Work,* Volume 2, eds. A. Minahan and R. Morris, pp. 1237-1245. New York: National Association of Social Workers.

Brower, A. M. and Garvin, C. D. (1989). Design issues in social group work research. *Social Work with Groups* 12(3):91-102.

Brown, A. and Mistry, T. (1994). Group work with "mixed membership" groups: Issues of race and gender. *Social Work with Groups* 17(3):5-21.

Brown, L. N. (1991). *Groups for Growth and Change.* White Plains, NY: Longman.

Cohen, M. B. (1994). Who wants to chair the meeting?: Group development and leadership patterns in a community action group of homeless people. *Social Work with Groups* 17(1/2):71-87.

Coyle, G. (1937). *Studies in Group Behavior.* New York: Harper.

_____. (1949). Definition of the function of the group worker. *The Group* 11(3): 11-13.

_____. (1959). Some basic assumptions about group work. In *Curriculum Study,* Volume 11, ed. M. Murphy, pp. 88-105. New York: Council on Social Work Education.

Davis, L. (1995). The crisis of diversity. In *Capturing the Power of Diversity,* eds. M. Feit and J. Ramey, pp. 47-58. Binghamton, NY: The Haworth Press.

Dewey, J. (1910). *How We Think.* Boston: Heath.

Ebenstein, H. (1998). Single-session groups: Issues for social workers. *Social Work with Groups* 21(1/2):49-60.

Falck, H. S. (1989). The management of membership: Social group work contributions. *Social Work with Groups* 12(3):19-33.

_____. (1995). Central characteristics of social work with groups—a sociocultural analysis. In *Group Work Practice in a Troubled Society: Problems and Opportunities,* eds. R. Kurland and R. Salmon, pp. 63-72. Binghamton, NY: The Haworth Press.

Feldman, R. A. (1986). Group work knowledge and research: A two-decade comparison. *Social Work with Groups* 9(3):7-14.

Finn, J. (1995). Computer-based self-help groups: A new resource to supplement support groups. *Social Work with Groups* 18(1):109-117.

Finnegan, E. (1987). The day the roof could have fallen in: Some naturalistic observations about board committees, professional behaviors, and the development of a working group. *Social Work with Groups* 10(2):69-78.

Galinsky, M. J. and Schopler, J. H. (1971). The practice of group goal formulation in social work practice. *Social Work Practice,* pp. 24-32.

_____. (1977). Warning: Groups may be dangerous. *Social Work* 22(2):89-94.

_____. (1980). Structuring co-leadership in social work training. *Social Work with Groups* 3(4):51-63.

_____. (1985). Patterns of entry and exit in open-ended groups. *Social Work with Groups* 8(2):67-80.

_____. (1989). Developmental patterns in open-ended groups. *Social Work with Groups* 12(2):99-114.

Garland, J. A. (1992). From the chairperson's pen: In defense of the larger group. *Social Work with Groups Newsletter* 8(2):1-2.

Garland, J. A. and Frey, L. A. (1976). Application of stages of group development to groups in psychiatric settings. In *Further Explorations in Group Work,* ed. S. Bernstein, pp. 1-33. Boston: Charles River Books.

Garland, J. A., Jones, H. E., and Kolodny, R. L. (1965). A model for stages of development in social work groups. In *Explorations in Group Work,* ed. S. Bernstein, pp. 17-71. Boston: Boston University School of Social Work.

Garland, J. A. and Kolodny, R. L. (1976). Characteristics and resolution of scapegoating. In *Further Explorations in Group Work,* ed. S. Bernstein, pp. 55-74. Boston: Charles River Books.

Garvin, C. (1969). Complementarity of role expectations in groups: The member-worker contract. *Social Work Practice,* pp. 127-145.

_____. (1987a). *Contemporary Group Work.* Englewood Cliffs, NJ: Prentice-Hall.

_____. (1987b). Group theory and research. In *Social Work Encyclopedia,* Volume 1, eds. A. Minahan and R. Morris, pp. 682-696. New York: National Association of Social Workers.

Gitterman, A. (1989). Building mutual support in groups. *Social Work with Groups* 12(2):5-21.

Gitterman, A. and Shulman, L., eds. (1994). *Mutual Aid Groups and the Life Cycle.* Itasca, IL: Peacock.

Glassman, U. (1996). "Approach to humanistic group work and short term designs." Paper presented at the Annual Symposium of the Association for the Advancement of Social Work with Groups (AASWG), Ann Arbor, Michigan, October.

Glassman, U. and Kates, L. (1983). Authority themes and worker-group transactions: Additional dimensions to the stages of group development. *Social Work with Groups* 6(2):33-52.

_____. (1986). Techniques of social group work: A framework for practice. *Social Work with Groups* 9(1):9-38.

_____. (1990). *Group Work: A Humanistic Approach.* Newbury Park, CA: Sage.

_____. (1993). Feedback, role rehearsal, and programming enactments: Cycles in the group's middle phase. *Social Work with Groups* 16(1/2):117-136.

Goldberg, A., Kestenbaum, S., and Shebar, V. (1987). Jerusalem, Arabs and Jews: What can group work offer? *Social Work with Groups* 10(1):73-84.

Goldberg, T. and Lamont, A. (1986). Do group work standards work?: Results from an empirical exploration. *Social Work with Groups* 9(3):89-110.

Goldstein, H. (1988). A cognitive-humanistic/social learning perspective on social group work practice. *Social Work with Groups* 11(1/2):9-32.

Gutierrez, L. (1990). Working with women of color: An empowerment perspective. *Social Work* 35(2):149-153.

Hartford, M. (1964). Frame of reference for social group work. In *Working Papers Toward a Frame of Reference for Social Group Work,* ed. M. Hartford, pp. 4-10. New York: National Association of Social Workers.

———. (1971). *Groups in Social Work.* New York: Columbia University Press.

———. (1976). Group methods and generic practice. In *Theories of Social Work with Groups,* eds. R. Roberts and H. Northen. New York: Columbia University Press.

———. (1978). Groups in the human services: Some facts and fancies. *Social Work with Groups* 1(1):7-13.

Heap, K. (1984). Purposes in social work with groups: Their interrelatedness with values and methods—a historical and prospective view. *Social Work with Groups* 7(1):21-34.

Heckman, T., Kalichman, S., Roffman, R., Sikkema, K., Heckman, B., Somlai, A., and Walker, J. (1999). A telephone-delivered coping improvement intervention for persons living with HIV-AIDS in rural areas. *Social Work with Groups* 21(4):49-62.

Henry, S. (1992). *Group Skills in Social Work: A Four Dimensional Approach.* Pacific Grove, CA: Brooks/Cole.

Holmes-Garrett, C. (1989). The crisis of the forgotten family: A single session group in the ICU waiting room. *Social Work with Groups* 12(4):141-157.

Jagendorf, J. and Malekoff, A. (2000). Groups-on-the-go: Spontaneously formed mutual aid groups for adolescents in distress. *Social Work with Groups* 22(4):15-32.

Kaiser, C. (1958). The social group work process. *Social Work* April:67-75.

Kaslyn, M. (1999). Telephone group work: Challenges for practice. *Social Work with Groups* 22(1):63-78.

Konopka, G. (1964). Introduction to definition of social group work. In *Working Papers Toward a Frame of Reference for Social Group Work,* ed. M. Hartford, p. 32. New York: National Association of Social Workers.

———. (1983). *Social Group Work.* Englewood Cliffs, NJ: Prentice-Hall.

———. (1990). Part II. *Social Work with Groups* 13(1):15-17.

Kosoff, Susan (2002). "Single session groups: Applications and areas of expertise." Unpublished paper. Professional Integrative Seminar, Hunter College School of Social Work, New York.

Kropotkin, P. (1908). *Mutual Aid: A Factor of Evolution.* London: William Heinemann.

Kurland, R. (1978). Planning: The neglected component of group development. *Social Work with Groups* 1(2):173-178.

Kurland, R. and Salmon, R. (1990). Self-determination: Its use and misuse in group work practice and social work education. In *Working from Strengths: The Essence of Group Work,* eds. D. Fike and B. Rittner, pp. 105-121. Miami Shores, FL: Center for Group Work Studies.

———. (1992). Group work vs. casework in a group: Principles and implications for teaching and practice. *Social Work with Groups* 15(4):3-14.

———. (1993). Not just one of the gang: Group workers and their role as an authority. *Social Work with Groups* 16(1/2):153-169.

_____. (1996). Making joyful noise: Presenting, promoting, and portraying group work to and for the profession. In *Social Group Work Today and Tomorrow: Moving from Theory to Advanced Training and Practice,* eds. B. Stempler and M. Glass, pp. 19-32. Binghamton, NY: The Haworth Press.

Lang, N. (1978). The selection of the small group for service delivery: An exploration of the literature on group use in social work. *Social Work with Groups* 1(3):247-264.

_____. (1986). Social work practice in small social forms: Identifying collectivity. *Social Work with Groups* 9(4):7-31.

Lee, J. A. B. (1988). Return to our roots. *Social Work with Groups* 11(4):5-9.

Lee, J. A. B. and Swenson, C. R. (1994). The concept of mutual aid. In *Mutual Aid Groups and the Life Cycle,* eds. A. Gitterman and L. Shulman, pp. 361-380. New York: Columbia University Press.

Levine, B. (1990). Part I. *Social Work with Groups* 13(1):3-12.

Levinson, H. M. (1973). Use and misuse of groups. *Social Work* January:66-73.

Lindeman, E. C. (1980). Group work and democracy—a philosophical note. In *Perspectives on Social Group Work Practice,* ed. A. S. Alissi, pp. 77-82. New York: Free Press.

Liu, F. W. C. L. (1995). Toward mutual aid in a Chinese society. In *Group Work Practice in a Troubled Society: Problems and Opportunities,* eds. R. Kurland and R. Salmon, pp. 89-100. Binghamton, NY: The Haworth Press.

Lowy, L. (1965). Decision-making and group work. In *Explorations in Group Work,* ed. S. Bernstein, pp. 107-136. Boston: Boston University School of Social Work.

_____. (1976). Goal formulation in social work with groups. In *Further Explorations in Group Work,* ed. S. Bernstein, pp. 116-144. Boston: Charles River Books.

Mackey, R. (1980). Developmental process in growth-oriented groups. *Social Work* January:26-29.

Malekoff, A. (1991). Difference, acceptance and belonging: A reverie. *Social Work with Groups* 14(1):105-112.

_____. (1994-1995). Decision Making. *Social Work with Groups Newsletter,* December-January: 6. Reprinted by permission of the author.

_____. (1999). Pink soap and stall doors. *Families in Society* May/June:219-220.

Meddin, B. (1986). Unanticipated and unintended consequences of the group process. *Social Work with Groups* 9(2):83-92.

Meier, A. (2000). Offering social support via the Internet: A case study of an online support group for social workers. *Journal of Technology in Human Services* 17(2/3):237-266.

Meier, A., Galinksy, M., and Rounds, K. (1995). Telephone support groups for caregivers of persons with AIDS. *Social Work with Groups* 18(1):99-108.

Meyer, C. H. (1987). Content and process in social work practice: A new look at old issues. *Social Work* September/October:401-404.

Middleman, R. (1974). *Social Service Delivery: A Structural Approach to Social Work Practice.* New York: Columbia University Press.

_____. (1978). Returning group process to group work. *Social Work with Groups* 1(1):15-26.

_____. (1982). *The Non-Verbal Method in Working with Groups.* Hebron, CT: Practitioner's Press.

_____. (1987). " 'Seeing' the group in group work: Skills for dealing with the groupness of groups." Paper presented at the Ninth Symposium for the Committee for the Advancement of Social Work with Groups, Boston, Massachusetts, October.

_____. (1989). "Skills for working with groups at the group level." Paper presented at the Eleventh Symposium for the Committee for the Advancement of Social Work with Groups, Montreal, Canada, October.

_____. (1990). Group work and the Heimlich maneuver: Unchoking social work education. In *Working from Strengths: The Essence of Group Work,* eds. D. Fike and B. Rittner, pp. 16-39. Miami Shores, FL: Center for Group Work Studies.

Middleman, R. and Rothman, B. (1988). Will the real group worker please stand up! *Social Work with Groups* 11(1/2):165-170.

Middleman, R. and Wood, G. G. (1990a). From social group work to social work with groups. *Social Work with Groups* 13(3):3-20.

_____. (1990b). *Skills for Direct Practice in Social Work.* New York: Columbia University Press.

_____. (1996). Constructivism, power, and social work with groups. In *From Prevention to Wellness through Group Work,* ed. J. Parry, pp. 1-14. Binghamton, NY: The Haworth Press.

Mondros, J. and Berman-Rossi, T. (1991). The relevance of stages of group development theory to community organization practice. *Social Work with Groups* 14(3/4):125-151.

Mordock, J. (1996). The road to survival revisited: Organizational adaptation to the managed care environment. *Child Welfare* 75(3):195-218.

Mullender, A. and Ward, D. (1991). Empowerment through social action group work: The "self-directed" approach. *Social Work with Groups* 14(3/4):125-139.

Newstetter, W. (1935). What is social group work? In *Proceedings of the National Conference of Social Work,* pp. 291-299. Chicago: University of Chicago Press.

Norman, A. (1991). The use of the group and group work techniques in resolving interethnic conflict. *Social Work with Groups* 14(3/4):75-86.

Northen, H. (1964). Working definition of social group work. In *Working Papers Toward a Frame of Reference for Social Group Work,* ed. M. Hartford, pp. 43-47. New York: National Association of Social Workers.

_____. (1976). Psychosocial practice in small groups. In *Theories of Social Work with Groups,* eds. R. Roberts and H. Northen. New York: Columbia University Press.

_____. (1987). Selection of groups as the preferred modality of practice. In *Social Group Work: Competence and Values in Practice,* eds. J. Lassner, K. Powell, and E. Finnegan. pp. 19-33. Binghamton, NY: The Haworth Press.

_____. (1988). *Social Work with Groups.* New York: Columbia University Press.

Northen, H. and Kurland, R. (2001). *Social Work with Groups.* New York: Columbia University Press.

Northen, H. and Roberts, R. W. (1976). The status of theory. In *Theories of Social Work with Groups,* eds. R. Roberts and H. Northen. New York: Columbia University Press.

Owen, A. (1991). Time and time again: Implications of time perception theory. *Lifestyles: Family and Economic Issues* 12(4):345-359.

Papell, C. and Rothman, B. (1980). Relating the mainstream model of social work with groups to group psychotherapy and the structured group approach. *Social Work with Groups* 3(2):5-23.

Pernell, R. B. (1986). Empowerment and social group work. In *Innovations in Social Group Work,* ed. M. Parnes. Binghamton, NY: The Haworth Press.

Phillips, H. U. (1954). What is group work skill? *The Group* 16(5):3-22.

_____. (1957). *Essentials of Social Group Work Skill.* New York: Association Press.

_____. (1964). A working definition of social group work practice. In *Working Papers Toward a Frame of Reference for Social Group Work,* ed. M. Hartford, pp. 48-51. New York: National Association of Social Workers.

Phillips, M. H. and Markowitz, M. A. (1990). *The Mutual Aid Model of Group Services: Experiences of New York Archdiocese Drug Abuse Prevention Program.* New York: Fordham University Graduate School of Social Work.

Pottick, K. J. (1988). Jane Addams revisited: Practice theory and social economics. *Social Work with Groups* 11(4):11-26.

Ramey, J. H. (1992). Group work practice in neighborhood centers today. *Social Work with Groups* 15(2/3):193-206.

Randall, E. and Wodarski, J. S. (1989). Theoretical issues in clinical social group work. *Small Group Behavior* 20(4):475-499.

Regan, S. (2002). Building bridges over troubled waters: A bridging model for teleconferencing group counseling. In *Social Work with Groups: Mining the Gold,* eds. S. Henry, J. East, and C. Schmidt, pp. 119-130. Binghamton, NY: The Haworth Press.

Rittner, B. (2001). "Re-conceptualizing group process: Computer-based chat rooms and discussion boards group development." Paper presented at the 23rd Annual Symposium of the Association for the Advancement of Social Work with Groups. Akron, OH, October.

Rittner, B. and Nakanishi, M. (1993). Challenging stereotypes and cultural biases through small group process. *Social Work with Groups* 16(4):5-24.

Roberts, R., and Northen, H., eds. (1976). *Theories of Social Work with Groups.* New York: Columbia University Press.

Robinson, V. P. (1942). *Training for Skill in Social Casework.* Philadelphia, PA: University of Pennsylvania Press.

Rooney, R. H., Rooney, G. D., and Herbst, A. P. (1981). Continuing education and graduate training needs for group work: Results of a survey of social workers who lead groups. *Journal of Continuing Social Work Education* Spring:11-34.

Rothman, B. and Fike, D. (1987). To seize the moment: Opportunities in the CSWE standards for group work research. *Social Work with Groups* 10(4):97-109.

Schiller, L. Y. (1995). Stages of developing women's groups: A relational group model. In *Group Work Practice in a Troubled Society: Problems and Opportu-*

nities, eds. R. Kurland and R. Salmon, pp. 117-138. Binghamton, NY: The Haworth Press.

Schmidt, J. T. (1969). The use of purpose in casework practice. *Social Work* 14(1): 77-84.

Schopler, J. H. and Galinsky, M. J. (1981). When groups go wrong. *Social Work* 26(5):424-429.

_____. (1984). Meeting practice needs: Conceptualizing the open-ended group. *Social Work with Groups* 7(2):3-22.

Schopler, J. H., Galinsky, M. J., and Abell, M. (1997). Creating community through telephone and computer groups: Theoretical and practice perspectives. *Social Work with Groups* 20(4):35-54.

Schwartz, W. (1959). Group work and the social scene. In *Issues in American Social Work,* ed. A. Kahn, pp. 11-37. New York: Columbia University Press.

_____. (1961). The social worker in the group. In *The Social Welfare Forum,* pp. 146-171. New York: Columbia University

_____. (1963). Small group science and group work practice. *Social Work* October:39-46.

_____. (1969). Private troubles and public issues: One job or two? In *Social Welfare Forum,* pp. 22-43. New York: Columbia University Press.

_____. (1976). Between client and system: The mediating function. In *Theories of Social Work with Groups,* eds. R. Roberts and H. Northen, pp. 44-66. New York: Columbia University Press.

_____. (1977). Social group work: The interactionist approach. In *Encyclopedia of Social Work,* ed. J. B. Turner, 2(16):1328-1338. New York: National Association of Social Workers.

_____. (1980). On the use of groups in social work practice. In *Perspectives on Social Group Work Practice,* ed. A. Alissi, pp. 268-284. New York: Free Press.

Schwartz, W. and Zalba, S. R. (1971). *The Practice of Group Work.* New York: Columbia University Press.

Schwartzben, S. (1989). The 10th floor family support group: A descriptive model of the use of a multi-family group in a home for the aged. *Social Work with Groups* 12(1):41-54.

Shalinsky, W. (1969). Group composition as an element of social group work practice. *Social Service Review* 43(1):42-49.

Shapiro, B. Z. (1990). The social work group as social microcosm: "Frames of reference" revisited. *Social Work with Groups* 13(2):41-46.

_____. (1991). Social action, the group and society. *Social Work with Groups* 14(3/4):7-22.

Shulman, L. (1967). Scapegoats, group workers, and pre-emptive interventions. *Social Work* 12(2):37-43.

_____. (1994). Group work method. In *Mutual Aid Groups and the Life Cycle,* eds. A. Gitterman and L. Shulman. New York: Columbia University Press.

_____. (1996). Social work with groups: Paradigm shifts for the 1990s. In *Social Group Work: Today and Tomorrow,* eds. B. Stempler and M. Glass, pp. 1-16. Binghamton, NY: The Haworth Press.

_____. (1999). *The Skills of Helping Individuals, Families, Groups, and Communities.* Itasca, IL: Peacock.

Shulman, L. and Gitterman, A. (1994). The life model, mutual aid, oppression, and the mediating function. In *Mutual Aid Groups and the Life Cycle,* eds. A. Gitterman and L. Shulman, pp. 3-22. New York: Columbia University Press.

Somers, M. L. (1976). Problem-solving in small groups. In *Theories of Social Work with Groups,* eds. R. Roberts and H. Northen, pp. 331-367. New York: Columbia University Press.

Steinberg, D. M. (1992). *The Impact of Group Work Education on Social Work Practitioners' Work with Groups.* New York: City University of New York.

_____. (1993). Some findings from a study of the impact of group work education on social work practitioners' work with groups. *Social Work with Groups* 16(3): 23-39.

_____. (1995). "A study of social work practitioners' responses to conflict in the small group: What's happening out there?" Paper presented at the Sixteenth Annual Symposium of the Association for the Advancement of Social Work with Groups, Hartford, Connecticut, October.

_____. (1996). She's doing all the talking, so what's in it for me? The use of time in groups. *Social Work with Groups* 19(2):5-16.

Toseland, R. W. and Rivas, R. F. (1995). *An Introduction to Group Work Practice.* New York: Allyn and Bacon.

Toseland, R. W., Rivas, R. F., and Chapman, D. (1984). An evaluation of decision making methods in task groups. *Social Work* 29:339-347.

Trecker, H. B. (1955). *Social Group Work: Principles and Practices.* New York: Whiteside.

Tropman, J. E. (1987). Effective meetings: Some provisional rules and needed research. *Social Work with Groups* 10(2):41-55.

Tropp, E. (1978). Whatever happened to group work? *Social Work with Groups* 1(1):85-94.

Wasserman, H. and Danforth, H. E. (1988). *The Human Bond: Support Groups and Mutual Aid.* New York: Springer.

Wayne, J. and Garland, J. (1990). Group work education in the field: The state of the art. *Social Work with Groups* 13(2):95-109.

Wheelan, S. and McKeage, R. L. (1993). Developmental patterns in small and large groups. *Small Groups Research* 24(1):60-83.

Whipp, R. (1994). A time to be concerned: A position paper on time and management. *Time and Society* 3(1):99-116.

Wiener, L., Spencer, E., Davidson, R., and Fair, C. (1993). National telephone support groups: A new avenue toward psychosocial support for HIV-infected children and their families. *Social Work with Groups* 16(3):55-71.

Wilson, E. (1979). *On Human Nature.* Cambridge, MA: Harvard University Press.

Wilson, G. (1976). From practice to theory: A personalized history. In *Theories of Social Work with Groups,* eds. R. Roberts and H. Northen, pp. 1-44. New York: Columbia University Press.

Wilson, G. and Ryland, G. (1949). *Social Group Work Practice: The Creative Use of the Social Process.* Boston: Houghton Mifflin.

Young, R. (1986). Collectivity vs. group: A framework for assessment. *Social Work with Groups* 9(4):33-44.

Index

Page numbers followed by the letter "f" indicate figures; those followed by the letter "t" indicate tables.

Advice, versus mutual aid, 35, 126
Advocacy, in mutual aid, 15
Affective ties
    in open-ended groups, 224
    in special groups, 189
Aggregation, versus community, 18
Aggregational therapy of individuals, 7, 28, 131
"All in the same boat," 4, 42-44. *See also* Common cause evaluation, 250t
Allies, group members as, 30
Amplifying, 181
"Assistant therapists," 46, 139
Authenticity, as group norm, 86
Authority
    decentralized, 88-89, 146
    group-specific skills for decentralization, 161-163
    legitimate uses of, 154, 155
    professional reflection on, 158-161
    sharing, 6
    in special groups, 187-189
Autonomy, in group building, 26

Balance, in mutual aid, 18
"Being there"
    in debate, 40-41
    in disagreement, 46, 169, 178-180
Bereavement support, open-ended group, 222

Bertcher, Harvey, 60
Biological evolution, and mutual aid, 14
Brainstorming, in mutual aid, 19
Breton, Margot, 25
Bridging theory, 1

Cancer-recovery group, 51
"Captive audience," and mutual aid, 60
Case examples
    "being there," 180
    common cause, 109
    conflict, 154-155, 173, 175, 176-177, 178
    data sharing, 98, 100
    differences, 40, 173, 174
    group time use, 126-127
    information sharing, 37
    mutual aid versus presenting approach, 134t-138t
    mutual demand, 47-48
    mutual support, 113
    reflections on authority, 159-160
    risk taking, 95-96
    self-determination, 148, 149, 150-151
    setting impact, 57-58
    sex-education myths, 107
    short-term groups, 209
    single-session group, 194, 195-196, 198

Case examples *(continued)*
   taboo discussions, 104, 105, 106
   taking sides, 179
   very large groups, 238
   work obstacles, 108
"Casework in a group," 7, 15, 17, 20,
   28, 128, 129, 131, 139, 174
Central authority, 146
Chronic illness, open-ended group, 222
Clarification, 47
Closed system, group restraint, 38
COCA (come one come all) groups,
   222-223
Colby, Frank Moore, 42
Collaboration
   as group norm, 85-86
   versus competition, 119
Collective interest, and time, 132
Commiseration, versus mutual aid, 35
Commitment
   and authority sharing, 150
   as group norm, 81-82
   modeling, 119-120
Common cause. *See also* Group
      purpose
   as group bond, 6, 16, 20-21
   worker's role in, 109-111
Common ground, 135t, 140
   and conflict, 169, 180-181
   in special groups, 189
Commonalities
   in group building, 26
   and mutual aid, 6, 17-18, 83, 141
   and pregroup planning, 59-60, 62-64
Communication, in pregroup planning,
   61-62
Community, and self-determination,
   150-151
Composition
   in pregroup planning, 59-60
   and taboos discussion, 105
Confidentiality, and safety, 82
Conflict, 154-155, 167
   acceptance of, 168, 172-174
   "being there," 169, 178-180
   and common ground, 169, 180-181

Conflict *(continued)*
   and commonalities, 63
   difference versus fault, 168,
      174-176
   in open-ended groups, 230
   personalizing, 175
   in short-term groups, 216-217
   in single-session group, 202-203
   smoothing over, 168-169
   in special groups, 190
   use of, 168, 169-172
   in very large groups, 242
   whole-group issue, 169, 177
   and work demand, 176
Conflict resolution, 168
Consensus, in mutual-aid group, 147,
   157-158
Content, versus purpose of group, 69
Contracting process, and mutual aid,
   142
Cooperation, versus competition,
   117-118
Corporate teamwork, and group work
     skills, 4
Courage, and connectedness, 50
Coyle, Grace, 26, 29
Creativity, and mutual aid, 19
Crisis management
   short-term groups, 208
   single-session groups, 194

Data sharing, 36-38, 83
   evaluation, 249t
   turning back to group, 98-100
Debate
   skills in, 39-40
   versus support, 5
Decision making
   and authority, 157-158
   process, 6
Democratic-humanistic culture, 3, 5, 7,
   157, 238
Descriptive attributes, and
     commonalities, 64
Development assessment, 30-31

Dialectic process, 38-41
   evaluation, 249t
   worker's role in, 101-104
Difference
   and conflict, 167-168, 170f
   exploration of, 24, 26, 38-39
   in open-ended groups, 229-230
   in pregroup planning, 59-60, 62-64
   in short-term groups, 216-217
   in single-session group, 202-203
   in special groups, 189-190
   in very large groups, 242
Discrepant perceptions, finding, 181
Dual focus, open-ended groups, 228
Dynamics, of mutual aid, 36, 52-63

Elaboration, 47
Empathy
   and conflict, 171
   in debate, 40
   and mutual aid, 16
   in mutual support, 45, 112, 113
   in story sharing, 139
Ending group
   and common cause, 110-111
   stepping back, 121
   term, 94
Equal-time approach, 130
Ethics, in group building, 26
Experiential links, 87

Facilitation, mature group, 118
Fairness, versus relevance, 129-131
Faults, use as strengths, 23-24
Feeling links, 87
Filled time, 133
First session
   introductions, 79-80
   norms establishment, 84-90
   sense of purpose, 80
Flexibility, in mutual aid, 19
Ford, Henry, on group work skills, 4

Formal entrance ritual, open-ended
   groups, 227
Free-floating communication, 17-18
Free-form interaction, 89-90

Galinsky, Maeda, 56
Gatekeeping, and obstacles to work,
   108
Generic interventions, 82
Generosity, and mutual aid, 18-19
Gitterman, Alex, 141, 142
Goodbye-time, open-ended groups, 229
Group, as second client, 22
Group building, 25-27, 30, 79
   in open-ended groups, 227-228
   in short-term groups, 214
   in single-session groups, 201
   in very large groups, 241
Group power, 51
Group process, 3
Group purpose. *See also* Common
   cause
   and composition, 61
   and introductions, 43
   mutual aid role, 64-68
   and mutual demand, 46
   in open-ended groups, 226-227
   in short-term groups, 208-209,
     211-212
   in single-session groups, 197,
     200-201
   skills for development of, 71-73
   in special groups, 188
   statement of, 69-71
   versus content, 69
   versus individual goals, 20, 68
   in very large groups, 240-241
"Groupness," 96
Group-specific skills, 6-7
   authority, 161-163
   conflict, 181-182
   evaluation, 253-254
   practice of, 28-31

Group-work skills, 4. *See also* Group-specific skills
Guidance, as worker's role, 153

Hartford, Margaret, 6, 20, 29, 30, 96, 120, 131
Hidden agenda, and authority, 149
Holistic use of groups, 15
Horizontal common ground, 225, 228
"Hot-seat" syndrome, 17, 45. *See also* "Casework in a group"
"Hourglass" approach, very large group, 240, 243
House meetings, and mutual aid, 57
Human connection, 79-80

Individual
    focus on in group, 7
    goal achievement versus group purpose, 20, 68
    problem solving and group purpose, 48-49
Individuality, in mutual aid, 19
Information
    exchange, 36
    linkage, 37, 161-162
    setting impact, 38
    sharing, 15
Insight, and mutual aid, 16
Interaction, and mutual aid, 18
Interpersonal difference, versus individual fault, 174
Intimacy, false state of, 105
Introductions
    in first session, 79-80
    and group purpose, 43, 80
    in open-ended groups, 227, 229
    and taboos discussion, 105, 106
    in very large groups, 240
Issues
    and conflict, 169
    cooperative working, 46

Issues *(continued)*
    individualization of, 48
    turning back to group, 88

Job preparation, single-session group, 194
Joke telling, and taboos, 41

Kaiser, Clara, 7, 97, 185

Language education, very large groups, 236
Leadership
    authority as, 146
    internal, 88
Linkage, 37, 87, 161-162
Listening skills, 24
Long-term members, as mentors, 225

Malekoff, Andrew, 210
Mandated juvenile-justice, open-ended group, 222
Maple, Frank, 60
Mature group
    and common cause, 110
    and professional authority, 154-155
    responsibility, 121
    term, 94
Maypole pattern, communication, 17
Medical support, open-ended group, 221
Membership
    and individual expression, 22
    selection, 60
Member-to-member communication, 17
"Me-too" syndrome, 28, 135t, 141
Middleman, Ruth, 96
Mistakes, acknowledging, 50
Modeling
    commitment, 81, 119-120, 161
    risk taking, 117

Modeling *(continued)*
   sensitive expression, 40
   support, 45
   taboos discussion, 41-42
   thinking-through, 47
Moratorium, conflict expression, 178
Multifamily, very large groups, 236
"Multilogue," 20
Mutual aid
   and authority, 146
   climate, 18-19
   and conflict, 168, 172
   and consensus, 157-158
   and decision making, 156-157
   description of, 3, 15-21
   development over time, 93-94
   differential nature of, 97
   group evaluation, 249t-252t
   as group norm, 83-84
   and group setting, 56
   and group size, 62
   implications for practice, 7-8
   incremental nature of, 97
   intervention examples, 2
   literature review, 14
   mind-set, 21-22, 185
   preparation for, 141
   skills for development, 142-143
   and systemic factors, 56-58
   term, 2, 14
   theoretical basis for, 4
   versus presenting approach,
      134t-138t
   worker's changing role in, 120-122
Mutual demand, 4, 45-48, 85, 108
   evaluation, 251t
   worker's role in, 113-114
Mutual support, 15, 44-45, 83
   evaluation, 250t
   worker's role in, 112-113
Mutual-aid practice, 1-2
   and autonomy, 21
   conditions for, 5-7
   consumer oriented, 247
   evaluation, 248, 249t-253t
   functions, 22-28

Mutual-aid practice *(continued)*
   group-specific skills, 30, 161-163
   implications of, 7-8
   open-ended group, 225-226,
      230-231
   short-term group, 207-208, 217-218
   single-session group, 195-196,
      203-204
   strength-centered approach, 23-24,
      25
   very large groups, 236, 239,
      243-244

New group
   and common cause, 109
   and mutual demand, 113, 114
   and professional authority, 154
   term, 94
Nonverbal reactions, 30, 37
Norms
   first session establishment, 78-79,
      84-90
   problem-solving, 116
   versus rules, 84
   worker's role in developing, 154

Obstacles
   extraordinary, 186
   to work, 108
Open-ended groups, 186
   conflict in, 230
   description, 221-222
   difference in, 224, 229-230
   group building, 227-228
   group purpose, 226-227
   mutual-aid practice in, 225-226,
      230-231
   preparation, 225, 226
   real talk, 228-229
   time and place issues, 222-225
Orientation
   short-term group, 208
   single-session group, 194
Ownership of time, 128

Pacing, 97, 109
Partializing time, 129
Participation, talkative member
    strength, 24
"Partnership," worker's role as, 146
Phillips, Helen, 28
Place
    and group experience, 95-98, 186
    in open-ended group, 222-225
    in short-term groups, 208-211
    in single-session group, 196-198
    in very large groups, 237-239
Plurality, and time, 132-133
Practitioner, as worker, 5, 26
Pregroup planning, 55
    communication, 61-64
    composition, 58-61
    group purpose development, 64-68
    short-term groups, 208
    for special groups, 190
    statement of purpose, 69-71
    systemic factors, 56-58
Preparation
    open-ended groups, 225, 226
    single-session groups, 198-200
Presenting approach. *See also*
        Aggregational therapy
        of individuals; "Casework in
        a group"
    and problem solving, 114-115, 126,
        129, 141
    versus mutual-aid approach
        134t-138t
Problem solving
    and collaboration, 85
    evaluation, 251t
    in mutual aid, 15, 128-129
    worker's role in, 114-116
Production-oriented group process, 6
Professional authority, 146
    in special groups, 187-188
Psychoeducation
    and mutual-aid groups, 57
    open-ended groups, 221
    single-session groups, 194
    very large groups, 236

Psychosocial perspective, 15
Purpose. *See also* Group purpose
    in mutual-aid group, 19
    worker's role in developing, 154
Purposeful use of self, 27-28, 30, 48,
        86-87

"Real say," 147-150, 158
Real talk
    norm establishment, 108-109
    in open-ended groups, 228-229
    in short-term groups, 215-216
    in single-session groups, 201-202
    in very large groups, 242
Reframing
    aggressive communication, 39
    faults into strengths, 23-24
Rehearsal, 49-50, 116-117
    evaluation, 252t
    and safety, 117
    worker's role in, 118
Relationship-building skills, 29
Relevance, versus fairness, 129-131
Residential treatment, open-ended
        group, 221
Results, of mutual aid, 16
Risk taking, 50
Robinson, Virginia, 27
Round robin, communication, 17, 18
Rules, versus norms, 84
Ryland, Gladys, 146

Safety
    as group norm, 83-84
    and mutual support, 112
    in open-ended groups, 224
    and rehearsal, 117, 118
    in special groups, 189
Scanning, visual, 26, 30, 37, 87
Schopler, Janice, 56
Schwartz, William, 2, 13
Self-determination, in helping process,
        147-150

Self-image, shaping, 152
Self-interest, and others, 25
Self-reference
    encouraging, 142
    and problem solving, 48, 139
    in purposeful use of self, 27-28, 87
Self-reflection
    and problem solving, 48, 139
    in purposeful use of self, 27, 86-87
Sensitivity, in debate, 39, 40
Setting, in pregroup planning, 55-56
Settlement houses, and mutual aid, 14
Shalinsky, William, 60
Shared leadership, 26
Sharing skills, 24
Short-term groups, 186
    conflict, 216-217
    description, 207
    difference in, 216-217
    group building, 214
    mutual-aid practice in, 207-208,
        217-218
    pregroup planning, 208
    real talk, 215-216
    realistic group purpose, 211-212
    structure, 212-214
    time and place issues, 208-211
Short-term mandates
    advocacy about, 210-211
    constraints, 209
Shulman, Lawrence, 35, 36, 38, 41, 43,
        44, 48, 49, 109
Single-session group, 186
    conflict, 202-203
    description, 193-194
    difference in, 202-203
    group building, 201
    mutual-aid practice in, 195-196,
        203-204
    predetermined group purpose, 197
    preparation, 198-200
    purpose relevance, 200-201
    real talk, 201-202
    time and place issues, 196-198
Small group
    dynamics, 3, 44
    professional impact, 2

Small group *(continued)*
    theories, 43
Social advancement, and mutual aid, 14
Social work, and mutual aid, 4, 14, 15
Social-action groups, 51, 119, 236
Socialization, very large groups, 236
Sounding board, for action, 49
Special groups
    mutual aid promotion in, 187-191
    types of, 185
"Squeaky wheel" approach, 130
Statement of purpose, 69-71
Stimulation, and group difference, 64
Story-sharing, 28, 135t
Strength
    and connectedness, 50
    exchange of, 3, 15, 151-152
    and group termination, 111
    in open-ended groups, 226
Strength-centered practice, 51
Strength-in-numbers, 50-51
    evaluation, 252t
    in special groups, 190
    worker's role in, 118-120
Strengths
    harnessing, 23-25, 30
    identification, 43
Structure
    short-term groups, 212-214
    in special groups, 187
Stylistic interventions, 82
Support
    and differences, 44-45
    in mutual aid, 15
Sympathy
    in mutual aid, 35
    in mutual support, 35, 112
System, group as, 22, 30
Systemic change, advocacy, 210-211
Systemic factors, in pregroup planning,
        56-58

Taboos
    discussing, 41-42
    discussion evaluation, 250t

Taboos *(continued)*
  and mutual aid, 15
  worker's role with, 101-109
Taking sides, 178, 179
Task-oriented group, 140
Teaching repertoire, 118
Teaching tool, authority use, 146, 153
Thinking-through skills, 47
Time
  and development of mutual aid, 93,
    94, 186
  and group experience, 95-98
  group sharing of, 128
  in open-ended groups, 222-225
  partializing, 129
  and plurality, 132
  in short-term groups, 208-211
  in single-session groups, 196-198
  in very large groups, 237-239
  as whole-group commodity, 131
Tone amplification, 37
Toning down, 181
Transition support, very large groups,
    236
Trecker, Harleigh, 26

Unfilled time, 133

Vertical common ground, 225, 228
Very large groups, 186
  conflict in, 242
  description, 235-237

Very large groups *(continued)*
  difference in, 242
  group building, 241
  group purpose, 240-241
  mutual-aid practice in, 236, 239,
    243-244
  preparation, 240
  real talk, 242
  small groups within, 239, 241, 242,
    243
  time and place issues, 237-239
Visual scanning
  in group building, 26, 30
  in mutual-aid maintenance, 142
Voting, in mutual-aid group, 147, 157,
    158

"We-ness," 25, 51, 118, 150
  in special groups, 190
Whole-group
  and conflict, 177-178
  and time, 131
Wilson, Gertrude, 146
Work
  and mutual demand, 46-48, 113-114
  obstacles to, 108
  and unidirectional approach, 113
Worker
  data sharing, 99
  dialectic development, 102-103
  mutual-aid role, 94
  in taboo discussion, 104-109
  versus leader, 26

CPSIA information can be obtained at www.ICGtesting.com
Printed in the USA
BVOW03s2130270813

329693BV00008B/244/P

9 780789 014627